1996/97 EDITION

The *Best* Resources

For College Choice & Admissions

SEATTLE

A RESOURCE PATHWAYS GUIDEBOOK

Published by:
Resource Pathways, Inc.
22525 S.E. 64th Place, Suite 253
Issaquah, WA 98027-5377

Publisher's Cataloging in Publication

The Best resources: for college choice and admissions.
    p. cm.
    Includes index.
    ISBN 0-9653424-0-9

    1. Universities and colleges--United States--Admission--
Directories I. Resource Pathways (Firm)

LB2351.2B47 1996   378.1'056'0973
                          QBI96-40208

Contents

Section **I** Introduction

Introduction

HOW TO USE THIS GUIDEBOOK

The College Choice Decision

Deciding which colleges to apply to is a process that millions of high school students undertake each year. Despite support from their parents, friends, fellow students, and counselors, it can still seem an overwhelming task.

Compounding this challenge is the fact that there are so many different resources available to help students and their parents do the research necessary to choose the right colleges to apply to! There are many more resources available offering advice on how to complete applications and compete for admission to those colleges, too!

As you might expect, the value these different resources bring to students and parents working on the college choice decision depends, in large part, on where you are in the decision-making process! Most resources will be very useful in helping one complete a single step in the process, but much less useful (or not useful at all) in other steps. No single resource can provide all the help or information one needs during each step.

So, what are you to do? The answer is simple – break this big decision into a number of smaller decisions, each supported by the best resources available!

Breaking The Process Into Steps

Just like any difficult decision, choosing colleges to apply to, and being successful in gaining admission to those colleges, can be broken down into more manageable steps. The benefit of taking this approach is twofold:

- The decisions to be made become less intimidating, it becomes easier to get started, and you can feel good about your progress as you complete each smaller step.

- You can take advantage of those resources which are **best** suited to help you with your research for **each** step. By doing so you'll make better decisions and have more confidence in the decisions you make.

What are the steps we've identified? They seem obvious once you think about it:

1. **Get an overview** of the entire college choice and admissions process, so you know what to expect and how to plan.

2. **Identify your priorities,** including, for some, **picking a major** area of concentration for your college studies.

3. For those focusing on a particular major area of study, **identify schools which have strong programs in that major** area of academics.

4.   Besides a major, decide on key criteria that can be used to **generate an initial list of colleges for further research.** These selection factors typically include geographic location, size, cost, student body profile, admissions selectivity, student life, available financial aid, special programs, and others.

5.   For some, colleges which support **specialized groups and programs** (for women, minorities, the arts, etc.) or address **specialized needs** (learning disabilities) need to be identified.

6.   Once an initial list of colleges meeting these criteria has been developed, then **do further research to create a final list of colleges** to which you'll submit applications.

7.   If you can, you'll want to **visit campuses and interview with admissions staff** before you make a final decision. These visits and interviews help you evaluate the colleges and help the colleges appreciate your unique qualities.

8.   Finally, you'll need to **complete applications,** including those essays!

If you approach the process of choosing a college using these steps, and you take advantage of the resources we've identified as the best to use each step of the way, then you'll find that you can complete these steps with confidence. We've made judgments about which resources you should use – your job is to do the research and make the decisions.

How This Book Is Organized

During the course of our ongoing research and analysis, we've identified the best resources to use each step of the way. We've grouped our recommendations together in the "Recommendations" section of this guidebook. Use this section to identify those resources which are best suited to help you complete the separate steps we've outlined above. We always recommend several that we believe can do the job well, so you'll have the freedom to choose resources that are convenient for you to find and that meet your specific requirements.

This guidebook also contains a complete listing of all the resources we've reviewed, in a section titled "Resource Reviews." In this section, we've organized our reviews by media type, so that those who might be interested in CD-ROM resources, for example, can find reviews of CD-ROMs that are available to support the college choice decision. These reviews are ranked by Overall Star Rating (1-4 Stars) within each media section, so that the best resources are always listed first.

We've also provided an index which lists all the resources reviewed, alphabetically by title, so those who might be interested in a title they've heard about can read our evaluation of that particular resource.

Keep These Tips In Mind

As good a tool as research can be in supporting your decision, don't forget to take advantage of the people around you who can help – your parents, college counselors and career advisors at your high school, friends already enrolled in college, and so on. Their experiences and perspective will help you as you go through the process and make the decisions you need to make.

Start early and stay on schedule! Your initial college research should begin no later than the spring quarter of your junior year. You should arrive at your summer vacation with your initial list of colleges, and you should spend the summer and early fall completing the research necessary to pick your final list (including campus visits if possible). You should have your applications complete by the end of the year, with only fall grades and teacher recommendations to be added before meeting the late January-early February application deadlines most colleges impose.

Don't panic. This should be a happy process of self-discovery and your first taste of adult decision-making. You'll do fine. Have fun!

Good luck with your research, and with the colleges to which you ultimately apply!

MEET RESOURCE PATHWAYS

As consumers in the Information Age, we all want to take advantage of the many sources of information available to help us make life's important decisions. Unfortunately, we don't always know where to find these sources of information. Often, we don't know very much about their quality, value, or relevance.

Resource Pathways' guidebooks solve the problem of "information overload" faced by consumers who want to learn about, or do some research on, a topic of importance (selecting a college, for example, can be a $100,000 decision with life-long implications). Consumers interested in doing such research typically:

- Don't know what resources are available, particularly those outside traditional print media.

- Don't know where to find most of those resources.

- Can't assess the quality or focus of those resources **before** spending time and money first finding, then evaluating, and perhaps buying them.

- Don't understand which resources will be particularly useful for each stage of a multi-step decision-making process. For example, choosing colleges to apply to involves decisions about major areas of study, creating an initial list of colleges (based on preferences for size, location, cost, department quality, specialized programs, etc.), reducing that initial list to a final list (through additional research, college visits, etc.), then creating applications (including those intimidating college essays). For **each** of these steps, certain resources will be very helpful, while others will be pretty much worthless.

This guidebook, which is focused on the best resources for college choice and admissions, will help you overcome these challenges. In this guidebook, you will find that:

- Virtually all available quality resources are reviewed, including those from all "modern, high-technology" media.

- Where to buy or how to access each resource is provided in each review, including ISBN numbers for obscure print media, direct order numbers for publishers, and URL "addresses" for sites on the World Wide Web.

- We make a reasoned judgment about the quality of each resource, and decide whether or not a resource should be recommended (only 20% are recommended).

- We take the time to define steps in the typical college selection process, and categorize each resource according to its primary focus. This helps ensure that you buy or access only the best resource for each step of the process.

After you have used this guidebook to learn which sources of information are best suited to help you make these important decisions, you can then acquire or access those sources with full assurance that your time and money will be well spent.

Our Quality Standards

Consumers turn to Resource Pathways guidebooks when they want to find the best sources of information on decisions having an important impact on their lives. To earn that trust, we've developed a proven set of policies which help ensure that the highest quality standards are met:

- We are independent from the publishers of products we review; we do not accept advertising or compensation of any kind from those companies.

- We employ Advisory Councils of independent professionals with many years of experience in each subject area we cover. These professionals help ensure that we are kept abreast of developments in the field, and that our evaluations meet their standards for accuracy and relevance.

- We review new products and editions as they become available, so that our guidebooks include the most up-to-date information about products available in various media. We revisit websites on the Internet and the online services frequently, to keep up with changes in those offerings as they are introduced.

How We Develop Our Reviews & Recommendations

This guidebook includes our reviews of over a hundred information sources that can help you select, and get admitted to, the right college for you.

Our Editors and Researchers have found virtually all sources of information focused on this topic, including books, the Internet, software, CD-ROMs, commercial online services, etc. We've created a concise, one-page review of each resource. Each review contains information about the resource (author, publisher, edition, etc.), describes the resource's content and focus, evaluates the quality, style, comprehensiveness, and effectiveness of the resource, and summarizes its findings in several graphic "Star" ratings (1-4 Stars). We expand these ratings with written evaluations explaining the rationale behind our ratings and providing guidance on how each source can be best applied. We also provide prices and "where to buy" information for each product.

We put a great deal of time and effort into reviewing and evaluating each source carefully. Here's what that process includes:

- **Printed Guidebooks:** For these resources, we read the book from cover to cover, identify the particular focus taken by each author, and make a judgment about how the book's contents could be best applied to the college choice and admissions process. Our judgment about the relative quality of each source is based upon readability, organization, depth, and style. We make every effort to ensure that the latest editions of books are reviewed.

- **Internet Websites & Online Services:** We review all websites and online services that have any significant amount of original material related to college choice and admissions. Our reviews include judgments about the site's graphic and navigation design, as well as the usefulness of material provided relative to that available in other media. We don't review "college-oriented" sites which don't have relevant material. We revisit sites frequently to stay abreast of changes and improvements.

- **CD-ROM & Software:** We carefully review each facet of each CD, including all branches and multimedia options, and thoroughly test software applications available on disk. Our reviews include judgments about the "cost/benefit" of multimedia additions, as well as the usefulness of the content provided relevant to the same offering in other media by the same publisher. We note technical problems in loading or using programs provided.

Because our mission is to help you find your way through this "forest" of information sources, we also provide you with our recommendations on which resources are best to help you each step of the way (roughly 20% of sources reviewed are recommended). Our recommendations are based upon our judgment of value, not only relative to alternatives in the same media, but against all available sources regardless of media.

Resource Pathways On The Internet

We maintain a website which can be accessed at http://www.sourcepath.com. There, you can browse or buy this and other directories, exchange views and comments with other parents and students, provide us with feedback, and take advantage of other services. Hope to see you online soon!

Section II Recommended Resources

Introduction

In this chapter, we take a thoughtful look at all the resources we've reviewed, and pick just a few that we think are the best for you. This section
provides you with our recommendations for resources we think you will
find particularly helpful as you work through the process of selecting colleges to apply to. Certain resources are more helpful early in that process
and others are more helpful later. We've categorized our suggestions accordingly.

In making these recommendations, we have attempted to err on the side
of providing too many choices rather than too few. In some cases we have
recommended additional sources to broaden representation from different
media. Take some time to read the full descriptions and evaluations for
each recommended source carefully; we're certain that you will discover
the right resources to best serve your needs.

GAINING AN OVERVIEW OF THE COLLEGE SELECTION & ADMISSIONS PROCESS

Well, here you are in the middle of your junior year of high school, and you want to go to college, and you haven't got a clue where to start. Or, you're the parent of this lucky high school student, and this is your first experience in helping a child work through this "college decision;" you may think you already know what's best for your child, or you may want to stand aside and let him (or her) make this decision his own by doing his own research.

In either case, this can be a pretty intimidating place to be. This is a "BIG" decision, one that carries a price tag that can range from $10,000 to ten times that amount. And, the popular perception is that one's choice of college can affect one's entire life thereafter. Certainly **everyone** wants to make the best possible decision.

Relax. Students, take these points to heart (parents, too!):

- Provided you don't put the whole thing off until late fall your senior year, you've got the time you need to do it right!

- There is a college that's just right for you, no matter what your grades, scores, activities, or interests; in fact, there are actually **several** (or more) colleges that are right for you! This "test" is easy because there is more than one right answer!

- Everything in life changes as we live it. Your feelings about that "perfect" major or that "perfect" college will probably change after you get there. And if it does, the good news is that you can change your mind. You can switch majors (most do, in fact). You can transfer to a different college or university (many do, in fact). The point is this: if you make the best decision you can **today** based on an honest assessment of your needs and plans, you will have made the best decision you can make. You **are** going to make the right decision for you at this point in time, so be happy about it going in!

- You don't have to do it by yourself. There are people who have been there before you who are happy to share what they know. Your parents, maybe. The college/career counselor at your high school. Your older friends or siblings. Ask, listen, learn!

- This isn't rocket science. When it's all over, you'll ask yourself what the fuss was all about.

To help ease your anxieties, we've selected several resources we think can be especially helpful to students and parents who are starting this process for the first time, and who would like to gain an overview of what the process entails, start to finish. Read these reviews, and pick the resource that sounds most helpful to you.

50 College Admission Directors Speak To Parents

Author/Editor: Sandra F. MacGowan and Sarah M. McGinty

Publisher: Books for Professionals, Inc.

Edition Reviewed: 1st (1988)

Internet URL:

Media Type: Print

Price: $8.95

ISBN: 0-15-601595-1

RATINGS (1-4 STARS):

Overall:	★★★★	Excellent general reference on admissions process
Breadth Of Content:	★★★★	Covers all elements, with emotional support for students and parents
Value Added:	★★★★	50 responses to questions posed to nationwide admissions directors
Ease Of Use:	★★★★	Very organized and easy to read; narratives are short and to the point

DESCRIPTION:

The authors compiled this book based upon questions from parents. These questions were then posed to 50 admission directors of colleges across the country. Each chapter of this 267 page book includes a 1 to 3 page overview by the authors on the subject matter and then several responses from the admissions directors to these questions. The first 2 chapters give a basic overview of what is included in the rest of the book. Chapters 3 and 4 deal primarily with selecting colleges and narrowing down the choices. Chapter 5 discusses what happens in the admission committees. Chapters 6, 7 and 8 discuss elements of the application, namely, the importances of test scores, the high school record, and the college essay. Chapter 9 then offers suggestions on how to make the most of interviews, campus visits and independent college consultants such as counselors. Chapter 10 relates financial aid advice and financing options. Chapter 11 highlights special schools and programs for special students, such as minorities, learning disabled, etc. Chapters 12, 13 and 14 then discuss acceptance and rejection offers, transfer possibilities, and how to ease the transition from high school to college.

EVALUATION:

This book should ease the minds of many parents. Many questions that arise during the arduous process of selecting and applying to colleges are answered here by authorities who make that all-important decision - the admissions directors. Responses to typical concerns are presented here in a non-condescending style; these admission directors genuinely want to help make a good match between their colleges and students. Too often, other books present check-off calendars and offer suggestions to parents without keeping in mind that students play an important role too. Throughout this book, both sides are given credibility and support. In particular, chapters 5 through 8 serve to make the application process a bonding opportunity between parents and student. Students are encouraged to take on more responsibility with the parent as a guide and model. Most books also neglect the impact on students and parents after the student enrolls at a given college. Chapter 13 is a must-read for all students and parents as it details how to make the college transition easier for all. In particular, the authors list for students certain routines and habits that will help start the school year right. The authors also help parents understand how to allow students to develop meaningful new adult relationships and life skills.

WHERE TO FIND/BUY:

Bookstores and libraries.

Getting Into College

★★★

Author/Editor: R. Fred Zuker (Consultant)
Publisher: College Admission Productions
Edition Reviewed: 1989
Internet URL: http://www.dn.net/NACAC

Media Type: Videotape
Price: $32.95
ISBN:

RATINGS (1-4 STARS):

Overall:	★★★	Good introduction to the process and terminology; positive tone & style
Breadth Of Content:	★★★	Strong on all elements of getting into college, except financial aid
Value Added:	★★★	Broad, effective coverage of college selection & admission
Ease Of Use:		Not applicable

DESCRIPTION:

This videotape runs roughly 45 minutes; it follows a high school student through the college selection and admissions process, A-Z (junior year through acceptance), with the student's college counselor giving advice and instruction throughout. Five "real" (not actors) college admission counselors also provide advice and counsel in short clips interspersed throughout the video. Subjects covered include the gamut: what's important during high school, how to decide which schools to apply to, the college visit and interview, the application (including what's important and how to write an effective essay), and how to make a final decision.

EVALUATION:

This videotape provides a very good overview of the college selection and admissions process. The narrative is well written and delivered at a pace which can be followed easily. The student, his family, and his high school counselor are presented in a positive, caring, constructive light. The information content of the video is thorough in its breadth, and provides many lists, tips, hints, questions, and instructions along the way. By its nature, however, the information provided is not as deep as can be provided by the better print options available. This video provides value as a "starting point" for students and families starting the college selection and admissions process. It includes a good overview of each stage of the process, introduces much of the terminology likely to be encountered, and provides reassurance, with its positive style, that "Getting Into College" can be a positive experience readily managed by the typical high school student.

WHERE TO FIND/BUY:

Order from the National Association Of College Admission Counselors @ 703-836-2222.

College Guide For Parents

★★★

Author/Editor: Charles J. Shields
Publisher: College Board Publications
Edition Reviewed: 3rd (1995)
Internet URL:

Media Type: Print
Price: $14
ISBN: 0-87447-474-4

RATINGS (1-4 STARS):

Overall:	★★★	A very helpful resource to parents of college-bound students
Breadth Of Content:	★★★★	Very broad in its treatment of the whole spectrum of issues
Value Added:	★★★	Some chapters stronger than others, but all have value
Ease Of Use:	★★★	Style and tone targeted at parents; lots of short chapters a helpful tool

DESCRIPTION:

This 180+ page book, written by an experienced high school counselor, provides a thorough overview of virtually the entire spectrum of issues involved in the decision to go to college: the high school years, the process of self-assessment and discovery involved in finding the right group of colleges to apply to, the application process itself, and other issues. The book is addressed to parents of students making these decisions, and reflects this perspective. After a chapter which offers methods to help crystallize reasons why college may or may not be the right next step after high school, the book offers two chapters focused on a college preparation calendar and on high school coursework. Several chapters are provided on the college choice process, including a chapter focused on athletes, minorities, and the disabled. The admissions process is given several chapters, including perspectives on admissions tests, applications, and how Admissions Committees work. A chapter is focused on a thorough treatment of the world of college financial aid. Finally, the book goes past getting admitted, with chapters discussing college housing issues, separation anxiety, and the first year at college.

EVALUATION:

This resource is addressed to parents of students considering going to college. It's writing style and reassuring tone reflects this point of view, and as such can be very helpful to "first-time" parents of college-bound students. Some chapters are more helpful than others, but all can be useful to parents intimidated by the process, the terminology, and the myths of the college search and admissions process. For example, the first chapter provides some useful aids to help parents and students decide why college might (or might not be) be the right step after high school. The chapter on making the right college choice is focused on issues the author believes are important in focusing the college search, including distance from home and admissions selectivity; particularly helpful to the parent is the reassurance that most students can get into most colleges, with only 200 or so brutally competitive. Chapters on applications, admissions, and financial aid are thin relative to more specialized books, but nonetheless provide a helpful overview. Most helpful are the final chapters which focus on such potentially troubling issues as college housing alternatives, and preparing for and dealing with separation anxiety. This book can be a reassuring companion to parents throughout this time of transition and decision-making for their sons and daughters.

WHERE TO FIND/BUY:

Bookstores and libraries, direct from the publisher by calling 800-323-7155, or on the World Wide Web at http://www.collegeboard.org.

Handbook For College Admissions

★★★

Author/Editor: Thomas C. Hayden

Publisher: Peterson's Guides

Edition Reviewed: 4th (1995)

Internet URL: http://www.petersons.com

Media Type: Print

Price: $14.95

ISBN: 1-56079-428-3

RATINGS (1-4 STARS):

Overall:	★★★	A useful overview resource, particularly for parents
Breadth Of Content:	★★★★	One resource that tries (and largely succeeds) to cover it all
Value Added:	★★★	Valuable perspectives and advice from this veteran of the process
Ease Of Use:	★★	Lots of small text, lots of topics, lots of reading

DESCRIPTION:

The author has extensive experience in admissions and counseling, on both the college side and the high school side. This 270+ page guidebook is made up of 10 chapters, covering the entire spectrum from college selection and admissions, to financial aid, to acceptance and freshman year adjustments. The book opens with some self-assessment exercises, then moves into the process of choosing colleges, including college visits. After a chapter explaining test (ACT/SAT) timing and test-taking strategy, the author focuses on college applications (including tips on creating a differentiating edge and constructing a powerful, integrated application). Financial aid gets a chapter, with the usual terminology explained and some aid evaluation tips included. The eighth chapter is for parents, offering some perspectives and advice on college choice and how/when to help and/or stay out of the process. The book closes with chapters devoted to the spectrum of outcomes and actions that can occur with acceptance and rejection by colleges; a final chapter offer perspectives and advice for the freshman year.

EVALUATION:

With breadth as a primary objective, most guidebooks have to trade off in-depth coverage; so it is with this book. The corollary questions which then pop up are: when can the book be valuable, and where should lack of depth be covered by other resources? We like this book's tone, which is serious, supportive, and addressed to parents as much as students; it could serve particularly well as a reference for parents to use to educate themselves broadly on the college search and admissions process. Strengths? The chapter on college visits gives two really helpful examples of effective and ineffective interviews. Chapters on test-taking and "developing an edge" in college applications are particularly strong. The chapter addressed to parents ("The Myth Of College & Success") provides some useful and frank opinions on parents' roles. Weaknesses? We've found other resources that do a better job of guiding students through the process of evaluating college decision factors; financing the costs of college is covered more thoroughly in books focused solely on that subject. All things considered, we'd recommend this resource to parents and students wanting a good overview and reference to go back to as the process unfolds.

WHERE TO FIND/BUY:

Bookstores and libraries, or direct from the publisher at 800-338-3282.

IDENTIFYING MAJORS & WHAT'S IMPORTANT TO YOU

Some high school juniors and seniors know what area of study they want to focus on in college, but the majority do not. In either case, that's perfectly OK!

For some of us, the process of self-discovery begins early (for some of us, it takes a lifetime). That includes, for those lucky enough to go to college, choosing a major area of study as initial preparation for our life's work. For some (accountants, engineers), a college major leads directly to specific skills essential for a chosen career. For others, college is simply a time for learning how to learn, how to think, how to communicate, how to make decisions – all these skills serve us well whatever our life's work becomes.

While still in high school, the most important thing to remember when deciding on a college major is: just **relax** a bit. While it can't hurt to have a focus on a specific major while generating your initial college list, it is not essential to have made a choice, either. You can change your mind after you get to college and sample some courses; in fact, **most** college students change their major while in college!

If you're a junior or senior in high school, an important point to keep in mind is that there really isn't a "minimum acceptable" state of thought about what you want to do with your life's work. It's OK if you haven't got a clue. Nonetheless, you'll benefit by giving it some thought before you begin to generate a list of colleges to look at more closely. When you think about it, some of the factors that will become important in choosing the right college for you may also influence your ultimate choice for your life's work and where you choose to live. Large university or small college? Engineering or liberal arts? Urban intensity or small town quiet for a campus setting? Liberal or conservative student body? Intense academic pressure or more relaxed "whole-man" approach?

If you think about these choices, and think about what they might imply for your life's work, you'll see that thinking about what's important to you during your college years is important (including a major area of academic study). So spend some time thinking about it. Make some tentative decisions. Sure, they're subject to change as you go through the process, but they will help you focus your search. You'll find it a worthwhile effort!

We've selected several resources that we think will be of particular help in focusing on what's important to you, including a possible major (or majors). Read these reviews and pick one or two. You'll be glad you took this extra step before you dive into the process of generating your initial list of colleges.

Guide To 150 Popular College Majors ★★★★

Author/Editor: Renee Gernand
Publisher: College Board Publications
Edition Reviewed: 1992
Internet URL:

Media Type: Print
Price: $16
ISBN: 0-87447-400-0

RATINGS (1-4 STARS):

Overall:	★★★★	Can't be beat for helping students understand their choices in majors
Breadth Of Content:	★★★	150 of the most common majors are included
Value Added:	★★★★	Descriptions are wholly original, readable, and very helpful
Ease Of Use:	★★★★	Well-organized, with good explanations of content and approach

DESCRIPTION:

This guidebook provides descriptions of the 150+ "most widely offered baccalaureate-level majors". The descriptions are written by professors teaching in each field, and are grouped under 17 general categories (humanities, physical sciences, engineering, etc.). An introduction to each of these broad categories provides an "overview of each field and describes differences between the various majors". The detailed description for each major follows a common format, describing interests and skills associated with success in the major, recommended high school education, typical courses, what the major is like, careers related to the major, and whom to contact for more information (associations, etc.). Two indexes are provided: a Careers index lists 150+ jobs and some of the majors that can be useful in preparing for a particular career; the Related Majors index provides an exhaustive list of other majors related to each specific major listed. An essay which puts choosing a major in perspective ("it's important enough to take seriously, but it's not irrevocable") is included, as are 12 anecdotal essays on choosing/changing majors, written by students.

EVALUATION:

This can be a wonderfully helpful book for high school students (and their parents) who are uncertain about picking a major as a point of focus for their college search. Most students in high school have some feelings about what they like and dislike, and this book can be very helpful in providing some definition to their college search plans. The introductory essay at the beginning of the book starts things out on the right foot by pointing out that the "major decision", while important, is not irrevocable and is, in fact, often changed during the course of getting a degree. The introductions to each broad category of majors provides a clear overview of fields of study within that general area of interest; this is useful reading, especially for those who haven't a clue about what they'd like to study. Profiles for each of the 150 majors are short, well-written, and provide helpful insights into what taking each major course of study will involve, what careers are typically related to each major, and what personal interests and skills are likely to match up well with each major. The Career index is also very helpful, showing in a very easy-to-use format which degrees most often lead to which jobs.

WHERE TO FIND/BUY:

Bookstores and libraries, direct from the publisher by calling 800-323-7155, or on the World Wide Web at http://www.collegeboard.org.

College Match

Author/Editor: Steven Antonoff, Ph.D. & Marie Friedemann Ph.D.
Publisher: Octameron Associates
Edition Reviewed: 4th (1996-97)
Internet URL:

Media Type: Print
Price: $7.50
ISBN: 1-57509-004-X

RATINGS (1-4 STARS):

Overall:	★★★★	Provides an excellent, and gentle, process of self-discovery and choice
Breadth Of Content:		Not applicable
Value Added:	★★★★	The authors' experience shows
Ease Of Use:	★★★	Worksheets and process require commitment but are worth it

---

DESCRIPTION:

The authors are experienced college admission officers and educational consultants; this book shares the methods they've developed over fifteen years of working with students making the college choice. The book follows a sequence of steps designed to lead students (and their parents) to suitable college choices. After a chapter which reassures the prospective college student about making this choice and debunks some myths, the authors provide a "self-survey" and three worksheets designed to help students develop their own admissions profile. This is followed by a chapter which identifies college characteristics that will be a good match to the personal profile just developed; thirteen factors such as size, student body qualities, academic environment, etc. are discussed and prioritized. Chapters follow which help students identify and compare college choices and manage college visits effectively. The chapters that follow deal with writing effective essays and understanding the admissions process. Appendices are provided suggesting college planning goals for each year in high school.

EVALUATION:

This book is an excellent choice for parents and students who want to take time for a thoughtful approach to the college selection process. The experience of these educational consultants shows through in the quality of their approach. We agree with the themes outlined in their preface; namely, that all students have colleges from which to choose, that the choice process does not have to be stressful, that a logical series of steps can make this process one of insight and discovery, and that choosing a college is a great "first test" of using personal values to make an important real-life choice. The writing style is gentle and easy to read. The worksheets, rankings, and questions are not overwhelming and can be completed easily. The process of self-discovery outlined in Chapter 2 is outstanding, and should really help students develop a picture of who they are and what's important to them. Chapter 3 is also very helpful in illuminating, and helping students rank, the typical college choice factors. After this preparatory work is done, the remaining research should be a much more positive and focused effort than it might otherwise be.

WHERE TO FIND/BUY:

Bookstores and libraries, or direct from the publisher by calling 703-836-5480.

FINDING COLLEGES BY MAJORS

Once you have a feeling for which major areas of study you're interested in, the next step is to identify some college alternatives that have strong programs in these areas of interest.

While it's relatively easy to generate lists of colleges which offer majors that you might be interested in, it's a bit bigger challenge to find out which colleges have particularly strong departments in selected academic areas. Many of the "all-inclusive" guidebooks provide indexes to colleges sorted by major. Most of the databases or CD-ROM based commercial programs purchased by many high schools can generate lists of colleges that offer selected majors, as do several online services and websites on the Internet.

But that's not good enough, unfortunately. What's necessary is to do a little more research to discover **which** of those colleges or universities have particularly **strong** academic departments. If you've taken the time to think about and decide on majors you're interested in, you don't want to stop short of doing this research.

So, here are some suggestions:

- Start with the college/career counselors at your high school. Their experience placing other students in prior years, along with the feedback they're received from those students, should generate some useful suggestions.

- If you, your family, and your friends have contacts having careers you're interested in, pick up the phone and do some networking. They'll be happy to talk to you and they'll give you an earful of opinions.

- Down the road, as you're making your final evaluations of schools on your preliminary list, be sure to ask for course catalogs and take a look at the courses that are actually offered by departments you're interested in. You'll be surprised at the range of quality and quantity of courses offered by different colleges **for the same major!**

- When you visit your "short list" of schools, be sure to make time to make an appointment with professors (and students!) who are active in the departments you're interested in. Ask them tough questions and listen to what they say.

We've included in the recommendations which follow a variety of resources that we've found particularly useful in helping students generate some initial lists of colleges with strong programs in selected majors. Good luck. And remember, you can **always** change your mind!

Rugg's Recommendations On The Colleges ★★★★

Author/Editor: Frederick E. Rugg

Publisher: Rugg's Recommendations

Edition Reviewed: 13th (1996)

Internet URL:

Media Type: Print

Price: $18.95

ISBN: 1-883062-09-8

RATINGS (1-4 STARS):

Overall:	★★★★	A "must have" for your first cut, if you know your planned major(s)
Breadth Of Content:	★★★	Includes 735 of the better schools in the country
Value Added:	★★★	Identifies the best departments at the quality colleges
Ease Of Use:	★★★★	Organized by major, college selectivity, and size

DESCRIPTION:

This guide, now in its 13th Edition, was developed to answer the question: "What are some good colleges that have strong programs in business, or engineering, or music (or whatever)?" 735 "quality" colleges are identified, including those with Phi Beta Kappa chapters, plus additional subjective choices (based on the author's, and his staff's, collective experiences). Ratings of the quality of various programs of study are primarily based on the input of current students (10,000+ interviews/surveys!), which the author argues is the most reliable source; he includes input from high school counselors, and the colleges themselves, as well. 39 undergraduate majors are listed separately, with 37 "miscellaneous" majors also listed. The listings are then organized into groups, based on college admissions selectivity (Most Selective - about 100 schools, Very Selective, and Selective); selectivity is determined on the measures of average high school GPAs and combined SAT scores. Finally, the size of each college is assigned to one of five categories, from Small (<1,000 students) to Extra Large (>20,000 students). An appendix provides average SAT-I scores for each college with a listing of its recommended majors.

EVALUATION:

For those students who have decided on, or have a strong inclination towards one or more possible majors in college, this guide is an excellent way to begin the process of creating that "first" list of alternatives. The guide includes a limited number of colleges, but includes enough high-quality choices to provide a good cross-section. Are their ratings of college degree programs reliable? Primarily based on input from current students, they're probably as good a place to begin as any; that this is the thirteenth edition is also of some comfort. What's particularly useful about this guide is that it is very easy to come up with an initial list of possible school choices, given some inkling of what majors you might be interested in, where your high school GPA and SAT score may place you on the "selectivity" scale, and how large an institution you want to attend. From this good start, other information sources can be used to learn more about each college alternative.

WHERE TO FIND/BUY:

Libraries and bookstores, or direct from the publisher at 805-462-2503.

College Finder

Author/Editor: Steven Antonoff, Ph.D.
Publisher: Ballantine Books
Edition Reviewed: 1993
Internet URL:

Media Type: Print
Price: $12.95
ISBN: 0-449-90772-4

RATINGS (1-4 STARS):

Overall:	★★★	An "alternative" resource for building an initial list for further research
Breadth Of Content:	★★★	There's a suggested list of colleges for virtually every interest or question
Value Added:	★★★	They're just lists, but a lot of thought and experience has built them
Ease Of Use:	★★★★	Well-organized, with helpful indexes

DESCRIPTION:

This 500 page guidebook contains 475 lists, principally rankings of colleges across the country against a huge variety of criteria. The lists are organized into 10 categories relevant to the student doing a preliminary search for colleges; the categories are admission, academics, quality, social, internationalism, careers, athletics, enrollment, cost, and "morsels." Lists provided range from "Great State Schools for the Student with Average Grades and Drive for College Success" to "Colleges That Own Their Own Golf Courses." The book's author is a 25-year veteran of the college selection & admission process, both as an Admissions Director and as a independent consultant; his stated goal for the book is "to expand the pool of schools that you should consider." The largely subjective lists were generated from a variety of sources: a survey of college counselors and consultants, college visits, previous students, college personnel, guidebooks, and his own experiences. A subject index which includes all specific topics covered is provided, as is an index of all colleges listed, with page references.

EVALUATION:

One of the big challenges facing students trying to generate their initial list of college alternatives, is that few resources exist to provide suggestions when certain criteria are of interest. This book can help solve that dilemma. The author's experience is extensive; many of these lists were developed while answering questions about prospective colleges posed by students and parents. While keeping in mind that the author's lists are highly subjective and therefore subject to debate, nonetheless his suggestions can be a helpful starting point for further research on college choices. The breadth of the topics covered by various lists should satisfy most inquiries. There are lists and more lists: "Best Colleges for Aspiring Artists" to "Hidden Treasures" ("..provide an excellent education and student experience but are not well known..") to "Colleges for the Shy Person" to "Colleges for the Fashion-Conscious Student" to "Top-Notch Low-Cost Colleges." There seems to be a list of suggested colleges satisfying virtually every question and interest, from campus safety to playing golf. We think this book, while now 3+ years old, is nonetheless a helpful resource for students facing the initially overwhelming variety of college choices.

WHERE TO FIND/BUY:

Bookstores and libraries. Amazon.com notice as of 8/96: "Though not officially "out of print," this item is "out of stock indefinitely" at the publisher."

National Review College Guide ★★★

Author/Editor: Charles Sykes & Brad Miner (Editors)
Publisher: Simon & Schuster (A Fireside Book)
Edition Reviewed: 2nd (1993)
Internet URL:

Media Type: Print
Price: $13
ISBN: 0-671-79801-4

RATINGS (1-4 STARS):

Overall:	★★★	A excellent resource, provided your focus is a liberal arts education
Breadth Of Content:	★★	Only 58 schools meet the editors' criteria
Value Added:	★★★★	The focus of the book, and the writing style, is original and evaluative
Ease Of Use:	★★★★	Listed alphabetically, with an index by state

DESCRIPTION:

In its second edition, the National Review guide takes a unique approach to the question of deciding where to go to college: it applies a narrow set of criteria to the universe of college alternatives, and comes up with a short list of just 58 schools it recommends for a quality liberal arts education. The criteria used are: faculty quality (they must actually teach undergraduates), quality of the core curriculum (courses focused on traditional language arts and sciences), and the quality of the intellectual environment (freedom from trendy, restrictive, or "politically correct" administrations or faculty). The profiles of schools recommended, each 3-4 pages, are focused on explaining how each school meets these criteria, giving frequent examples of their successes (such as acceptance rates in graduate programs averaging over 90%!). Also included is a explanation of why some 12 "famous" schools did not make the cut (they call it the "Academic Gulag"). Some essential statistics for each school are also included.

EVALUATION:

This guidebook is unique. It is focused solely on recommending only the very best schools for getting an liberal arts education. The editors are straightforward and precise about their criteria for selection, and stick to those criteria while rejecting such alternatives as Harvard and Yale. The 10 page preface is worth reading if for no other reason than to understand why a liberal arts education is an important alternative in this age of specialization, and why we should focus on schools where the faculty actually does the undergraduate teaching (as opposed to graduate student teaching assistants). The writing style is sophisticated and focused solely on how each school meets their criteria; no insight into student life or campus "feel" is offered. The schools selected are, for the most part, both private and expensive (the editors point out how far these schools will go with financial aid to attract the best students). If a liberal arts education is your priority, you can't go wrong using this as a resource; if not, its tight focus may not be particularly useful.

WHERE TO FIND/BUY:

Bookstores and libraries.

Cass & Birnbaum's Guide To American Colleges ★★★

Author/Editor: Julia Cass-Liepmann
Publisher: HarperCollins Publishers
Edition Reviewed: 17th
Internet URL:

Media Type: Print
Price: $19.95
ISBN: 0062734040

RATINGS (1-4 STARS):

Overall:	★★★	Among the better of the large, all-inclusive guides
Breadth Of Content:	★★★★	Typically strong, with 1,500 colleges profiled
Value Added:	★★★	Largely based on input from the colleges themselves; some innovations
Ease Of Use:	★★★	Well-organized, with useful indexes

DESCRIPTION:

This guidebook is a large one, with 1/2 page descriptions of some 1,500 colleges. Information included in these brief descriptions is similar to that typically supplied by colleges to all-encompassing guidebooks of this nature, including the usual summary statistics. Unique to this guide, and new to this edition, is a "College Selection Index." This index, organized by state, compares the colleges using a number of factors relating to four key questions: "What kind of education will I receive?" -- liberal arts, business, etc. "Can I get in?" -- "non-selective" to "most selective." "Can I afford it?" -- average annual cost, % of students receiving aid. "What will it be like when I get there?" -- comparisons shown for campus setting, undergrad enrollment, male/female mix, and campus life. Indexes are also supplied for religious orientation and for college majors, the latter including the unique feature of showing how many students recently received degrees.

EVALUATION:

This guidebook is one among roughly a half-dozen that are useful in generating that initial list of college alternatives. The descriptions of colleges are typical, based on material provided by the colleges themselves. But this guide has several wrinkles which set it apart somewhat from its crowd. First is an index based on religious orientation, with additional comments in the profiles on intensity of religious focus. They also include the typical index organized by college major, but add the very useful useful element of showing how many students received degrees in each major; this can help indicate the relative strength of major departments. Their "College Selection Index," listing colleges by state, is a useful way to compare some of the statistics (in this case roughly a dozen) that can be relevant to initial college selection -- it's easier to use this index than flip back and forth between pages of the profiles. The authors also provide a well-written introduction that explains why these particular statistics may be important to prospective college students as they create their initial list of alternatives.

WHERE TO FIND/BUY:

Libraries and bookstores.

MAKING YOUR INITIAL LIST OF COLLEGES

Anyone going to college can create an initial list of colleges to research further, based on their ideas about what they want to get out of their investment in college. Besides possible majors, before you begin you'll need to take some time to think carefully about what qualities (both tangible and intangible) this "home away from home" should have to make your next 4+ years happy and productive. Use your parents and your college counselor as a sounding board throughout this process, of course.

Think about these issues before you begin:

- **Selectivity.** Consider this an issue worth studying, but don't be too hard on yourself. Set your sights on a mix of alternatives that include "stretch" (more selective) schools, "safety" (less selective) schools, and colleges whose admission criteria seem well matched to your accomplishments.

- **Location & Surrounding Area.** Do you want to live close to home? Within driving distance? Want to try living in another part of the country or experiencing another climate? Do you want to go to school in the city, a suburb, or in the country?

- **Size.** The size of school can dramatically effect your experience. How about class size? Who teaches lower level classes? How much housing is provided? How many students commute?

- **Student Characteristics.** Coed? Conservative or liberal? Minorities? Large concentration of fraternity/sorority types? Religious affiliation?

- **Programs.** Sports programs? Faculty strength and teacher/student ratios? ROTC? Specialized degrees? Study abroad?

We've not ignored college cost or financial aid, critical issues for many families. However, if you're an above average student, you should place less emphasis on costs while making your initial choices, because many selective colleges compete using financial aid offers which fill the financing gap for good prospects. If you're an average student, you'll need to look at this factor more carefully before you set your sights on some private college alternatives.

If you're lucky, your high school has already invested in one of the better commercial college search programs. If so, give that a try first to see if its search capabilities are sufficient for your needs. If not, we've included a number of recommended resources in the section that follows. We've included quality choices from a variety of media (the Internet, CD-ROM, etc.). If you're interested in building a list of colleges offering programs to specialized **groups** (like women's or minority colleges, etc.) or assistance with specialized **needs** (learning disabled, etc.), please see the recommended resources in the next section, "Resources For Specialized Programs or Needs."

Just remember, when you're done creating an initial list, you'll still need to do more research to reduce this initial list down to a manageable number to first visit (if possible) and then complete applications for. Have fun!

Ivy League Programs At State School Prices   ★★★★

Author/Editor: Robert R. Sullivan   **Media Type:** Print
Publisher: Arco/Prentice Hall   **Price:** $15
Edition Reviewed: 1st (1994)   **ISBN:** 0-671-87426-8
Internet URL:

RATINGS (1-4 STARS):

Overall:	★★★★	Illuminating insights into Honors Programs at state universities
Breadth Of Content:	★★	Covers programs at just 55 state universities
Value Added:	★★★★	The profiles are wholly original, including program quality judgments
Ease Of Use:	★★★★	Easy to use and to read

DESCRIPTION:

This guidebook provides information on Honors Programs at 55 state universities (the "flagship" state universities, with some exceptions). An introductory chapter explains that these programs offer small classes, taught by professors, to a small number of academically qualified students. The result, according to the author: a "quality education at low prices." The author cautions that academically qualified usually means a B or better high school GPA and scores of 1,100+ on the SAT or 26+ on the ACT. A summary of basic information about each program is provided, along with 1-2 pages of narrative describing the program and its strengths and weaknesses. The process of application and selection is outlined, as are the courses offered, and how the program fits within the institution as a whole. The summary information includes subjective judgments by the author on factors he considers important to the quality of the various programs: town and campus settings, intellectual setting (including student diversity), the relative competitiveness of admission to the program, and the quality of the program itself. An overall rating of each program is provided (one to three Stars).

EVALUATION:

As the author states in the first sentence of his introduction, "This book is for academically talented high school juniors and seniors from families with moderate incomes." If this description fits you, then the universities and programs described in this book are worthy of review. The author makes a convincing argument that admission to one of these programs can result in an educational experience equal to or better than that available from more expensive private institutions. This book is a sincere and serious effort to both identify these programs nationally, and provide some evaluative judgments on the relative quality of the various programs profiled; the profiles are based on lengthy phone interviews and research. The profiles provided are written in an engaging, easy-to-read style.

WHERE TO FIND/BUY:

Find at bookstores and libraries.

College Board Online

★★★★

Author/Editor:

Publisher: The College Board

Edition Reviewed:

Internet URL: http://www.collegeboard.org

Media Type: Internet

Price:

ISBN:

RATINGS (1-4 STARS):

Overall:	★★★★	A "must-see" site for their ExPAN college database
Breadth Of Content:	★★★★	The ExPAN database includes all 2 and 4 year colleges
Value Added:	★★★	Value concentrated in ExPAN and college information therein
Ease Of Use:	★★★★	A well-designed website; nice graphics, well organized

DESCRIPTION:

This is a large website, second only in breadth to Peterson's site. The site has been developed with the Educational Testing Service, and thus emphasizes services like SAT preparation and registration. As for offerings related to the process of selecting colleges, the site provides a page of services for students and parents (largely services related to SAT preparation and financial aid); a comprehensive college search facility, using their "ExPAN" system, is included. Multiple criteria are available for searches: geographic, majors, general (size, setting), student life (housing, etc.), admissions/aid, special programs, advanced placement, and sports. An exhaustive list of choices is available for each criteria, and all can be combined in a search. Information provided for each college is generous, roughly a dozen pages of stats and basic information, some reprinted from their guidebook, "The College Handbook." The site provides an extensive online store, which contains thumbnail descriptions of the complete line of College Board publications (including software and video titles); these books can be ordered online with a credit card (secure if a Netscape browser is used), or by calling an 800 number.

EVALUATION:

The best feature of this site is the The College Board's ExPAN database (ExPAN is one of the better commercial systems sold to high school career/counseling centers). It's been implemented recently, and the site notes that its career-planning module will be added in the future. In a word, the ExPAN database as implemented here is the most comprehensive college search facility available online. That comprehensiveness extends to the number of colleges in the database (all 2/4 year schools), the number of search variables and values available, and the amount of information provided for each school. This said, users of this facility have to be careful in using the power of their search engine: specify too many variables, and it eliminates all the colleges. But, if used with care, this site can be used to generate a pretty good initial list of colleges of interest (with the caveat, of course, to do lots more research using evaluative guidebooks, campus visits, talks with counselors and others, etc.). Additional value on the site is concentrated in services related to SAT preparation. The comprehensive online store offers the broad line of College Board books, videos, and software, which can be valuable if one can't find their resources elsewhere. They use Netscape's SSL protocol for encryption of credit card information; for other browsers, an 800 number is offered. This site really shows the value of the Internet realized in practical, time and money saving terms.

WHERE TO FIND/BUY:

Find on the WorldWideWeb using the URL: http://www.collegeboard.org. Orders from the online bookstore can be placed online (securely, with Netscape browsers), or are available direct at 800-323-7155.

Four-Year Colleges

★★★

Author/Editor: Peterson's Guides
Publisher: Peterson's Guides
Edition Reviewed: 1995
Internet URL: http://www.petersons.com

Media Type: Print
Price: $19.95
ISBN: 1-56079-364-3

RATINGS (1-4 STARS):

Overall:	★★★	Among the better of the all-inclusive tomes, but no subjective assessments
Breadth Of Content:	★★★★	Contains basic profiles on 2,000+ colleges and supplements on 800+
Value Added:	★★★	They've got more goodies and indexes than most, but nothing evaluative
Ease Of Use:	★★★	If you can carry it, you can use it easily

DESCRIPTION:

Peterson's Four-Year Colleges is one of a half-dozen all-inclusive guidebooks, in this case covering 2,000 four year colleges. At the core of the guidebook are roughly 1/2 page (VERY small type) profiles of each college, supplied by the colleges, which contain basic information and statistics. Supplements to these profiles are also included, for some 800+ colleges. These supplements provide 1-2 pages of additional descriptive information, also supplied by the schools, containing descriptive information about each school, its location, majors and degrees, academic facilities, faculty, and a number of other topics. Peterson's also includes four indexes: a state-by state summary table (enrollment, SAT/ACT scores, etc.), the colleges' self-ranking (from Most Difficult to Non-Competitive), a listing of the colleges by cost (from <$2,000 to >$20,000), and a listing of all colleges offering each of 450+ majors). Inside the covers, Peterson has also bound a 12-page color magazine ("Inside College") and a 3-1/4" DOS disk (the "college application planner") which includes the basic college profiles.

EVALUATION:

There are roughly a half-dozen large, all-inclusive printed college guides out there, each of which contains basic information and stats about the four-year colleges, in every case supplied by the colleges themselves and in no case providing any evaluative input. They're all useful for constructing a first cut at possibilities for colleges, and Peterson's, in our opinion, is one of the better from this group. Why? Because it does provide some supplemental information on some 800+ colleges, and it has most of the indexes that can prove useful in comparing colleges to your academic interests and profiles. Just recognize that when it comes down to paring your list down to those schools meriting further research, you'll need to go elsewhere to find someone willing to state an opinion about a school or provide some original insight.

WHERE TO FIND/BUY:

Bookstores and libraries, or direct from the publisher at 800-338-3282.

College Handbook

★★★

Author/Editor: The College Entrance Examination Board
Publisher: College Board
Edition Reviewed: 1996
Internet URL:

Media Type: Print
Price: $20
ISBN: 0-87447-506-6

RATINGS (1-4 STARS):

Overall:	★★★	One of the better of the all-inclusive guides, particularly for its indexes
Breadth Of Content:	★★★★	It's got all accredited two and four year colleges listed
Value Added:	★★	Not much; the usual basic facts provided by the schools themselves
Ease Of Use:	★★★	Very large, but well organized; many useful indexes

---

DESCRIPTION:

The College Handbook is one of the half-dozen or so all-inclusive guidebooks; this one contains all the accredited two and four year colleges in the country (3,215!), as well as the largest number of indexes of any in this class of guidebook. The information shown for each college, listed by state, is typical to this kind of guidebook, a half page or so of basic descriptive text and the usual statistics. This guide includes 20+ pages of essays on choosing a college and paying for college; the essays are supplemented with short profiles written by students about their recent experiences in selecting their college. 30+ indexes are included in the guidebook: 6 focused on general colleges (two year vs. four year, men/women only, etc.), 9 focused on specialized colleges (agricultural, art/music, business, engineering, etc.), 8 organized by campus environment (small, medium, large, etc.), ROTC indexes, Hispanic/black indexes, and more. A glossary and a "How to use The College Handbook" section are included as well.

EVALUATION:

This is one of the more useful of the all-inclusive guides, which as a group are helpful early in the college selection process. The many indexes are useful in creating an initial list of college selections, provided you have some strong feelings about a factor addressed by one of the indexes (small or large, men/women only, those specializing in certain degrees, ROTC, etc.). The "Choosing A College" essay, 15 pages long, is particularly useful in helping get the initial search process organized. A number of helpful checklists/questionaire's are included in this essay, as are a number of insightful profiles written by students about their own reasons for picking the college they selected. This is one of the better of the large guides; just remember that you'll need to consult with other resources to find original insight into what life might really be like at the schools you're interested in.

WHERE TO FIND/BUY:

Bookstores and libraries, direct from the publisher by calling 800-323-7155, or on the World Wide Web at http://www.collegeboard.org.

Kaplan On Campus '96 ★★★

Author/Editor:	**Media Type:** CD-ROM
Publisher: Meetinghouse Technologies	**Price:** $49.95
Edition Reviewed: 1996	**ISBN:** 0-671-05323-X
Internet URL:	

RATINGS (1-4 STARS):

Overall:	★★★	A useful CD-ROM; easy-to-use search engine helps with initial picks
Breadth Of Content:	★★★★	Basic information on 1,700 colleges provided, with 300 video clips, etc.
Value Added:	★★★	Great search engine; college data provided is limited
Ease Of Use:	★★★★	A really well-designed CD-ROM; effective use of multimedia

DESCRIPTION:

For Mac (7.1+; 68030+) and Windows (3.1+; 486/25+). This is Kaplan's new 5-disk CD-ROM set, with a database of 1,700 schools accessible by state, alpha, or search (5 regions are on different CDs). The search engine uses up to nine variables (selectivity, majors, location, cost, affiliation, size, setting, athletics, special services); choices are explained with a short video. As choices are made, the number of schools meeting the criteria are indicated. A separate facility is available to help select a major; nine major "clusters" are described, as are 100+ individual majors. Selecting personal abilities/tasks builds a list of suggested majors; a similar process is used to suggest career choices. Over 300 videos are available, as are campus maps. A financial aid reference includes an overview, details of federal and state sources of aid (for states, a listing of agencies is provided), and financial planning tools for estimating financial aid, loans, etc. Software to produce the Common Application (accepted at many schools) is included. Kaplan's "Guide To College Admissions" (print guidebook) is included.

EVALUATION:

This is an excellent tool for developing an initial list of college choices. The program indicates how many schools meet the criteria specified, an excellent way to fine-tune a search: for example, selecting no majors is better than two or three majors as possibilities, as the latter case requires that schools have ALL majors chosen to be listed. The videos are fun to watch, but basically convey no real information (not enough time); same for the campus maps (not enough detail); with a database this size, little else should be expected. Maneuvering within the database is eased by clicking on states or an alpha listing. College data provided is limited to statistics and lists. The processes provided to help identify majors or careers should be used just as a starting point at best; books focused on majors or careers will probably be more helpful. The financial aid section provides useful, but limited overviews. The financial aid estimator is a good tool for generating a quick estimate of expected student and parent contribution, given input for income, assets, etc. Helpful documentation is provided, as is online, context-sensitive video help. The "Guide To College Admissions" booklet is a useful additional resource; it's well organized, easy to read, and provides a lot of helpful information on essays, recommendations, interviews, etc.

WHERE TO FIND/BUY:

Bookstores and libraries, direct from the publisher at 800-527-4836, or on the Web at http://www.kaplan.com.

CollegeXpress

★★★

Author/Editor:

Publisher: Carnegie Communications, Inc.

Edition Reviewed:

Internet URL: http://www.collegexpress.com

Media Type: Internet

Price:

ISBN:

RATINGS (1-4 STARS):

Overall:	★★★	A good source for basic information about 400+ private institutions
Breadth Of Content:	★★★	400+ private college/university profiles and data offered
Value Added:	★★★	Useful essays, helpful information provided
Ease Of Use:	★★★	Nicely designed website, with good tools to get to lots of information

---

DESCRIPTION:

This is a large website that is the online counterpart of the magazine, Private Colleges & Universities (various editions of this magazine profile some 400+ institutions; it's distributed to 1.3 million college-bound high school students each spring). The site includes a comprehensive (but optional) registration form that is used to fulfill requests for college information made on the site. The principal feature of the site is a database of the college profiles included in their magazine, searchable by region, alphabetically, or keyword, or with a "profile search" (uses major, region, size, tuition, sports, and religious affiliation as variables). For each college found, a two page narrative (provided by the college) is provided, with pictures of campus scenes. Complete statistical information (from the College Board database) for each college is also available (degrees and majors offered, data on admissions, athletics, expenses, financial aid, etc.). A number of essays are offered on admissions topics, as are threaded discussion forums with counselors. Several books, and the magazines themselves, are featured as well, with ordering information included.

EVALUATION:

If you're interested in attending a private college or university, you'll want to visit this website. On this site you'll find profiles (written by the colleges themselves, and thereby promotive in tone) and data (from the College Board database) on some 400+ private colleges and universities across the country. The search facilities to find colleges of interest works well. Registration, while comprehensive, is optional; it's used by the company to forward requests for more information to colleges of interest to the student. The numerous essays, on a variety of topics relevant to the college search and admissions process, are useful and well written (even those that promote private institutions over the public school alternatives). Additional information from schools can be requested easily. The negatives? Well, the universe of institutions covered is limited, and to private colleges and universities at that, excluding the very worthwhile universe of public school alternatives. The college profiles provided are, of course, universally flattering. And there are some gaps in coverage, too. Nonetheless, we're recommending this resource because it's free and easy to use. Treat it as just one source of information to generate an initial list of colleges that interest you, however.

WHERE TO FIND/BUY:

On the World Wide Web, using the URL: http://www.collegexpress.com.

Peterson's College Database

Author/Editor: Peterson's Guides

Publisher: Peterson's

Edition Reviewed:

Internet URL:

Media Type: Online Service

Price:

ISBN:

RATINGS (1-4 STARS):

Overall:	★★★	Helpful to the initial search process; minimal college info provided
Breadth Of Content:	★★★★	Includes all 3,400 U.S. and Canadian two and four year colleges
Value Added:	★★★	Information provided is minimal; the search engine is really helpful
Ease Of Use:	★★★	Text-based with some improvements needed, but great search selectivity

DESCRIPTION:

Found on: CompuServe. This online site provides the same basic college profile information contained in Peterson's printed guidebooks on Two-Year and Four-Year Colleges. What's unique about this service is its ability to support searches of this large database, using up to 38 college characteristics, grouped within 8 primary categories: Location, Costs, Admission Difficulty, Majors Offered, Number of Students, Type of College (2/4 year, public/private), Campus Setting, and Student Mix (ethic, gender). Using this ability, you can produce as large or as small a list as you wish. For each college returned by a search, the database provides basic information on the college, its academic program, student life and housing, athletics, cost, and financial aid. None of the typical statistics or indexes are provided.

EVALUATION:

We've reviewed the printed version of this database, and Peterson's Internet Web Site as well. Of the three, this product is perhaps most limited in features. The printed version, for example, provides supplemental information on some 800+ colleges; these profiles enhance the limited pictures drawn by the basic information provided through this service. The printed version also provides numerous indexes and other materials. What distinguishes this service, and strongly recommends it, is the ability it provides for a college-bound student to spend some time building a list of choices on location, size, admissions difficulty, campus setting, etc. -- the resulting listing of colleges then produced by the database can save a student hours of flipping through pages, reading indexes, and creating list after list of alternatives. What this database provides is a shortcut to a student's initial list of target schools. That's very helpful. Nonetheless, when it's time to cut this initial list down to size, you'll still need to go other sources which provide some evaluative feedback on the college choices they review.

WHERE TO FIND/BUY:

Find on Compuserve, in the Education subject area.

CollegeAssist

★★★

Author/Editor:

Publisher: edworks, inc.

Edition Reviewed:

Internet URL: http://www.edworks.com

Media Type: Internet

Price:

ISBN:

RATINGS (1-4 STARS):

Overall:	★★★	Definitely worth a visit; an ambitious site focused on college admissions
Breadth Of Content:	★★★	Very broad subject coverage, sometimes not deep without paying the fee
Value Added:	★★★	The searchable database is as useful as we've seen; no evaluative comments
Ease Of Use:	★★★	Quick navigation, well designed and useful

DESCRIPTION:

This is a large website, focused almost exclusively on the process of selecting and applying to colleges. As such, it's practically unique. Its Home Page has six principle areas: College Research, Personal Organizer, Financial Aid, Personal Profile, Admission Test, and Application Essays. Each area has features available to "guests," and each page has additional services available for a single $39 fee (good for 12 months). The "free" features for the College Research area are substantial: guests can search a database (supplied by College Research Group) of 3,000 colleges using a number of criteria "sets" (admissions, sports, costs, majors, etc.), with results available by region. The facts provided for each college by CRG are comprehensive. Links to college home pages are provided (and organized by state). The free areas for the remainder of the site consist largely of lists of tips and short essays (tips on writing essays, descriptions of types of financial aid, etc.); taking advantage of the full complement of features in these areas requires payment of the fee. Several features profiled (essay evaluation, scholarship search) require additional fees. Some links to related websites are provided.

EVALUATION:

This comprehensive website is worth a visit for sure, simply because such a large percentage of its content is focused on selecting and getting into colleges. The college database output (statistics) is quite comprehensive, well formatted, and easy to navigate, equal to alternatives we've found anywhere else; the trick is that the search engine is much less flexible (and results can't be saved) in the "free" area. After payment of the fee, search "sets" can be retained, refined, and compared. The Personal Organizer is virtually unavailable without payment of the fee, but when paid for provides a comprehensive integrated planning and reminder calendar. The Personal Profile area, after payment of the fee, provides a very useful tool for building a documented profile of the student, all retained by the CollegeAssist database for later use (an online common application form is planned, for example). The principal value-added feature of the paid portion of the "Essays" section is a $49 service of essay evaluation. The Financial Aid section's principal feature is material provided by the National Scholarship Research Service (which costs $75). Too commercial? Sometimes. Do we recommend paying the fee? It's too close to call -- the database facilities and the personal organizer would be worth it to some, while other features may lack practical application for others. But, visit this fine site and decide for yourself!

WHERE TO FIND/BUY:

On the Internet at the URL: http://www.edworks.com.

CollegeNet   ★★★

Author/Editor: **Media Type:** Internet
Publisher: Universal Algorithms, Inc.   **Price:**
Edition Reviewed: **ISBN:**
Internet URL: http://www.collegenet.com

RATINGS (1-4 STARS):

Overall:	★★★	A site worth visiting for its search capabilities and specialized lists
Breadth Of Content:	★★★	Comprehensive database, limited information on non-linked colleges
Value Added:	★★	Additional value provided by search engine and supplemental college data
Ease Of Use:	★★	Well-organized; response time OK

DESCRIPTION:

Much is included in this website; the publishers have a database of about 3,000 colleges. With this as a foundation, the site supports searches, with up to four variables: state, enrollment size, tuition range, and majors; you can also search for a college by name. The search pulls up a listing of schools with basic contact information; links are provided to college home pages if available. "Featured" schools (currently 8) provide additional admissions-oriented information; schools with home pages are linked as well. An online application to selected schools is being developed, but is still noted as being for "demonstration purposes only." The site offers listings of specialized schools (Catholic, Ivy League, Women's, Historically Black, etc.). Listings of academic resource links and information about financial aid are included also. Users of the site can also complete a request form which will bring more information from selected colleges and advertisers. Recent additions to the site include a planetarium, a notice about impending college-oriented magazines, a search capability for schools in Canada/New Zealand/Australia, and a $5,000 scholarship.

EVALUATION:

This is a useful site, particularly for its ability to search its database, for example, for all undergraduate colleges in Oregon that have less than 5,000 students and cost no more than $10,000/year. The listing returned from such a search is a useful beginning but provides just basic contact information. The links to colleges' home pages are helpful as well, with the usual variations in quality and relevance found in those home pages (some colleges provide additional information focused solely on admissions). The listings of specialized schools and graduate programs are helpful (although just a list of colleges names by state), too, as are hypertext links to financial aid information resident on the Internet. The site is managed as a commercial site by Universal Algorithms, a provider of scheduling software to colleges; the site is supported by colleges' purchases of additional listings and services. The value of this site is concentrated in its database, search engine, and specialized listings -- the information gleaned from time spend "on site" is just a starting point for college research.

WHERE TO FIND/BUY:

Find on the WorldWideWeb using the URL: http://www.collegenet.com

RESOURCES FOR SPECIALIZED PROGRAMS OR NEEDS

One of the wonderful aspects of the American system of higher education is the amazing diversity of alternatives that are available to high school students from all walks of life, having diverse interests and aspirations. To this potential demand for a variety of college alternatives, add the capacity of educational institutions to supply specialized programs to meet this demand, and you have a happy match!

If you're one of those students interested in pursuing a highly focused higher education (in filmmaking or dance, for example), or a minority student interested in a college environment made up of your peers, or an athlete that wants to maximize the return on your athletic skills, you should feel confident that you can find a number of college alternatives that are right for you. If you need to find out about colleges with particularly helpful programs for learning disabled students, you'll be successful in your search, too.

The good news is that publishers of college guides and resources have responded well to these specialized interests and needs, and have published a number of guidebooks addressed to these groups of college students.

You should include additional time in your college search schedule to allow for extra research into these specialized programs and environments. You'll need to spend more time on the phone and more time on campus to help you understand the differences between colleges that **say** they have the specialized commitment you need, and those that have **proven** they do. Ask for the names of currently enrolled students, or students that have recently graduated. Call them up and ask them how their experiences matched their expectations. Visit campuses if you can, and talk to currently enrolled students; compare the printed hype with the in-person realities you find.

We've reviewed a number of resources that are focused on specialized programs (women's, black, or native American colleges, colleges with strong performing arts programs, etc.) or specialized needs (colleges with programs for the learning disabled, etc.). You can find the best of those resources in the pages that follow. We've included as many quality resources as we could find, to help ensure sufficient coverage for as many interests and needs as possible.

Performing Arts Major's College Guide   ★★★★

Author/Editor: Carol J. Everett	**Media Type:** Print
Publisher: Macmillan USA	**Price:** $20.00
Edition Reviewed: 2nd (1994)	**ISBN:** 0-671-88417-4
Internet URL:	

RATINGS (1-4 STARS):

Overall:	★★★★	Comprehensive resource for aspiring performers
Breadth Of Content:	★★★	Covers 300+ programs worldwide
Value Added:	★★★★	The author's experience with Julliard School shows
Ease Of Use:	★★★★	Easy to read with a handy index

DESCRIPTION:

This guidebook, written by the former Director of Admissions for The Julliard School, provides information on 300+ colleges, universities and conservatories worldwide with a focus on performance in Dance, Drama, and Music. This is the second edition and includes a new section on "How to Evaluate Your Talent". The first half of this guidebook outlines the process of applying to and auditioning for programs in these disciplines. Each discipline is covered in its own chapter with the music section being further divided by instrument. The chapters cover advanced study, how to handle auditions (including what to wear and what not to do), and an admissions checklist. The author provides progam rankings in Part 5, based on surveys and interviews with performers, faculty, and students. Part 6 contains college profiles arranged alphabetically; the information here is also survey-based. The profiles range in length from one paragraph to two pages and the amount of information given depends on how thoroughly the institution filled out the survey. Each contains the usual stats as well as deadline information, information for international students and an author's comment.

EVALUATION:

The major strength of this book is the author's in-depth experience with applications and auditions. She has "seen it all" and wants to make sure that you benefit from her learning experiences. Although the different chapters for music, dance, and drama cover the same overall points, each one contains specific tips and details to help students in those disciplines get into the program of their choice. The weaker part of this book is the section which covers 300+ programs and institutions. It is not nearly as comprehensive as the first half and it is evident that the author's main focus was on how to get in, not where to go. This book won't tell you everything you need to know about all of the programs out there, but you will get a general feel of who you want to call for more information. This resource is recommended for students who wish to pursue a career in the performing arts.

WHERE TO FIND/BUY:

Bookstores and libraries.

Winning Edge: The Student Athlete's Guide To College Sports

Author/Editor: Frances & James Killpatrick
Publisher: Octameron Associates, Inc.
Edition Reviewed: 4th (1995)
Internet URL:

Media Type: Print
Price: $7.50
ISBN: 0-945981-99-6

RATINGS (1-4 STARS):

Overall:	★★★★	Covers college sports thoroughly
Breadth Of Content:	★★	Hundreds of colleges listed, minimum information is given
Value Added:	★★★★	Important statistics listed for the serious athlete
Ease Of Use:	★★★	Colleges listed by sport and State; an index is needed

DESCRIPTION:

In its fourth edition, this book is a guide to all levels of college sports for the serious and not-so-serious high school athlete. The first section provides basic information on applications, financial aid, and campus visits (with a slant toward the high school athlete), as well as the other steps that student athletes need to take in order to continue their sport in college. The differences between amateur and professional sports are outlined. How to appraise your skill and getting help from your coach are also discussed. The second section of the book is a listing of winning teams (organized by sport and division); this includes essays written by top coaches in baseball, basketball, crew, field hockey, football, golf, ice hockey, lacrosse, skiing, soccer, softball, swimming, tennis, track, and volleyball. The third section lists NCAA Divisions IA, I, II, and III, by State. The listings for NCAA IA and I include graduation statistics for each school. All division rankings are for the 1994-95 season. The book concludes with a sample sports resume, college checklist, and sample letters.

EVALUATION:

One drawback of this guidebook is that its focus is so narrow. Hundreds of colleges are listed in this slim 136 page guide, but aside from the sports statistics and contact information, there is no other information given about the colleges and universities listed here. On the upside, the essays by the top coaches in the country are insightful and replete with important tips on how to continue your achievements in your sport at the college level. A wide variety of sports are covered and we were happy to see that equal weight was given to women's sports. The chapter overview of NCAA recruiting rules and regulations was particularly useful, with simple, everyday terms to explain regulations that are sometimes tricky and hard to understand. Used in conjunction with other guidebooks, this book will be very useful to high school athletes and their parents. It is recommended to the serious athlete for help you decide on your initial list of schools.

WHERE TO FIND/BUY:

Find in Libraries or Bookstores, or call the publisher direct at 703-836-5480.

College Guide For The Learning Disabled ★★★★

Author/Editor: Charles T. Straughn II

Publisher: Lovejoy's Educational Guides / Prentice Hall

Edition Reviewed: 3rd (1993)

Internet URL:

Media Type: Print

Price: $22.00

ISBN: 0-671-84771-6

RATINGS (1-4 STARS):

Overall:	★★★★	Full of important information for students with learning disabilities
Breadth Of Content:	★★★	270+ colleges and universities profiled
Value Added:	★★★★	Author's experience and compassion shines throughout
Ease Of Use:	★★★	Well organized, but small type makes profiles hard to read

DESCRIPTION:

This 177 page guidebook, now in its third edition, profiles 270 colleges and universities in the United States with support services for Learning Disabled (LD) students. The author talks about his own LD and that of his daughter and how this influenced him to write this book. Section III offers techniques on developing coping skills for the LD student's college experience. Section IV describes what an LD student needs to look for in a college and what the college looks for in the admissions process. Colleges and universities included in this guide responded to a survey sent out by Lovejoy's; they were asked to read the definition of LD and state whether or not they should be included in this guide. Those who answered "yes" were included in this book. Each profile is approximately 3/4 of a page long and includes general information about the campus, a checklist of support services available, admissions requirements, and special comments on services for LD students. Each college is given a ranking of L, LL, or LLL based on the level of support available to LD students. The schools are listed alphabetically by State, by career curricula, special programs, and sports.

EVALUATION:

This guidebook is a valuable resource for students with LDs and their parents. The author's experiences show in the compassionate tone of the opening sections of this book; written in the first person, they will help make parents and students feel comfortable immediately. It is nice to see a specialized guidebook that assumes that all students, regardless of their particular disability, are interested in knowing what academic programs are available and what sports the college participates in, as well as the services they provide. The profiles themselves contain more information than we have seen in other guidebooks for LD students. The information about admissions and services for LD students are listed at the beginning of each profile and is followed by useful information on campus life and housing; graduate/enrollment statistics are included. Type in this section is quite small, making it a little difficult to read. Some of the information may be dated, since this edition was published in 1993, but the contact information and the sections on what to expect and how to prepare should be current. This resource should help the LD student determine which of those institutions offer the level of support required.

WHERE TO FIND/BUY:

Bookstores and libraries.

Multicultural Student's Guide To Colleges ★★★★

Author/Editor: Robert Mitchell
Publisher: The Noonday Press
Edition Reviewed: 2nd (1996)
Internet URL:

Media Type: Print
Price: $25.00
ISBN: 0374524769

RATINGS (1-4 STARS):

Overall:	★★★★	Extensive review of colleges by multicultural demographics and issues
Breadth Of Content:	★★★	Profiles 200+ colleges with pertinent details on social and academic life
Value Added:	★★★★	Narrative information takes into account student opinion
Ease Of Use:	★★★★	Very well laid out and explained; format is easy to read

DESCRIPTION:

In its 839 pages, this book takes a critical look at 200+ prominent colleges around the country. The book includes an introduction, 4 brief sections, and then the body of colleges profiled. Within these 4 sections, you will find information about how to use the contents of this book, the application process (9 pages), avenues for financial aid (7 pages), and a section citing pros and cons of selecting a predominately black college. The remainder of the book then lists college and university information alphabetically by state. Within each profile, you will find the following information: tuition, room and board, freshman characteristics, history of non-white enrollment, geographic distribution, top majors, retention rate of non-white students, scholarships available for non-white students, remediation programs, academic support services, ethnic studies programs, courses, and organizations, notable non-white alumni, faculty information, and recent non-white speakers. Following this statistical information is a narrative that discusses the social, academic life along with the geographic setting of the college. Information for the narratives was obtained from students through phone, mail surveys and in-person interviews.

EVALUATION:

Any student looking for a college to support their ethnic identity will find this useful book of great interest. Statistics such as the history of non-white students enrolled, the breakdown of the current student population by ethnic group (African, Hispanic, Asian, Native American), the ethnic make-up of the administration, and the retention rate of non-white students (those who return a second year, and graduate) help protray the underlying philosophy and climate of these colleges. Additionally, the presence or absence of organizations, programs, support services, and recent speakers that administer to the needs of these groups is enlightening. It is also refreshing to have students' opinions taken into account when discussing these colleges; other guidebooks often omit this. The narratives are upbeat, yet critical when needed. The author also states that colleges are not ranked because such rankings can be misleading and are usually subjective based upon input from college presidents, admissions deans, etc. We like this approach because it emphasizes the need for students to develop their own rating system given their individual situation. Although this book is written primarily for the non-white student, any student interested in attending a culturally diverse college will find helpful information here.

WHERE TO FIND/BUY:

Bookstores and libraries.

K&W Guide To Colleges For The Learning Disabled

★★★

Author/Editor: Marybeth Kravets & Imy F. Wax

Publisher: Educators Publishing Service, Inc.

Edition Reviewed: 3rd (1995)

Internet URL:

Media Type: Print

Price: $28.00

ISBN: 0838822495

RATINGS (1-4 STARS):

Overall:	★★★	Specific information of interest to students with learning disabilities
Breadth Of Content:	★★	Profiles just 265 colleges and universities
Value Added:	★★★★	Brings together information not readily available elsewhere
Ease Of Use:	★★★	Easy to use; well organized visually

DESCRIPTION:

This guidebook profiles 265 colleges and universities in the United States with reference to the services and programs available to students with learning disabilities (LDs).   The profiles are listed alphabetically by State. The colleges and universities have been grouped into three categories: Structured Programs, those campuses which offer the most comprehensive services for students with LDs and have special admission requirements, Coordinated Services, those campuses which offer services which are not as comprehensive and which may not offer help in the admissions process, and Services, those campuses which provide the least amount of services and may require documentation of the disability in order for the students to receive accommodations. Each profile is two pages long and includes information on: LD programs and services (special centers for students with LDs, etc.) , LD admissions information, LD services (such as, note takers and the # of LD specialists on campus), general admissions information, college graduation requirements, and additional information. A contacts list and an alphabetical list of colleges by degree of level of support is included as well.

EVALUATION:

This resource starts with "thoughts from. . . ", a series of essays written by various people on what it means to be a college student with an LD. While self-congratulatory in tone, this section of the book provides useful and positive perspectives on the issues surrounding higher education for LD students. The information provided in the profiles comes from a survey conducted by the authors and contains valuable information not likely to be readily available elsewhere. The profiles are accessible by State, level of services, and by school name. Since the information provided in these profiles is so specific, this listing can be used to determine which schools you want to contact for further information. If you are more interested in pursuing a particular course of study or living in a particular geographic area, than you may want to use this book to see which of the campuses you are already considering offer the types of services needed for LD students.

WHERE TO FIND/BUY:

Find in libraries and bookstores or call the publisher at 800-225-5750.

Women's Colleges

Author/Editor: Joe Anne Adler
Publisher: ARCO/Prentice Hall, Inc.
Edition Reviewed: 1994
Internet URL:

Media Type: Print
Price: $15.00
ISBN: 0-671-86706-7

RATINGS (1-4 STARS):

Overall:	★★★	An excellent resource for those seeking a women's college
Breadth Of Content:	★★★★	Profiles virtually all women's colleges in the United States
Value Added:	★★★★	Descriptions are wholly original and informative
Ease Of Use:	★★★	Needs to be properly indexed

DESCRIPTION:

This guidebook provides profiles of 76 women's colleges in the United States. The author visited all 76 campuses and conducted interviews with the students, faculty and administration. The book begins with a foreword by Linda Koch Lorimer, the Secretary of Yale University, followed by a brief history of women's colleges in the United States. In a "Note from the Author" it is explained that Radcliffe, Sophie Newcomb College and West Hampton were omitted from this book because they are considered undergraduate schools within Harvard, Tulane, and University of Richmond and not separate colleges. The rest of the book is taken up by the profiles which are listed alphabetically. Each college is given three and a half pages and the following points are covered: school history, academics (including core requirements and majors offered), students and student life (demographics, sports, clubs, sororities and campus traditions), campus and community, an admissions note, and a list of academic programs. A chart, listing the colleges alphabetically , lists tests required, application deadlines, expenses, and percentage of students receiving financial aid.

EVALUATION:

The lack of indexing is the only significant shortcoming for this book. The profiles are listed alphabetically, as is the "Guide to Women's Colleges" chart at the back of the book;, but the book's utility would be improved with indexes by State or academic program. It is not the author's intent for anyone to use this book as their sole guide to getting into college; the reader should find information on financial aid and the application process elsewhere. The point of this book is to give an overview of women's colleges and this is accomplished with excellence. The profiles written by the author contain a good deal of useful information for women who wish to continue their education in a same sex environment and are interested in evaluating their alternatives. The author provides some compelling rationale in the introduction as to why women should attend women's colleges. Several of the colleges listed have close relationships with all-male campuses in their community and it is noted when classes are coed. The colleges profiled are not ranked. This book is recommended for the college bound student interested in women-only institutions.

WHERE TO FIND/BUY:

Find at bookstores and libraries.

Making A Difference College Guide   ★★★

Author/Editor: Miriam Weinstein
Publisher: Sageworks Press
Edition Reviewed: 4th (1995)
Internet URL:

Media Type: Print
Price: $16.00
ISBN: 0963461834

RATINGS (1-4 STARS):

Overall:	★★★	A good resource that targets students seeking alternative programs
Breadth Of Content:	★★	Only 100 schools meet the editor's criteria
Value Added:	★★★	Essays a useful perspective; profiles provided by colleges
Ease Of Use:	★	Listed alphabetically by school, state index; some material incomplete

DESCRIPTION:

Weinstein, an environmental and social activist, compiled this resource guide highlighting colleges with innovative programs. These programs offer hands-on experiences for students who are concerned with social and environmental responsibility. The first section consists of several essays written by students, graduates, professors, and environmentalists, outlining serious questions facing today's students. Two of the essays address concerns a worried parent may have regarding their child's choice of these programs. Two other essays discuss college choices for a quality education. In particular the chapter entitled "What is education for?" sums up Weinstein's premise to rethink education. The second section lists, in alphabetical order, colleges and field programs that offer "relevant, values-based education." Within each college's description, an individual will find the following: the number of students attending, the degree of selectivity of applicants, a description of the educational atmosphere and of the community, and finally the college's philosophy. Also included is a list of "making a difference studies." Finally there are statistics included which list the profiles of the student and faculty populations, tuition costs, and a condensed version of the school's attributes. An index of all of the colleges and programs listed alphabetically by state is also provided.

EVALUATION:

Weinstein's book is of particular use to students and parents seeking an alternative education. The colleges described within her book place emphasis on meaningful career-oriented studies and hands-on training for future jobs. Weinstein successfully captures the questions many students have in this time of social and environmental awareness. The programs of the nearly 100 colleges outlined in the guide attempt to address these questions. The essays in the first half of the book are useful for those parents and students who have not quite decided if an innovative college program will suit their needs; these narratives serve to convince one of the need to offer alternatives to traditional college courses. What remains unclear in the guide is whether or not the lists of studies are one-time courses or entire programs; are there degree options if an individual wishes later on to pursue more study? Weinstein mentions that the schools categorized their own degree of selectivity, and asks the reader to be aware that selectivity is based upon rather faulty premises. This guidebook will be useful for students who are seeking choices different than those offered by the traditional college institutions.

WHERE TO FIND/BUY:

Bookstores and libraries.

Complete Guide To American Film Schools   ★★★

Author/Editor: Ernest Pintoff
Publisher: Penguin Books
Edition Reviewed: 1994
Internet URL:

Media Type: Print
Price: $16.95
ISBN: 0140172262

RATINGS (1-4 STARS):

Overall:	★★★	An excellent initial resource for this area of focus
Breadth Of Content:	★★★	Variety of listings, both two year schools and four year institutions
Value Added:	★★★	Guide POV, listing of alumni, and anecdotes all add interest
Ease Of Use:	★★★	Organized alphabetically by state

DESCRIPTION:

In this 510 page resource, Pintoff has compiled a state-by-state listing of American schools for those seeking a career in television, the cinema, or video. The author himself has been involved in animation, television and film directing, and writing; he currently is a professor of film at the University of Southern California. Each school listing includes the location of the school (rural, suburban, urban), the number of students, the academic calendar (quarter, semester), entrance requirements, degrees offered, curricular emphasis, special activities, facilities and equipment that are available to students, names of well-known alumni, and a "Guide POV" (point of view). The POV is a subjective overview of each program and is based upon input from departments, catalogs, and students. At the end of each state section is an anecdote from students, graduates and professionals who reflect upon their own experiences in school and offer advice to someone embarking upon a career in these fields. At the end of the book are two glossaries outlining academic and technical terms.

EVALUATION:

This guide addresses many of the important points important to making an initial decision as to which schools to consider for a future career in the cinema and television media. Each school's important features are highlighted, enabling the reader to make cross-comparisons of schools (missing is the cost of tuition). Pintoff does a fine job presenting various types of schools, both two and four-year institutions. Although the "Guide POV" may read as an advertisement for a particular school, the POV and the listing of recognized alumni add interest and personalization to the book. Pintoff and many of the anecdotal authors reflect upon the importance of gaining "a broad-based background"; they advise that the humanities should not be overlooked. Therefore, a student might consider institutions that not only offer general education courses but also offer specialized fields of study in the television and film industry. While this guide will be helpful in selecting alternatives, students should seek information from professionals in the field and others to find out how these schools are perceived in the industry.

WHERE TO FIND/BUY:

Bookstores and libraries.

Campus Opportunities For Students With Learning Differences

★★★

Author/Editor: Judith M. Crooker	**Media Type:** Print	
Publisher: Octameron Associates	**Price:** $5.00	
Edition Reviewed: 4th (1994)	**ISBN:** 0-945981-93-7	
Internet URL:		

RATINGS (1-4 STARS):

Overall:	★★★	Well-written specifically for the student with learning differences (LD)
Breadth Of Content:	★★★	Covers all the bases for an LD student deciding to go to college
Value Added:	★★★	Personal comments from an LD college students are included
Ease Of Use:	★★★	Short chapters and sections which don't waste words or confuse

DESCRIPTION:

In its fourth edition, this 41 page pamphlet sets out to reassure the student with a learning difference (LD) that there are opportunities for them at a post-secondary level. The book addresses the LD student with supportive information for parents. The book is organized into nine chapters, the first three of which explain what learning differences are, and how parents can help their LD child maximize their potential by possibly setting their sights on college. Chapters 4 and 6 focus on basic personal and study skills that are necessary to survive and succeed in college. Chapter 5 discusses the process used in choosing a college or an alternative school. Advice is given on how to obtain information about schools, questions to ask of admissions personnel, a self-assessment inventory to see if the LD student is ready, and finally how to apply to the school. Chapter 7 lists some LD "success stories" while Chapter 9 provides an annotated list of resources which include books, hardware/software, and organizations that can help to inspire and support the LD student. Chapter 8 highlights some summer programs for LD students to ease their transition from high school into a post-secondary situation.

EVALUATION:

This book fulfills a need for both parents and LD students alike. It reads comfortably and with a great deal of emphathy for the student with learning differences. Each chapter is short, to the point, and well-organized in format. In particular Chapters 4 and 6 are helpful for an LD student in making the decision whether or not college is right for them. Chapter 4 gives pointers on how to prepare for college while in high school in terms of academic skills , practical skills and personal skills. This chapter also gives the LD student a checklist to help them get ready during high school - a "year by year plan." Chapter 6 gives many suggestions on taking notes, preparing for class, taking tests, writing papers, organizing yourself and your time, and how to find supportive services on campus. Throughout the book are boxed-in comments from a student with learning differences who "survived his college years." In general, any parents of an LD child will find the information in this book useful in helping their child succeed during their college experience. In particular, this book is helpful in encouraging and supporting the LD student's decision to pursue a college education.

WHERE TO FIND/BUY:

Bookstores and libraries or directly from the publisher at 703-836-5480.

Guide To Nursing Programs

★★★

Author/Editor:
Publisher: Peterson's Guides
Edition Reviewed: 2nd (1996)
Internet URL: http://www.petersons.com

Media Type: Print
Price: $24.95
ISBN: 1-56079-565-4

RATINGS (1-4 STARS):

Overall:	★★★	Lots of information; take the in-depth profiles with a grain of salt
Breadth Of Content:	★★★★	Lists all accredited and chartered nursing programs in the U.S. and Canada
Value Added:	★★	No evaluative information provided
Ease Of Use:	★★★★	Very well organized and easy to use

DESCRIPTION:

This is one of Peterson's specialized guides, listing more than 2,000 nursing programs at over 625 schools in the United States and Canada. All of the programs profiled in this guide are four-year and graduate level programs; no comparative or evaluative information is provided. The programs are all accredited or have candidate-for-accreditation status in the U.S., and Canadian programs are all chartered or accredited. The first section includes articles on nursing careers today, how to finance your education, and tips for returning students. Section two contains the profiles, organized alphabetically by State and Province. The profiles range in length from 1/4 of a page to a page and a half and contain information on enrollment, academic facilities, student life, contact information, expenses and programs offered. In-depth descriptions of the nursing programs, written by the schools are provided in section three. These essays are approximately two pages long and Peterson's does not take responsibility for their content (not all of the schools chose to be included in this section). The final section is a series of indexes by institution name, type of program, masters level programs, area of study and concentration.

EVALUATION:

Peterson's has written several very good guidebooks and this is no exception. This is an impressive tome, at 688 pages, and it contains a lot of information focused on college nursing programs. Peterson's does not evaluate the colleges they profile; information included is provided by the colleges and universities and consists largely of statistics on enrollment and basic information on the programs, expenses and student life. The information is helpful in deciding which schools to contact for further information and it will give you a good idea of what to expect in course load and expenses. One the strengths Peterson's provides is a variety of indexes that make it possible to find exactly the information you are looking for. The in-depth profiles of the programs were provided by the schools and should be read with the same caution used when reading official school publications; it's important to look elsewhere for an evaluative opinion or original insight into the relative quality these programs.

WHERE TO FIND/BUY:

Bookstores and libraries, or see Peterson's website at the URL: http://www.petersons.com.

Colleges With Programs For Students With Learning Disabilities

★★★

Author/Editor: Charles T. Mangrum II, Ed.D.
  & Stephen S. Strighart, Ph.D.
Publisher: Peterson's Guides
Edition Reviewed: 4th (1994)
Internet URL: http://www.petersons.com

Media Type: Print
Price: $32.95
ISBN: 1-56079-400-3

RATINGS (1-4 STARS):

Overall:	★★★	An all-inclusive specialized guide; focus is on LD programs & services
Breadth Of Content:	★★★	800+ programs, including those in Canada
Value Added:	★★★	Good section on "College Opportunities" but little else that is novel
Ease Of Use:	★★	Small type and amount of information presented makes it difficult to read

---

DESCRIPTION:

In its fourth edition, this 674 page guide profiles 800+ programs that focus on the needs of students with learning differences (LD). The list was compiled by mailing questionnaires to all accredited two-year and four-year U.S./Canadian colleges and universities (3,300+) to identify programs or services for LD students. This edition consists of 6 parts. One part describes learning disabilities and characteristics of LD students, and explains assistance colleges can provide for these students. Two sections deal with selecting a college (visits, creating a comparative checklist of LD programs, etc.). The 5th part includes testing accommodations and highlights organizations for LD students. The last two sections focus on specific college programs that are available. One of these sections is a quick-reference chart listing colleges and includes a column which ranks entrance difficulties (based upon both entering freshmen's high school rank and SAT/ACT scores); the other profiles each of the 800+ programs. These profiles have two parts; the first describes colleges that offer "programs" for students with LD, the other, colleges that have "services" for LD students. Within each profile, specific information on the LD program (fees, admission requirements, staffing, LD student population, support services,etc.), general college information (student/faculty population, expenses, financial aid, housing, college life, majors, etc.), etc., are provided.

EVALUATION:

This edition offers some value for parents of LD students in their search to find the right college program. The editors, who have worked in special education programs and with students of learning disabilities, attempt here to present an "end-all" guide to colleges for students with LD. The book is often difficult to wade through because of small type and the variety of information presented. Most of the schools seem to have close to the same opportunities available, and no attempt is to rank LD programs. The method used to rank schools in the chapter entitled "Quick-Reference Chart of Colleges", as with many other college guides, is suspect. Simply ranking schools based upon entering freshmen's high school ranking and test scores provides only a hint of relative "quality" and no evidence of "fit". The section entitled "College Opportunities for Students with Learning Disabilities" can be valuable because it highlights special needs that may arise in college, such as counseling, tutoring, special courses, auxiliary aids and services, and so on.

WHERE TO FIND/BUY:

Bookstores and libraries.

I Am Somebody: College Knowledge For The First-Generation Campus Bound ★★★

Author/Editor: Anna Leider
Publisher: Octameron Associates
Edition Reviewed: 6th (1994)
Internet URL:

Media Type: Print
Price: $6.00
ISBN: 0-945981-94-5

RATINGS (1-4 STARS):

Overall:	★★★	A positive approach for first generation college-bound students
Breadth Of Content:		Not applicable
Value Added:	★★★	Provides clear answers to tough questions
Ease Of Use:	★★★	Worksheets require commitment but are worth it

DESCRIPTION:

This book outlines the process of getting into college for the first generation college-bound student. A foreword to parents asks them to encourage their children to go to college and is provided in English and Spanish. Several education counselors, high school counselors , college admission offices, and financial aid officers cooperated in the production of this book. Chapter one tells the stories of several famous minorities and explains how their stories should inspire students to pursue a college education. Chapter two lists composite descriptions of first generation college students written by HS counselors and based on students they have helped in the past. These profiles illustrate the different financial, academic, and social standing of these students; it's the author's intent that students reading this book will see themselves and be encouraged. Chapters three and four list reasons a student should go to college and refute myths that keep students from going to college. A brief overview of the selection and admissions process is followed by information about financial aid (what financial aid is, how to get it,several sources of aid described). The last third of the book includes a senior year timetable, several worksheets and a glossary .

EVALUATION:

Although addressed to all first generation students going to college, this book focuses on first generation minority students -- the listing of scholarship providers lists only those who provide scholarships to minorities, such as the American Indian College Fund, and the profiles of first generation college students are all of minorities. Nonetheless, the positive message of this book help ensure its value to all first generation college bound students. The strongest section of this book is Chapter 6: Financial Aid. It includes several mathematical examples that are easy to follow and understand. The emphasis is on applying correctly and on time, with several easy-to-use worksheets are included to help students gather information to get the aid they need. The senior year timetable in Chapter 7 contains references back to other chapters to help students complete the right step at the right time. The author encourages students to continue their education in a way that is positive and tries to help students see the rewards and not the obstacles. This book is recommended for all first generation college bound students.

WHERE TO FIND/BUY:

Find in Libraries or Bookstores, or call the publisher direct at 703-836-5480.

Guide To Architecture Schools

Author/Editor: Richard E. McCommons
Publisher: Association of Collegiate Schools of Architecture
Edition Reviewed: 5th (1994)
Internet URL:

Media Type: Print
Price: $19.95
ISBN: 0-935502-06-8

RATINGS (1-4 STARS):

Overall:	★★★	Brief descriptions of ACSA architecture programs and worldwide programs
Breadth Of Content:	★★★	118 U.S. and Canadian schools described
Value Added:	★★★	Charts in each profile listing degrees, admission requirements,etc. helpful
Ease Of Use:	★★	Alphabetically by school; map at beginning needed to find schools by state

DESCRIPTION:

This 297+ page resource guide was developed for prospective architecture students and professionals in the field. There are 7 sections at the very beginning of the book. The first section gives a brief overview of the history of architecture education. The second and third sections outline ways a student may prepare in high school before they select an appropriate school. Section 4 details the practice of architecture. Sections 5 - 7 explain accreditation methods, locations of architecture schools (a U.S. map is illustrated), and a list of affiliate members of the Association of Collegiate Schools of Architecture (ACSA).   There is an appendix that lists degree types, specializations within the architecture degree, related degree programs, scholarships, organizations, and a list of abbreviations. The remainder of the book includes profiles of 118 schools arranged alphabetically by school.   Within each profile, you will find: tuition and fees, degrees offered, number of years to complete the degrees, school population demographics, special activities, opportunities, resources and programs, description of the facilities, scholarships available, philosophy statements from the undergraduate and graduate programs, etc.

EVALUATION:

The author's purpose in this book is to describe the opportunities available in the field of architecture so that students can match their potential and interests with an appropriate program. This book does conveniently provide students and professionals with information that can be used to compare one school with another. However, since the information contained within profiles is supplied by the schools themselves, there is little feel for the actual school and the climate of learning within. The philosophy statements read as a marketing brochure would - too vague, without any specific goals. Additionally, there is no real idea of how the schools are perceived by students in attendance or architecture professionals. Although specific programs of study are shown to be accredited or not, some comments about the programs from professionals in the field would be helpful. The author does, however, make some useful suggestions in the beginning sections of his book concerning architecture education. Any prospective architecture student should in particular read sections 2 - 4 that describe the "real" picture of what is involved with becoming an architect and what the field of architecture is really like. This book can give you a start on deciding which schools of architecture might serve your needs, but further research will be also needed.

WHERE TO FIND/BUY:

Bookstores and libraries.

PICKING YOUR FINAL LIST OF COLLEGES

In the spectrum of things to do when choosing colleges to apply to, this step is perhaps the toughest. It's tough because what's needed is insight into the realities of attending one college versus another college. Gaining that insight is not easy.

You'll want to take your initial list of 10-20 schools, and winnow it down to maybe 5-10 schools that feel "right" and provide a good match to your criteria. Then, you'll need to make like a sponge and try to soak up as much feedback on each of these alternatives as possible, with the objective of constructing a "short list" of 4-6 schools you'll apply to.

You'll want to visit as many schools in person as time and budgets allow. There is no substitute for this. For schools you can't visit, try browsing their web pages or viewing tour videos. Call their alumni office and get names of local, recent graduates; call them up and ask them lots of questions.

As your opinions evolve, test them on your parents and your counselors. Their responses to your reasoning will be helpful as your thinking evolves.

Work on this. It's important. Agonize over it a bit. But recognize that ultimately, you're going to make good college choices and most of those choices are going to invite you to enroll. So, be confident in your judgments and make the decisions you need to make!

Any resource which rates colleges will be subject to some criticism from some professionals in the college counseling business. They will argue that each student must construct his or her own individual "reality" of each school being considered, and that because this is true, no subjective opinion (constructed from others' feedback) can be relied on to pick the best alternatives for that individual.

While this basic point is valid, not every student can visit every school being considered. Not every college visit can be relied on as being representative of what will be experienced. Well-intentioned feedback from friends, relatives, and counselors is based on **their** individual (and biased) experiences.

Thus, subjective guidebooks exist, along with various statistical rankings. We don't think much of statistical rankings. But we do like a number of the subjective guidebooks, particularly those based on feedback from large numbers of currently enrolled or recently graduated students. We feel they can help provide a "feel" for the student body and the overall campus experience; this can supplement other impressions gathered while researching college alternatives. We've recommended the best of these in the pages that follow. Recognize that not every college is represented in these guidebooks; they're generally focused on the more selective colleges.

Fiske Guide To Colleges

 ★★★★

Author/Editor: Edward B. Fiske
Publisher: Times Books (Division Of Random House, Inc.)
Edition Reviewed: 1997
Internet URL:

Media Type: Print
Price: $19
ISBN: 0812927575

RATINGS (1-4 STARS):

Overall:	★★★★	One of the best to help you get to your final list
Breadth Of Content:	★★★	Only 315 colleges and universities covered
Value Added:	★★★★	Really outstanding insight; wholly original writing
Ease Of Use:	★★★★	Listed alphabetically; indexes by alpha, state, and price

DESCRIPTION:

Published annually since 1982, this 800+ page guidebook is one of the few available which offers original, evaluative essays on each of the 300+ colleges and universities covered. The essays are based primarily on in-depth feedback from students, supplemented by additional research, including campus visits. All "selective admission" colleges and universities are included (175 by their definition), with the remainder providing geographic diversity and a balance of public/private schools. Each write-up (2-4 pages in length) includes comments on academics, the student body, financial aid, housing, food, social life, and extracurricular activities, with summary ratings (1-5 Stars) for Academics, Social Life, and Quality of Life. At the beginning of each article, typical statistics about the school are listed (location, enrollment, size, M/F ratio, SAT/ACT ranges, number of applicants/accepted/enrolled). Each school's admissions practices, policies, and deadlines are summarized as well. In addition, 42 institutions are highlighted as "Best Buys" -- "remarkable educational opportunities at a relatively modest cost."

EVALUATION:

This guidebook is among the best, if not the best, source of original descriptions on the colleges included. Its writing style is entertaining, thorough, and refreshingly free of the promotional prose parroted by many guides. The research done and questions asked of students and administrators alike are focused on issues that are relevant to selecting a college, and are responsive to the focus of parents and prospective students alike. For example: strong (and weak) academic departments are noted, student housing is discussed in detail, the origin, focus, and interests of typical students are described -- as a result, the descriptive "feel" of each campus really helps a prospective student visualize what it would be like to attend. Student social life - what students do when they're not in classes - is discussed in some detail, as is the surrounding community and the quality of life it offers. If you've got some of its 300+ schools on your list to evaluate, this guidebook will be among the best resources you can use to pare down your list.

WHERE TO FIND/BUY:

Bookstores and libraries, or order direct from the publisher by calling 800-793-BOOK.

Insider's Guide To The Colleges

★★★★

Author/Editor: Staff of The Yale Daily News
Publisher: St. Martin's Press
Edition Reviewed: 1995
Internet URL:

Media Type: Print
Price: $14.99
ISBN: 031213522X

RATINGS (1-4 STARS):

Overall:	★★★★	Useful student perspective on colleges included
Breadth Of Content:	★★★	Limited to 300+ colleges included
Value Added:	★★★★	Excellent insight into student body taken as a whole
Ease Of Use:	★★★★	Easy to use format and indexes

DESCRIPTION:

Published since the early '70's, this guidebook provides original profiles on 300+ of the "best and most noteworthy" colleges. It's written by the staff of the Yale Daily News, based on input from college students across the country. Colleges profiled are included primarily on academic quality, with others added to provide balance in size and geographic distribution; some specialized schools are also included (technical institutes and creative/performing arts). Each 2 page essay focuses on student-centered issues such as: which departments are strong, class size and teaching quality, academic focus and approach, popular extracurricular activities, school traditions, student body characteristics as a whole, living/dining facilities and quality, and student social life. A good selection of useful statistics is included for each school as well. This guidebook also includes some comprehensive essays on the admissions process and which factors are important to consider when choosing among schools; perspectives for international and disabled students are included, as well as several useful indexes based on selected college attributes.

EVALUATION:

This publication provides useful insight on the 300+ colleges included, taken primarily from the focus of currently enrolled students. This focus, while a bit narrow, can be very helpful in gaining a "feel" for an institution before deciding on a short list for visits or applications. The writing style is original, entertaining, and easy to read. The essays are short, which means that a more comprehensive picture will have to be filled in from other sources, but they provide a unique perspective drawn exclusively from students; descriptions of the character of the student body taken as a whole are particularly useful. The comprehensive essays that describe the entire college selection/admission process (17 pages) and discuss factors to consider when selecting a college (10 pages) are very helpful and are alone worth the price of this guidebook.

WHERE TO FIND/BUY:

National distribution through bookstores, libraries, etc., or order direct from Publisher's Books at 800-288-2131.

Best 309 Colleges

Author/Editor: Meltzer/Knower/Custard/Katzman
Publisher: Princeton Review/Random House, Inc.
Edition Reviewed: 1997
Internet URL:

Media Type: Print
Price: $18
ISBN: 0679771220

RATINGS (1-4 STARS):

Overall:	★★★★	Easy-to-use format; provides a quick but original look at some good schools
Breadth Of Content:	★★★	Only 309 schools covered; only 2 pages allotted per school
Value Added:	★★★★	A comprehensive survey forms the basis for some interesting observations
Ease Of Use:	★★★★	Very easy to use; well-organized visually

DESCRIPTION:

This guidebook is based largely on surveys from some 56,000 students at the 309 colleges reviewed (70 multiple-choice questions on a variety of subjects, and free-form comments,too). The authors polled 50 independent college counselors to help generate their list of the nation's best colleges. Each school reviewed gets two pages, organized to combine statistics with commentary; survey input finds its way into both. The usual stats are included, supplemented by summary ratings on campus life, academics, admissions, and financial aid, as well as survey-based facts on "what's hot & not," ratings on professors, popular majors, and others. Commentaries include observations on student life, academic environment, and types of students enrolled. Next, the authors focus on each school's admissions process; this is supplemented by observations from the admissions office and independent counselors. Requirements for financial aid are spelled out in a separate section, as are comments from each admissions office. Separate rankings for 61 categories (selected mostly for fun) are included, as are a listing of independent college counselors.

EVALUATION:

We like the general tone of this guidebook, which doesn't take itself too seriously. The authors have done a good job weaving a largely survey-based database and some student comments into a useful tapestry of observations about each school. Their stats are easy to use, with visual summaries indicating relative rank within the group. The survey generates some interesting input on campus life ("What's Hot & What's Not"), input on the quality of teaching, popular majors, etc. The written commentary is livened up with frequent quotations from students, and provides useful perspectives on the typical student, campus life, and the academic environment. Most admissions offices provide some useful insight on the kind of student they're looking for, in a section where they're invited to "speak directly to the readers". The summary ratings provided for campus life, academics, admissions, and financial aid are useful in comparing each college within this select group. Finally, the authors lighten things up by providing survey-based rankings on 61 wildly divergent categories. They close this guidebook with some funny and irreverent quotes gathered from their survey, in a section titled "My Roommate's Feet Really Stink".

WHERE TO FIND/BUY:

Bookstores and libraries, or order direct by calling 800-793-BOOK.

Barron's Top 50   ★★★

Author/Editor: Tom Fischgrund (Editor)
Publisher: Barron's
Edition Reviewed: Third
Internet URL:

Media Type: Print
Price: $14.95
ISBN: 0-8120-9053-5

RATINGS (1-4 STARS):

Overall:	★★★	A useful resource, if you're targeting any of these schools.
Breadth Of Content:	★★	Covers only 50 schools.
Value Added:	★★★★	Comprehensive (10+ pages each) profiles based on standard format.
Ease Of Use:	★★★★	Listed alphabetically; easy to use.

DESCRIPTION:

This guidebook takes a highly focused approach and provides comprehensive essays on the "Top 50" schools in the nation. Essays (10-15 pages each) are written by recent graduates of the school. The schools reviewed are selected based on SAT I scores, % of applications accepted, and % of those accepted who enrolled, cut off after the top 50 are calculated. The profiles follow a standard format, which includes sections on: the education program (educational philosophy, strongest majors, defining characteristics), getting in/financial aid, the academic environment (requirements, atmosphere, teaching methods, class size), social life, extracurricular activities (what's available, what's popular, what's the housing like), graduates (what do students do after graduation), and a summary overview (summary, strengths and weaknesses). Short essays ("tips") are also provided on: selecting top colleges, getting in, filling out applications, financing, and succeeding while enrolled. "Insider's Perspectives" on the applications process, written by three admissions directors from these schools, are also included.

EVALUATION:

This guidebook takes a straightforward approach to selecting its "Top 50" -- simply ranking colleges based on SAT scores, % of applications accepted, and % enrolled of those accepted. Some would argue that other criteria are more appropriate, but at least these are straightforward and completely objective. Given this list, the approach taken by this resource is to have a recent graduate (recommended by the school) write a comprehensive essay about the school, following a standard format which includes short "chapters" on most issues of importance to the college selection process. The essays are long (10-15 pages) and well written; they provide some useful insights not generally available from other guides. One comes away from reading these essays with a genuine feeling that one knows the school a lot better -- that's good. That the writing is uniformly promotive in nature (somewhat like the smiling guides that you tour campuses with), and that it reflects the particular experience of a single student -- that's probably a little too subjective, so look for other opinions, too. The "Tips" essays are OK -- good summaries but no extraordinary insights. The 3 essays written by admissions directors are useful.

WHERE TO FIND/BUY:

Bookstores and libraries.

Collegiate Choice Walking Tours

Author/Editor: **Media Type:** Internet
Publisher: **Price:**
Edition Reviewed: **ISBN:**
Internet URL: http://www.register.com/collegiate/

RATINGS (1-4 STARS):

Overall:	★★★	A pretty good idea, one that may help families save some time and $
Breadth Of Content:	★★	Just 400+ college videos are available, concentrated in the East
Value Added:	★★★	The advisors ask the questions and provide an "informal" look at colleges
Ease Of Use:		Not applicable

DESCRIPTION:

This is a service set up by several independent college advisors "who work with families in Bergen County, New Jersey." Since 1988, these advisors have taken amateur videos of the tours offered by some 400+ colleges throughout the country. Their intent in doing so has been to provide those families they work with an opportunity to "visit" colleges of interest that they aren't able to visit in person. They charge $15 per video plus a $6 handling/shipping fee per order (videos are ordered via mail or toll phone call; the website does not support online purchases). The website includes information explaining the service; these pages make it clear that these videos have been made by amateurs using hand-held video cameras, and that they are not intended to replace viewbooks and catalogs available from the colleges. Their value, the site explains, is found in the experience of the advisors taking the college tours -- in the questions asked, and the "feel" for the school created by an informal, unbiased approach. The videos vary in length from 20-100 minutes in length (average roughly 60+ minutes). A brief essay on making a college visit is included on the site, as are simple lists of "best colleges" from U.S. News, Money Magazine, etc.

EVALUATION:

This is a useful service. We've ordered and viewed several sample tapes. Each tape provides a "real" tour of the college, lasting roughly 60 minutes. You get to see lots of buildings and classrooms, students in informal, unrehearsed settings, and hear the Q&A of the tour participants and the guide. The questions asked by these college advisors are useful (and consistent from tour to tour); no subjective commentary is added (judgments are left to the viewers). The video quality is quite good, the audio quality less so. Guides can be good (enthusiastic, well-informed) or bad (dull, ill-informed). One video we saw on a college we know well was 4 years out-of-date and the answers given by the guide in some cases were inaccurate. The price of $15/video may seem steep, but value added, measured by an unbiased view of the schools toured, should be higher than the standard "canned" college viewbook. When each video was taken is not revealed in their listing, but an email inquiry brought a response that they try to update each video at least every 5 years. There are a healthy number of colleges from each state listed (albeit with an East Coast concentration), and these videos could serve as a practical alternative to a college visit for those families whose budgets or schedules prohibit a visit to all colleges of interest.

WHERE TO FIND/BUY:

Find on the Web at the URL: http://www.register.com/collegiate/; order videos by calling 201-871-0098.

Interactive Fiske Guide To Colleges   ★★★

Author/Editor: Edward B. Fiske

Publisher: Interactive Education, Inc. (Random House, Inc.)

Edition Reviewed: 1996

Internet URL:

Media Type: CD-ROM

Price: $49.99

ISBN: 0812-927-44-3

RATINGS (1-4 STARS):

Overall:	★★★	A great CD-ROM for evaluative input on colleges
Breadth Of Content:	★★★	Only 300+ colleges and universities covered
Value Added:	★★★★	Really outstanding insight; wholly original writing
Ease Of Use:	★★★	Excellent search engine, not deep on navigation design or multimedia

DESCRIPTION:

For Mac (System 7.0+, 68030+) & Windows (3.1+). The same product, less video clips, is available on floppy disk. The 800+ page guidebook contained on this CD-ROM offers original, evaluative essays on each of the 300+ colleges and universities covered, based primarily on in-depth feedback from students, supplemented by additional research, including campus visits. Each write-up (2-4 pages in length) includes comments on academics, the student body, financial aid, housing, food, social life, and extracurricular activities, with summary ratings (1-5 Stars) for Academics, Social Life, and Quality of Life. Typical statistics about the school are included; admissions practices, policies, and deadlines are summarized as well. Roughly 200 schools have short videos clips. A highly flexible search engine using 15 variables is available to generate a scored ranking of 10, 25, or all colleges. Choices within each variable can be expressed as positive (important to you), indifferent, or negative; rankings can exclude schools if they have any negatives. Criteria used in generating these ranked listings can be modified, saved, and printed.

EVALUATION:

This CD-ROM contains among the best, if not the best, source of original descriptions on the colleges included. The research done and questions asked of students and administrators alike are focused on issues that are relevant to selecting a college, and are responsive to the focus of both parents and prospective students. If you've got some of its 300+ schools on your list to evaluate, these profiles will be among the best resources you can use to pare down your list. That said, should you buy the CD-ROM or the printed guidebook? On the plus side, having a search engine this good and this flexible is a blessing. But, search engines can be misleading if not used with a great deal of care -- potentially great choices might be excluded inadvertently. So start with just a few criteria and refine the rankings carefully. The videos clips don't add much value: too small, too short, sometimes just pictures, frequently no narrative. Would we recommend the CD-ROM over the book? Probably not. The big minus is increased cost; the big plus is the search engine, if used carefully. But for refining a initial college list down to a dozen or so finalists, you'll have what you need in the print version.

WHERE TO FIND/BUY:

Bookstores or computer stores selling CDs, or direct from the publisher by calling 800-793-2665.

CAMPUS VISITS & INTERVIEWS

Once you've done enough research to come up with a final list of colleges you think you might want to apply to, you're not yet finished with your research! Most college counselors recommend on-campus visits with your "final" list, since there is nothing like "being there" to help form the impressions that may prove most valuable in deciding which colleges to apply to. And, being there gives you the opportunity to meet face to face with a member of the admissions staff.

For most high school students, college visits are an **adventure.** For some, this may be a rare occasion to travel out of town (usually with parents in tow) to visit several colleges, each having the potential to be a new "home" for 4+ years! This is great fun. On the other hand, for many students, the "interview" with the admissions office is approached with much **trepidation.**

We would counsel you to try to attenuate both these emotional extremes. A visit to a college campus has a serious purpose and should be approached with specific objectives in mind. Namely:

- Learn enough about the campus setting ("look and feel') to make judgments about how you'd like living there.

- Learn enough about the composition, interests, academic acuity, and beliefs of the student body to decide if you'd feel comfortable with them.

- Ask questions about specific courses and majors, to draw a conclusion on the relative strength of academic departments you're interested in.

- Check out special programs and facilities of interest (sports, fine arts, etc.).

To accomplish these goals will require that you do more than passively join a tour led by a student. Schedule appointments ahead of time with professors, coaches, etc. Spend some time talking to students; drop in on some dorms. Go to your interview prepared to ask the questions you need answers to; the interview is used by the college to sell itself just as much as by you to sell yourself. Finally, write down your impressions immediately after each visit. You'll need them later to compare visits which may otherwise blend together.

As luck would have it, there are some great resources which are focused just on preparing for campus visits and interviews! Read one of these cover to cover and you be both prepared and confident for those visits and interviews!

Campus Pursuit ★★★★

Author/Editor: G. Gary Ripple, Ph.D.

Publisher: Octameron Associates

Edition Reviewed: 6th (1995)

Internet URL:

Media Type: Print

Price: $5

ISBN: 1575090031

RATINGS (1-4 STARS):

Overall:	★★★★	Very focused, very effective; the author's experience shows
Breadth Of Content:		Not Applicable
Value Added:	★★★★	Very thorough treatment of two important subjects
Ease Of Use:	★★★	Well organized, well written, mercifully concise

DESCRIPTION:

This 32 page guidebook is in its 6th edition; it's written by an experienced college admissions director. The chapter on "Visiting A College" begins with an overview of college handbooks and ratings, and the role parents should play in a visit. The remaining sections provide advice on planning college visits, including objectives for each visit, and suggestions for followup. The final two chapters, and the two appendices following, focus on college interviews. Overviews are provided on the interview's importance, and what admissions staff are looking for in the students they interview, and how an interview is normally conducted. The remainder of the chapter, and the appendices, then focus on questions that are likely, as well as questions that prospective students should ask of their interviewer. A short chapter then discusses common questions (and answers) which prospective students typically have about the interview process.

EVALUATION:

This is a short, focused little book that may provide you all you need to know about the importance of, and objectives for, visiting colleges and about handling the typical college interview to your benefit. The experience of the author really shows through in the insights provided throughout each chapter. The objectives described for college visits should help ensure they provide maximum benefit. Reading the thorough treatment of interviews will provide prospective college students with much reassurance about what's typically going to happen during such interviews, how to best prepare for the experience, which classic mistakes to avoid, and how to ensure that the communication process works to the benefit of interviewer and interviewee. A study of the list of questions likely to be asked, and those that should be asked by the student, will be of great benefit in calming the inevitable trepidation felt by college applicants.

WHERE TO FIND/BUY:

Bookstores and libraries, or direct from the publisher by calling 703-836-5480.

Campus Visits & College Interviews   ★★★★

Author/Editor: Zola Schneider
Publisher: College Board Publications
Edition Reviewed: 1987
Internet URL:

Media Type: Print
Price: $9.95
ISBN: 0-87447-260-1

RATINGS (1-4 STARS):

Overall:	★★★★	Very thorough treatment of two important topics
Breadth Of Content:		Not applicable
Value Added:	★★★★	Lots of detailed suggestions
Ease Of Use:	★★★	Well-organized; useful checklists

DESCRIPTION:

This 120+ page book dedicates half its pages to campus visits, half to college interviews. Chapters on campus visits cover preparations including deciding when/where to visit, planning the visit, making preparations; other chapters focus on what to accomplish during the visit. One chapter suggests dividing the campus exploration into five areas: students, social life, facilities, outside community, and academics. This portion of the book closes with a college evaluation checklist. The chapters on interviewing include putting the interview into perspective, how to approach and prepare for the interview, and questions likely to be asked and that should be asked by the student. A separate chapter is devoted to helping the "shy" person get through the experience successfully. The author places fictional high school students in scenarios which give a feel for how a campus visit might go; these chapters are usually followed by more detailed lists of things to think about, and suggestions on what to accomplish. Key points made in each chapter are summarized in checklists.

EVALUATION:

Campus visits and admissions interviews are critical elements in the college admissions process, yet most information sources focus on other elements. A campus visit and interview can tell things to a student that nothing in print can; thankfully, this book takes a very detailed look at these important steps in selecting a college home. Particularly useful among the chapters on campus visits is the first, which gives some convincing advice on when to visit (and when NOT to), and shows how this can be managed. Indicative of the author's experience are the detailed questions included in the chapter which suggest dividing the campus visit into five areas of inquiry; also useful is the detailed college evaluation checklist, which can be used to evaluate alternatives within a common framework. The author puts the admissions interview into a relaxed context, making the point that it is simply a two-way information exchange. She nonetheless provides thorough advice on getting ready for such interviews: "knowing thyself," practice, planning, and preparing to both answer and ask questions; a separate chapter is devoted to helping the "shy" person cope. The writing style is enlivened by placing fictional high school students in the various situations discussed.

WHERE TO FIND/BUY:

Bookstores and libraries, direct from the publisher by calling 800-323-7155, or on the World Wide Web at http://www.collegeboard.org.

COMPLETING APPLICATIONS

Now you're ready to complete the applications! Congratulations on the hard work you've done and the good decisions you've made to arrive at this point. Do the **best** job you can with your applications, and get them in before the deadline. Then relax, wait, and enjoy your break before you hear from your colleges later in the spring. Or, help your parents finish those financial aid applications (our directory "The Best Resources: For College Financial Aid" can help with that process)!

There's lots of advice out there on writing applications and completing essays, including the great advice contained in the resources we've recommended in the pages that follow, so we won't try to restate it all here.

Remember these points about applications, though:

- A **completed** application requires input from teachers, counselors, and registrars, but don't assume they'll remember. Create a checklist and followup until you **know** all required components have been sent to each college to which you've applied.

- **Don't** put them off until January. Get them done, absent fall grades and recommendations, **before** the end of the year. Think how great you'll feel.

- Read about how to do a good essay, and then think about what you've read, **before** you begin writing. You'll write with much more confidence, and you'll produce a much better product.

- Believe in yourself. You're a unique person with a wonderful set of talents, and you've got special gifts to give to whatever college environment you join.

Attacking this last college admission task can be made much easier by using one or more of the resources recommended here. In this section, we've also included the best resources we've encountered that are focused on the applications process **as a whole.**

Good luck, and congratulations on completing the process!

Writing Your College Application Essay

Author/Editor: Sarah Myers McGinty
Publisher: College Board Publications
Edition Reviewed: 1992
Internet URL:

Media Type: Print
Price: $9.95
ISBN: 0-87447-429-9

RATINGS (1-4 STARS):

Overall:	★★★★	An excellent resource to help students over the college essay hurdle
Breadth Of Content:		Not applicable
Value Added:	★★★★	Just the right amount of depth, balanced with encouragement
Ease Of Use:	★★★	Well written; takes focus and discipline to get through

---

DESCRIPTION:

The author is an experienced English teacher and college admissions director. The focus of this 120+ page book is, as the title states, solely on the college application essay. The first chapter is an overview of the college selection process, and positions the importance of the essay within this context. Chapter Two reassures by reviewing the basics of writing essays (structure, style, etc.) that students already know as high schools students. Chapter Three, the meat of the book, is a review course in essay writing: prewriting (brainstorming, organizing), drafting (topic sentences, development, clincher, conclusion), and editing. Chapter Four describes and discusses the types of questions typically asked on college applications, with expansion in the following chapter on two key types of questions: "Tell us about yourself..." and "Why do you want to come here...". The book closes with an analysis of six actual essays.

EVALUATION:

The experience of the author on "both sides of the fence" shows through brightly in this book. It is both methodical and precise in helping students revisit and understand the process of writing essays, and empathetic and encouraging in tone, providing a positive "you can do it" push to students intimidated by the process. For example, it's useful that the author takes some time to bring the reader up to the point of detailed advice on the essay, by placing its importance within the context of the whole application, and by restating what high school students already know about writing -- this all should serve to relax anxieties somewhat and help the student focus on the details which follow. The chapters on essay writing are a very readable (and detailed) dissection of the writing process, giving particular focus on the kinds of questions typically asked by colleges. The author effectively leads the reader through the process of creating good college essays; all that's required to succeed is for students to stay confident, think carefully about the processes and observations laid out in this book, and implement them in their writing.

WHERE TO FIND/BUY:

Bookstores and libraries, direct from the publisher by calling 800-323-7155, or on the World Wide Web at http://www.collegeboard.org.

College Applications & Essays

Author/Editor: Susan D. Van Raalte
Publisher: Arco
Edition Reviewed: 2nd (1994)
Internet URL:

Media Type: Print
Price: $9
ISBN: 0-671-86644-3

RATINGS (1-4 STARS):

Overall:	★★★★	The best resource on essay writing we've seen
Breadth Of Content:		Not applicable
Value Added:	★★★★	The author's experience shows; the forms and processes used are polished
Ease Of Use:	★★★	An easy-to-use format for an intimidating topic

---

DESCRIPTION:

This book captures a course in college applications/essays taught by the author for 15 years, and is targeted at high school seniors: "they will be coaxed and prodded..through a step-by-step system designed to break down application writing into manageable pieces." The book is organized into twelve chapters, with most focused on writing essays;throughout, lots of forms and checklists are included so processes suggested can be implemented as the book is read. The second chapter provides forms and suggestions for organizing the admissions process. Chapters follow which explain typical essay questions asked, and walk the student through a personal inventory process (with input, suggestions, and insights by the author throughout). Focusing on the process of writing essays, the book provides chapters and exercises on generating and refining ideas for essays, structuring essays to be readable, creating great "beginnings" and "endings," using tone and style to improve readability, overcoming "writer's block," and adapting essays to different questions. The book closes with the author's analysis of three "good essays."

EVALUATION:

In 130+ very easy-to-use pages, the author walks a student through the application and essay writing process as painlessly as possible. Particularly helpful is the author's organized approach. The chapter on understanding essay questions, for example, walks the student through a process which illustrates overlaps in questions asked by various colleges (many essays can be used in more than one application), then categorizes and explains the intent of typical essay topics -- these thoughtful steps really can help break down what can be an overwhelming task into less threatening components. The book's layout, which includes many well-designed forms and matrices interspersed with the author's tips and insights, helps guide the reader through the necessary steps in as entertaining and understandable a process as we're seen. There's enough thoughtful detail here to draw excellent essays out of the most challenged student (intimidated by writing, concerned about a lack of subject matter, etc.). The process flows logically from chapter to chapter, with reinforcement and explanation helpful in providing continuing encouragement that the process IS working and WILL achieve the desired result. As good a resource as we've seen.

WHERE TO FIND/BUY:

Find at bookstores and libraries.

Scaling The Ivy Wall In The '90's   ★★★★

Author/Editor: Howard Greene and Robert Minton
Publisher: Little, Brown and Company
Edition Reviewed: 2nd (1994)
Internet URL:

Media Type: Print
Price: $12.95
ISBN: 0-316-32736-0

RATINGS (1-4 STARS):

Overall:	★★★★	Comprehensive overview of the admissions process
Breadth Of Content:	★★★★	Hits all areas of the college process; places student in a proactive role
Value Added:	★★★	Sections on marketing yourself, financial aid, chances of admission
Ease Of Use:	★★★★	Well-organized and easy to read; good student examples

DESCRIPTION:

The authors, a veteran admissions counselor and university administrator, have rewritten their book to include current trends in the college world, up-to-date statistics, and comments from students, admission directors, and counselors. The book begins with an introductory chapter that gives an overview of the book's purpose and defines selective colleges. The remainder of the book consists of 12+ chapters that detail the authors' 12-step method of gaining admission into these selective colleges. These 12 steps include the following areas: the admissions process, a self-analytical study, high school prep, testing, extracurricular activities, getting acquainted with the colleges, determining your chances of gaining admission, writing the essay, financial aid, marketing yourself to these colleges, and enrolling. Also included in the book are a 20- month calendar of the admissions process, a section explaining the importance of the liberal arts, a chapter focusing on how to apply from abroad, an appendix containing sample worksheets, a bibliography and an index. Within each of the 12-step chapters, you will find anecdotes from accepted students, statistics, questionnaires, etc. At the end of each chapter is a summary/checklist.

EVALUATION:

It's often misleading to believe that anything can be reduced to a simple process. At first glance, this book seems no exception. However, upon closer investigation the authors give many atypical suggestions throughout their book. One underlying theme running through this book is that students can take the initiative, determine their strengths, and market themselves to selective colleges such as Harvard, Yale, Stanford, etc. In particular, we liked the steps entitled "Determining Your Strengths", "Excel Outside Class", "Find Your Place in the Class Pie Charts", and "Market Your Strengths". These chapters help students find their own potential and future possibilities aside from their GPA, high school rank, or testing scores. Additionally, the chapter entitled "Plan Your Selective College Finances" highlights information and statistics (number of scholarships funded by given institutions, etc.) not usually encountered in other guide books. Finally, the worksheets explained throughout and provided at the back of the book (college requirements, college visits, financial aid, self-analysis, etc.) are also an asset. This book may not be for everyone but it certainly has much to offer to the student who is driven, organized and adventurous.

WHERE TO FIND/BUY:

Bookstores and libraries.

Behind The Scenes: An Inside Look At The Selective College Admission Process ★★★

Author/Editor: Edward B. Wall
Publisher: Octameron Associates
Edition Reviewed: 10th (1994)
Internet URL:

Media Type: Print
Price: $4.00
ISBN: 0-945981-89-9

RATINGS (1-4 STARS):

Overall:	★★★	Great suggestions and examples from a veteran admissions director
Breadth Of Content:	★★	Narrow focus on admissions process, using Liberal Arts examples
Value Added:	★★★	Profiles provided of students who were accepted and rationale as to why
Ease Of Use:	★★★	Chapter headings, Q&A format make it an easy read

DESCRIPTION:

This 7-chapter, 36 page book, written by a 30+ year veteran in student admissions and counseling, outlines the admissions process. Chapter 1, dedicated to dean of admissions at Amherst, gives you a history of admissions' policies. Chapter 2 answers the most common questions about selective admission. Chapter 3 outlines strategies for the student when interviewing with prospective colleges. Information is also given about choosing schools, contacting and applying to schools, facing a personal interview, financial aid, and summer programs. Chapter 4 outlines the "mechanics of selection" and Chapter 5 answers the questions of "what are you looking for? what kinds of applicants are accepted?" by presenting profiles of 18 students who were admitted and enrolled at Amherst. Chapter 6 lists several arguments in support of a liberal arts education. Finally, chapter 7 is a one-page statistical profile of a class from the "most competitive year at Amherst". Information is listed such as: the volume of applicants ("accepted", "early decision matriculated", etc.), college board aptitude scores from those who applied, were accepted, were matriculated, rankings of students (public schools, private schools), etc.

EVALUATION:

This little book covers the important aspects of the admissions process. Within its cover you will find pertinent advice concerning contact with a college, how to prepare in your high school years, the worthiness of test scores, and how to supply useful information that gives colleges a true picture of yourself. In particular, chapter 1 gives a dean of admissions' point of view to exemplify what decisions are used to accept or reject applicants. Chapter 2 at first glance seems to have a hodgepodge of questions, but there are several suggestions here which should be taken seriously as students prepare for their college years. Chapter 3 also offers great advice on how to conduct yourself with the college of choice, including interview questions that might be asked of any applicant. Additionally, specific advice on the application process, from when to apply to what to include, is also supplied. Of particular interest are chapters 4 and 5 which give you an inside look into the admissions officers' thought processes. Chapter 4 outlines what actually goes on as the finalist list is narrowed down and chapter 5 profiles a variety of students and explains why they were accepted to Amherst. In all, this book does a great job of summing up the important points of the admissions process in a neat little package.

WHERE TO FIND/BUY:

Bookstores and libraries or through the publisher at 703-836-5480.

Section **III** Resource Reviews

Introduction

In this chapter, we provide you with reviews of all the resources we've encountered in our search for the best information focused on college choice and admissions. These reviews are organized by media, and within each media type, by overall "Star" rating.

In a few cases, we've included resources that we have not rated, but which we feel are worthwhile for you to know about. These will be listed at the end of each section.

PRINT RESOURCES 68

These reviews are focused primarily on printed guidebooks. Some of the guidebooks are hundreds of pages long; some just dozens of pages. We work hard to ensure that we've reviewed the latest version of guidebooks that are reissued once/year. Many guidebooks are not issued annually, however; the edition date included in each review shows when the most recent edition was issued or the latest copyright date.

We don't review guidebooks that are no longer in print or not readily available from bookstores.

RESOURCES ON THE INTERNET'S WORLD WIDE WEB 139

These reviews include all the websites that we've been able to find on the web. Our criteria for selecting a website for review include these requirements:

- A substantial portion of its content must be focused on college choice and admissions. Thus, sites that have currently-enrolled college students as their focus are generally excluded.
- It must be substantially complete, not substantially under construction.
- Commercial sites that have products or services for sale to visitors are reviewed, provided they also contain some relevant, free content.
- We don't review sites which have as their primary focus simply providing links to other sites, particularly since most of those linked sites will be included in our reviews.

CD-ROM RESOURCES 167

These reviews include all the CD-ROMs we've found that are focused on selecting colleges. In several cases, CD-ROMs we've reviewed are made up primarily of material duplicated elsewhere, usually in a printed guidebook; in these cases, we comment on the additional value provided by the CD-ROM's multimedia features relative to its higher cost.

We don't review CD-ROM based products that are sold primarily to high schools and libraries as commercial products; they usually cost several hundred dollars and up.

SOFTWARE RESOURCES 173

These reviews include software applications that are focused on college selection or admissions. They include software programs for different operating systems (Mac OS, Windows); availability for different operating systems, and minimum system requirements, are noted.

VIDEOTAPE RESOURCES   176

These reviews include videotape products that are focused on college selection or admissions, or on companies that sell videotapes of colleges, either produced by the colleges or by independent counselors.

RESOURCES ON THE COMMERCIAL ONLINE SERVICES   179

These reviews include forums or special interest areas containing proprietary or sponsored content focused on college selection or admissions. Online services include America Online, The Microsoft Network, Compuserve, and Prodigy. Content offered by these companies through their websites are reviewed in the Internet section.

MISCELLANEOUS RESOURCES   183

These reviews are of products or services that do not readily fit within one of the previous categories, such as annual magazine issues focused on college ratings.

Fiske Guide To Colleges

★★★★

Author/Editor: Edward B. Fiske
Publisher: Times Books (Division Of Random House, Inc.)
Edition Reviewed: 1997
Internet URL:

Media Type: Print
Price: $19
ISBN: 0812927575

RATINGS (1-4 STARS):

Overall:	★★★★	One of the best to help you get to your final list
Breadth Of Content:	★★★	Only 315 colleges and universities covered
Value Added:	★★★★	Really outstanding insight; wholly original writing
Ease Of Use:	★★★★	Listed alphabetically; indexes by alpha, state, and price

DESCRIPTION:

Published annually since 1982, this 800+ page guidebook is one of the few available which offers original, evaluative essays on each of the 300+ colleges and universities covered. The essays are based primarily on in-depth feedback from students, supplemented by additional research, including campus visits. All "selective admission" colleges and universities are included (175 by their definition), with the remainder providing geographic diversity and a balance of public/private schools. Each write-up (2-4 pages in length) includes comments on academics, the student body, financial aid, housing, food, social life, and extracurricular activities, with summary ratings (1-5 Stars) for Academics, Social Life, and Quality of Life. At the beginning of each article, typical statistics about the school are listed (location, enrollment, size, M/F ratio, SAT/ACT ranges, number of applicants/accepted/enrolled). Each school's admissions practices, policies, and deadlines are summarized as well. In addition, 42 institutions are highlighted as "Best Buys" -- "remarkable educational opportunities at a relatively modest cost."

EVALUATION:

This guidebook is among the best, if not the best, source of original descriptions on the colleges included. Its writing style is entertaining, thorough, and refreshingly free of the promotional prose parroted by many guides. The research done and questions asked of students and administrators alike are focused on issues that are relevant to selecting a college, and are responsive to the focus of parents and prospective students alike. For example: strong (and weak) academic departments are noted, student housing is discussed in detail, the origin, focus, and interests of typical students are described -- as a result, the descriptive "feel" of each campus really helps a prospective student visualize what it would be like to attend. Student social life - what students do when they're not in classes - is discussed in some detail, as is the surrounding community and the quality of life it offers. If you've got some of its 300+ schools on your list to evaluate, this guidebook will be among the best resources you can use to pare down your list.

WHERE TO FIND/BUY:

Bookstores and libraries, or order direct from the publisher by calling 800-793-BOOK.

Insider's Guide To The Colleges

Author/Editor: Staff of The Yale Daily News	**Media Type:** Print
Publisher: St. Martin's Press	**Price:** $14.99
Edition Reviewed: 1995	**ISBN:** 031213522X
Internet URL:	

RATINGS (1-4 STARS):

Overall:	★★★★	Useful student perspective on colleges included
Breadth Of Content:	★★★	Limited to 300+ colleges included
Value Added:	★★★★	Excellent insight into student body taken as a whole
Ease Of Use:	★★★★	Easy to use format and indexes

DESCRIPTION:

Published since the early '70's, this guidebook provides original profiles on 300+ of the "best and most noteworthy" colleges. It's written by the staff of the Yale Daily News, based on input from college students across the country. Colleges profiled are included primarily on academic quality, with others added to provide balance in size and geographic distribution; some specialized schools are also included (technical institutes and creative/performing arts). Each 2 page essay focuses on student-centered issues such as: which departments are strong, class size and teaching quality, academic focus and approach, popular extracurricular activities, school traditions, student body characteristics as a whole, living/dining facilities and quality, and student social life. A good selection of useful statistics is included for each school as well. This guidebook also includes some comprehensive essays on the admissions process and which factors are important to consider when choosing among schools; perspectives for international and disabled students are included, as well as several useful indexes based on selected college attributes.

EVALUATION:

This publication provides useful insight on the 300+ colleges included, taken primarily from the focus of currently enrolled students. This focus, while a bit narrow, can be very helpful in gaining a "feel" for an institution before deciding on a short list for visits or applications. The writing style is original, entertaining, and easy to read. The essays are short, which means that a more comprehensive picture will have to be filled in from other sources, but they provide a unique perspective drawn exclusively from students; descriptions of the character of the student body taken as a whole are particularly useful. The comprehensive essays that describe the entire college selection/admission process (17 pages) and discuss factors to consider when selecting a college (10 pages) are very helpful and are alone worth the price of this guidebook.

WHERE TO FIND/BUY:

National distribution through bookstores, libraries, etc., or order direct from Publisher's Books at 800-288-2131.

Best 309 Colleges

Author/Editor: Meltzer/Knower/Custard/Katzman	**Media Type:** Print
Publisher: Princeton Review/Random House, Inc.	**Price:** $18
Edition Reviewed: 1997	**ISBN:** 0679771220
Internet URL:	

RATINGS (1-4 STARS):

Overall:	★★★★	Easy-to-use format; provides a quick but original look at some good schools
Breadth Of Content:	★★★	Only 309 schools covered; only 2 pages allotted per school
Value Added:	★★★★	A comprehensive survey forms the basis for some interesting observations
Ease Of Use:	★★★★	Very easy to use; well-organized visually

DESCRIPTION:

This guidebook is based largely on surveys from some 56,000 students at the 309 colleges reviewed (70 multiple-choice questions on a variety of subjects, and free-form comments,too). The authors polled 50 independent college counselors to help generate their list of the nation's best colleges. Each school reviewed gets two pages, organized to combine statistics with commentary; survey input finds its way into both. The usual stats are included, supplemented by summary ratings on campus life, academics, admissions, and financial aid, as well as survey-based facts on "what's hot & not," ratings on professors, popular majors, and others. Commentaries include observations on student life, academic environment, and types of students enrolled. Next, the authors focus on each school's admissions process; this is supplemented by observations from the admissions office and independent counselors. Requirements for financial aid are spelled out in a separate section, as are comments from each admissions office. Separate rankings for 61 categories (selected mostly for fun) are included, as are a listing of independent college counselors.

EVALUATION:

We like the general tone of this guidebook, which doesn't take itself too seriously. The authors have done a good job weaving a largely survey-based database and some student comments into a useful tapestry of observations about each school. Their stats are easy to use, with visual summaries indicating relative rank within the group. The survey generates some interesting input on campus life ("What's Hot & What's Not"), input on the quality of teaching, popular majors, etc. The written commentary is livened up with frequent quotations from students, and provides useful perspectives on the typical student, campus life, and the academic environment. Most admissions offices provide some useful insight on the kind of student they're looking for, in a section where they're invited to "speak directly to the readers". The summary ratings provided for campus life, academics, admissions, and financial aid are useful in comparing each college within this select group. Finally, the authors lighten things up by providing survey-based rankings on 61 wildly divergent categories. They close this guidebook with some funny and irreverent quotes gathered from their survey, in a section titled "My Roommate's Feet Really Stink".

WHERE TO FIND/BUY:

Bookstores and libraries, or order direct by calling 800-793-BOOK.

Guide To 150 Popular College Majors

Author/Editor: Renee Gernand
Publisher: College Board Publications
Edition Reviewed: 1992
Internet URL:

Media Type: Print
Price: $16
ISBN: 0-87447-400-0

RATINGS (1-4 STARS):

Overall:	★★★★	Can't be beat for helping students understand their choices in majors
Breadth Of Content:	★★★	150 of the most common majors are included
Value Added:	★★★★	Descriptions are wholly original, readable, and very helpful
Ease Of Use:	★★★★	Well-organized, with good explanations of content and approach

DESCRIPTION:

This guidebook provides descriptions of the 150+ "most widely offered baccalaureate-level majors". The descriptions are written by professors teaching in each field, and are grouped under 17 general categories (humanities, physical sciences, engineering, etc.). An introduction to each of these broad categories provides an "overview of each field and describes differences between the various majors". The detailed description for each major follows a common format, describing interests and skills associated with success in the major, recommended high school education, typical courses, what the major is like, careers related to the major, and whom to contact for more information (associations, etc.). Two indexes are provided: a Careers index lists 150+ jobs and some of the majors that can be useful in preparing for a particular career; the Related Majors index provides an exhaustive list of other majors related to each specific major listed. An essay which puts choosing a major in perspective ("it's important enough to take seriously, but it's not irrevocable") is included, as are 12 anecdotal essays on choosing/changing majors, written by students.

EVALUATION:

This can be a wonderfully helpful book for high school students (and their parents) who are uncertain about picking a major as a point of focus for their college search. Most students in high school have some feelings about what they like and dislike, and this book can be very helpful in providing some definition to their college search plans. The introductory essay at the beginning of the book starts things out on the right foot by pointing out that the "major decision", while important, is not irrevocable and is, in fact, often changed during the course of getting a degree. The introductions to each broad category of majors provides a clear overview of fields of study within that general area of interest; this is useful reading, especially for those who haven't a clue about what they'd like to study. Profiles for each of the 150 majors are short, well-written, and provide helpful insights into what taking each major course of study will involve, what careers are typically related to each major, and what personal interests and skills are likely to match up well with each major. The Career index is also very helpful, showing in a very easy-to-use format which degrees most often lead to which jobs.

WHERE TO FIND/BUY:

Bookstores and libraries, direct from the publisher by calling 800-323-7155, or on the World Wide Web at http://www.collegeboard.org.

College Match

★★★★

Author/Editor: Steven Antonoff, Ph.D. & Marie Friedemann Ph.D.
Publisher: Octameron Associates
Edition Reviewed: 4th (1996-97)
Internet URL:

Media Type: Print
Price: $7.50
ISBN: 1-57509-004-X

RATINGS (1-4 STARS):

Overall:	★★★★	Provides an excellent, and gentle, process of self-discovery and choice
Breadth Of Content:		Not applicable
Value Added:	★★★★	The authors' experience shows
Ease Of Use:	★★★	Worksheets and process require commitment but are worth it

---

DESCRIPTION:

The authors are experienced college admission officers and educational consultants; this book shares the methods they've developed over fifteen years of working with students making the college choice. The book follows a sequence of steps designed to lead students (and their parents) to suitable college choices. After a chapter which reassures the prospective college student about making this choice and debunks some myths, the authors provide a "self-survey" and three worksheets designed to help students develop their own admissions profile. This is followed by a chapter which identifies college characteristics that will be a good match to the personal profile just developed; thirteen factors such as size, student body qualities, academic environment, etc. are discussed and prioritized. Chapters follow which help students identify and compare college choices and manage college visits effectively. The chapters that follow deal with writing effective essays and understanding the admissions process. Appendices are provided suggesting college planning goals for each year in high school.

EVALUATION:

This book is an excellent choice for parents and students who want to take time for a thoughtful approach to the college selection process. The experience of these educational consultants shows through in the quality of their approach. We agree with the themes outlined in their preface; namely, that all students have colleges from which to choose, that the choice process does not have to be stressful, that a logical series of steps can make this process one of insight and discovery, and that choosing a college is a great "first test" of using personal values to make an important real-life choice. The writing style is gentle and easy to read. The worksheets, rankings, and questions are not overwhelming and can be completed easily. The process of self-discovery outlined in Chapter 2 is outstanding, and should really help students develop a picture of who they are and what's important to them. Chapter 3 is also very helpful in illuminating, and helping students rank, the typical college choice factors. After this preparatory work is done, the remaining research should be a much more positive and focused effort than it might otherwise be.

WHERE TO FIND/BUY:

Bookstores and libraries, or direct from the publisher by calling 703-836-5480.

Campus Pursuit

★★★★

Author/Editor: G. Gary Ripple, Ph.D.
Publisher: Octameron Associates
Edition Reviewed: 6th (1995)
Internet URL:

Media Type: Print
Price: $5
ISBN: 1575090031

RATINGS (1-4 STARS):

Overall:	★★★★	Very focused, very effective; the author's experience shows
Breadth Of Content:		Not Applicable
Value Added:	★★★★	Very thorough treatment of two important subjects
Ease Of Use:	★★★	Well organized, well written, mercifully concise

DESCRIPTION:

This 32 page guidebook is in its 6th edition; it's written by an experienced college admissions director. The chapter on "Visiting A College" begins with an overview of college handbooks and ratings, and the role parents should play in a visit. The remaining sections provide advice on planning college visits, including objectives for each visit, and suggestions for followup. The final two chapters, and the two appendices following, focus on college interviews. Overviews are provided on the interview's importance, and what admissions staff are looking for in the students they interview, and how an interview is normally conducted. The remainder of the chapter, and the appendices, then focus on questions that are likely, as well as questions that prospective students should ask of their interviewer. A short chapter then discusses common questions (and answers) which prospective students typically have about the interview process.

EVALUATION:

This is a short, focused little book that may provide you all you need to know about the importance of, and objectives for, visiting colleges and about handling the typical college interview to your benefit. The experience of the author really shows through in the insights provided throughout each chapter. The objectives described for college visits should help ensure they provide maximum benefit. Reading the thorough treatment of interviews will provide prospective college students with much reassurance about what's typically going to happen during such interviews, how to best prepare for the experience, which classic mistakes to avoid, and how to ensure that the communication process works to the benefit of interviewer and interviewee. A study of the list of questions likely to be asked, and those that should be asked by the student, will be of great benefit in calming the inevitable trepidation felt by college applicants.

WHERE TO FIND/BUY:

Bookstores and libraries, or direct from the publisher by calling 703-836-5480.

Campus Visits & College Interviews ★★★★

Author/Editor: Zola Schneider
Publisher: College Board Publications
Edition Reviewed: 1987
Internet URL:

Media Type: Print
Price: $9.95
ISBN: 0-87447-260-1

RATINGS (1-4 STARS):

Overall:	★★★★	Very thorough treatment of two important topics
Breadth Of Content:		Not applicable
Value Added:	★★★★	Lots of detailed suggestions
Ease Of Use:	★★★	Well-organized; useful checklists

DESCRIPTION:

This 120+ page book dedicates half its pages to campus visits, half to college interviews. Chapters on campus visits cover preparations including deciding when/where to visit, planning the visit, making preparations; other chapters focus on what to accomplish during the visit. One chapter suggests dividing the campus exploration into five areas: students, social life, facilities, outside community, and academics. This portion of the book closes with a college evaluation checklist. The chapters on interviewing include putting the interview into perspective, how to approach and prepare for the interview, and questions likely to be asked and that should be asked by the student. A separate chapter is devoted to helping the "shy" person get through the experience successfully. The author places fictional high school students in scenarios which give a feel for how a campus visit might go; these chapters are usually followed by more detailed lists of things to think about, and suggestions on what to accomplish. Key points made in each chapter are summarized in checklists.

EVALUATION:

Campus visits and admissions interviews are critical elements in the college admissions process, yet most information sources focus on other elements. A campus visit and interview can tell things to a student that nothing in print can; thankfully, this book takes a very detailed look at these important steps in selecting a college home. Particularly useful among the chapters on campus visits is the first, which gives some convincing advice on when to visit (and when NOT to), and shows how this can be managed. Indicative of the author's experience are the detailed questions included in the chapter which suggest dividing the campus visit into five areas of inquiry; also useful is the detailed college evaluation checklist, which can be used to evaluate alternatives within a common framework. The author puts the admissions interview into a relaxed context, making the point that it is simply a two-way information exchange. She nonetheless provides thorough advice on getting ready for such interviews: "knowing thyself," practice, planning, and preparing to both answer and ask questions; a separate chapter is devoted to helping the "shy" person cope. The writing style is enlivened by placing fictional high school students in the various situations discussed.

WHERE TO FIND/BUY:

Bookstores and libraries, direct from the publisher by calling 800-323-7155, or on the World Wide Web at http://www.collegeboard.org.

Ivy League Programs At State School Prices ★★★★

Author/Editor: Robert R. Sullivan

Publisher: Arco/Prentice Hall

Edition Reviewed: 1st (1994)

Internet URL:

Media Type: Print

Price: $15

ISBN: 0-671-87426-8

RATINGS (1-4 STARS):

Overall:	★★★★	Illuminating insights into Honors Programs at state universities
Breadth Of Content:	★★	Covers programs at just 55 state universities
Value Added:	★★★★	The profiles are wholly original, including program quality judgments
Ease Of Use:	★★★★	Easy to use and to read

DESCRIPTION:

This guidebook provides information on Honors Programs at 55 state universities (the "flagship" state universities, with some exceptions). An introductory chapter explains that these programs offer small classes, taught by professors, to a small number of academically qualified students. The result, according to the author: a "quality education at low prices." The author cautions that academically qualified usually means a B or better high school GPA and scores of 1,100+ on the SAT or 26+ on the ACT. A summary of basic information about each program is provided, along with 1-2 pages of narrative describing the program and its strengths and weaknesses. The process of application and selection is outlined, as are the courses offered, and how the program fits within the institution as a whole. The summary information includes subjective judgments by the author on factors he considers important to the quality of the various programs: town and campus settings, intellectual setting (including student diversity), the relative competitiveness of admission to the program, and the quality of the program itself. An overall rating of each program is provided (one to three Stars).

EVALUATION:

As the author states in the first sentence of his introduction, "This book is for academically talented high school juniors and seniors from families with moderate incomes." If this description fits you, then the universities and programs described in this book are worthy of review. The author makes a convincing argument that admission to one of these programs can result in an educational experience equal to or better than that available from more expensive private institutions. This book is a sincere and serious effort to both identify these programs nationally, and provide some evaluative judgments on the relative quality of the various programs profiled; the profiles are based on lengthy phone interviews and research. The profiles provided are written in an engaging, easy-to-read style.

WHERE TO FIND/BUY:

Find at bookstores and libraries.

Writing Your College Application Essay

Author/Editor: Sarah Myers McGinty **Media Type:** Print
Publisher: College Board Publications **Price:** $9.95
Edition Reviewed: 1992 **ISBN:** 0-87447-429-9
Internet URL:

RATINGS (1-4 STARS):

Overall:	★★★★	An excellent resource to help students over the college essay hurdle
Breadth Of Content:		Not applicable
Value Added:	★★★★	Just the right amount of depth, balanced with encouragement
Ease Of Use:	★★★	Well written; takes focus and discipline to get through

---

DESCRIPTION:

The author is an experienced English teacher and college admissions director. The focus of this 120+ page book is, as the title states, solely on the college application essay. The first chapter is an overview of the college selection process, and positions the importance of the essay within this context. Chapter Two reassures by reviewing the basics of writing essays (structure, style, etc.) that students already know as high schools students. Chapter Three, the meat of the book, is a review course in essay writing: prewriting (brainstorming, organizing), drafting (topic sentences, development, clincher, conclusion), and editing. Chapter Four describes and discusses the types of questions typically asked on college applications, with expansion in the following chapter on two key types of questions: "Tell us about yourself..." and "Why do you want to come here...". The book closes with an analysis of six actual essays.

EVALUATION:

The experience of the author on "both sides of the fence" shows through brightly in this book. It is both methodical and precise in helping students revisit and understand the process of writing essays, and empathetic and encouraging in tone, providing a positive "you can do it" push to students intimidated by the process. For example, it's useful that the author takes some time to bring the reader up to the point of detailed advice on the essay, by placing its importance within the context of the whole application, and by restating what high school students already know about writing -- this all should serve to relax anxieties somewhat and help the student focus on the details which follow. The chapters on essay writing are a very readable (and detailed) dissection of the writing process, giving particular focus on the kinds of questions typically asked by colleges. The author effectively leads the reader through the process of creating good college essays; all that's required to succeed is for students to stay confident, think carefully about the processes and observations laid out in this book, and implement them in their writing.

WHERE TO FIND/BUY:

Bookstores and libraries, direct from the publisher by calling 800-323-7155, or on the World Wide Web at http://www.collegeboard.org.

College Applications & Essays

★★★★

Author/Editor: Susan D. Van Raalte

Publisher: Arco

Edition Reviewed: 2nd (1994)

Internet URL:

Media Type: Print

Price: $9

ISBN: 0-671-86644-3

RATINGS (1-4 STARS):

Overall:	★★★★	The best resource on essay writing we've seen
Breadth Of Content:		Not applicable
Value Added:	★★★★	The author's experience shows; the forms and processes used are polished
Ease Of Use:	★★★	An easy-to-use format for an intimidating topic

DESCRIPTION:

This book captures a course in college applications/essays taught by the author for 15 years, and is targeted at high school seniors: "they will be coaxed and prodded..through a step-by-step system designed to break down application writing into manageable pieces." The book is organized into twelve chapters, with most focused on writing essays;throughout, lots of forms and checklists are included so processes suggested can be implemented as the book is read. The second chapter provides forms and suggestions for organizing the admissions process. Chapters follow which explain typical essay questions asked, and walk the student through a personal inventory process (with input, suggestions, and insights by the author throughout). Focusing on the process of writing essays, the book provides chapters and exercises on generating and refining ideas for essays, structuring essays to be readable, creating great "beginnings" and "endings," using tone and style to improve readability, overcoming "writer's block," and adapting essays to different questions. The book closes with the author's analysis of three "good essays."

EVALUATION:

In 130+ very easy-to-use pages, the author walks a student through the application and essay writing process as painlessly as possible. Particularly helpful is the author's organized approach. The chapter on understanding essay questions, for example, walks the student through a process which illustrates overlaps in questions asked by various colleges (many essays can be used in more than one application), then categorizes and explains the intent of typical essay topics -- these thoughtful steps really can help break down what can be an overwhelming task into less threatening components. The book's layout, which includes many well-designed forms and matrices interspersed with the author's tips and insights, helps guide the reader through the necessary steps in as entertaining and understandable a process as we're seen. There's enough thoughtful detail here to draw excellent essays out of the most challenged student (intimidated by writing, concerned about a lack of subject matter, etc.). The process flows logically from chapter to chapter, with reinforcement and explanation helpful in providing continuing encouragement that the process IS working and WILL achieve the desired result. As good a resource as we've seen.

WHERE TO FIND/BUY:

Find at bookstores and libraries.

Performing Arts Major's College Guide ★★★★

Author/Editor: Carol J. Everett
Publisher: Macmillan USA
Edition Reviewed: 2nd (1994)
Internet URL:

Media Type: Print
Price: $20.00
ISBN: 0-671-88417-4

RATINGS (1-4 STARS):

Overall:	★★★★	Comprehensive resource for aspiring performers
Breadth Of Content:	★★★	Covers 300+ programs worldwide
Value Added:	★★★★	The author's experience with Julliard School shows
Ease Of Use:	★★★★	Easy to read with a handy index

DESCRIPTION:

This guidebook, written by the former Director of Admissions for The Julliard School, provides information on 300+ colleges, universities and conservatories worldwide with a focus on performance in Dance, Drama, and Music. This is the second edition and includes a new section on "How to Evaluate Your Talent". The first half of this guidebook outlines the process of applying to and auditioning for programs in these disciplines. Each discipline is covered in its own chapter with the music section being further divided by instrument. The chapters cover advanced study, how to handle auditions (including what to wear and what not to do), and an admissions checklist. The author provides progam rankings in Part 5, based on surveys and interviews with performers, faculty, and students. Part 6 contains college profiles arranged alphabetically; the information here is also survey-based. The profiles range in length from one paragraph to two pages and the amount of information given depends on how thoroughly the institution filled out the survey. Each contains the usual stats as well as deadline information, information for international students and an author's comment.

EVALUATION:

The major strength of this book is the author's in-depth experience with applications and auditions. She has "seen it all" and wants to make sure that you benefit from her learning experiences. Although the different chapters for music, dance, and drama cover the same overall points, each one contains specific tips and details to help students in those disciplines get into the program of their choice. The weaker part of this book is the section which covers 300+ programs and institutions. It is not nearly as comprehensive as the first half and it is evident that the author's main focus was on how to get in, not where to go. This book won't tell you everything you need to know about all of the programs out there, but you will get a general feel of who you want to call for more information. This resource is recommended for students who wish to pursue a career in the performing arts.

WHERE TO FIND/BUY:

Bookstores and libraries.

Winning Edge: The Student Athlete's Guide To College Sports

Author/Editor: Frances & James Killpatrick

Publisher: Octameron Associates, Inc.

Edition Reviewed: 4th (1995)

Internet URL:

Media Type: Print

Price: $7.50

ISBN: 0-945981-99-6

RATINGS (1-4 STARS):

Overall:	★★★★	Covers college sports thoroughly
Breadth Of Content:	★★	Hundreds of colleges listed, minimum information is given
Value Added:	★★★★	Important statistics listed for the serious athlete
Ease Of Use:	★★★	Colleges listed by sport and State; an index is needed

---

DESCRIPTION:

In its fourth edition, this book is a guide to all levels of college sports for the serious and not-so-serious high school athlete. The first section provides basic information on applications, financial aid, and campus visits (with a slant toward the high school athlete), as well as the other steps that student athletes need to take in order to continue their sport in college. The differences between amateur and professional sports are outlined. How to appraise your skill and getting help from your coach are also discussed. The second section of the book is a listing of winning teams (organized by sport and division); this includes essays written by top coaches in baseball, basketball, crew, field hockey, football, golf, ice hockey, lacrosse, skiing, soccer, softball, swimming, tennis, track, and volleyball. The third section lists NCAA Divisions IA, I, II, and III, by State. The listings for NCAA IA and I include graduation statistics for each school. All division rankings are for the 1994-95 season. The book concludes with a sample sports resume, college checklist, and sample letters.

EVALUATION:

One drawback of this guidebook is that its focus is so narrow. Hundreds of colleges are listed in this slim 136 page guide, but aside from the sports statistics and contact information, there is no other information given about the colleges and universities listed here. On the upside, the essays by the top coaches in the country are insightful and replete with important tips on how to continue your achievements in your sport at the college level. A wide variety of sports are covered and we were happy to see that equal weight was given to women's sports. The chapter overview of NCAA recruiting rules and regulations was particularly useful, with simple, everyday terms to explain regulations that are sometimes tricky and hard to understand. Used in conjunction with other guidebooks, this book will be very useful to high school athletes and their parents. It is recommended to the serious athlete for help you decide on your initial list of schools.

WHERE TO FIND/BUY:

Find in Libraries or Bookstores, or call the publisher direct at 703-836-5480.

Rugg's Recommendations On The Colleges   ★★★★

Author/Editor: Frederick E. Rugg
Publisher: Rugg's Recommendations
Edition Reviewed: 13th (1996)
Internet URL:

Media Type: Print
Price: $18.95
ISBN: 1-883062-09-8

RATINGS (1-4 STARS):

Overall:	★★★★	A "must have" for your first cut, if you know your planned major(s)
Breadth Of Content:	★★★	Includes 735 of the better schools in the country
Value Added:	★★★	Identifies the best departments at the quality colleges
Ease Of Use:	★★★★	Organized by major, college selectivity, and size

DESCRIPTION:

This guide, now in its 13th Edition, was developed to answer the question: "What are some good colleges that have strong programs in business, or engineering, or music (or whatever)?" 735 "quality" colleges are identified, including those with Phi Beta Kappa chapters, plus additional subjective choices (based on the author's, and his staff's, collective experiences). Ratings of the quality of various programs of study are primarily based on the input of current students (10,000+ interviews/surveys!), which the author argues is the most reliable source; he includes input from high school counselors, and the colleges themselves, as well. 39 undergraduate majors are listed separately, with 37 "miscellaneous" majors also listed. The listings are then organized into groups, based on college admissions selectivity (Most Selective - about 100 schools, Very Selective, and Selective); selectivity is determined on the measures of average high school GPAs and combined SAT scores. Finally, the size of each college is assigned to one of five categories, from Small (<1,000 students) to Extra Large (>20,000 students). An appendix provides average SAT-I scores for each college with a listing of its recommended majors.

EVALUATION:

For those students who have decided on, or have a strong inclination towards one or more possible majors in college, this guide is an excellent way to begin the process of creating that "first" list of alternatives. The guide includes a limited number of colleges, but includes enough high-quality choices to provide a good cross-section. Are their ratings of college degree programs reliable? Primarily based on input from current students, they're probably as good a place to begin as any; that this is the thirteenth edition is also of some comfort. What's particularly useful about this guide is that it is very easy to come up with an initial list of possible school choices, given some inkling of what majors you might be interested in, where your high school GPA and SAT score may place you on the "selectivity" scale, and how large an institution you want to attend. From this good start, other information sources can be used to learn more about each college alternative.

WHERE TO FIND/BUY:

Libraries and bookstores, or direct from the publisher at 805-462-2503.

College Guide For The Learning Disabled   ★★★★

Author/Editor: Charles T. Straughn II
Publisher: Lovejoy's Educational Guides / Prentice Hall
Edition Reviewed: 3rd (1993)
Internet URL:

Media Type: Print
Price: $22.00
ISBN: 0-671-84771-6

RATINGS (1-4 STARS):

Overall:	★★★★	Full of important information for students with learning disabilities
Breadth Of Content:	★★★	270+ colleges and universities profiled
Value Added:	★★★★	Author's experience and compassion shines throughout
Ease Of Use:	★★★	Well organized, but small type makes profiles hard to read

DESCRIPTION:

This 177 page guidebook, now in its third edition, profiles 270 colleges and universities in the United States with support services for Learning Disabled (LD) students. The author talks about his own LD and that of his daughter and how this influenced him to write this book. Section III offers techniques on developing coping skills for the LD student's college experience. Section IV describes what an LD student needs to look for in a college and what the college looks for in the admissions process. Colleges and universities included in this guide responded to a survey sent out by Lovejoy's; they were asked to read the definition of LD and state whether or not they should be included in this guide. Those who answered "yes" were included in this book. Each profile is approximately 3/4 of a page long and includes general information about the campus, a checklist of support services available, admissions requirements, and special comments on services for LD students. Each college is given a ranking of L, LL, or LLL based on the level of support available to LD students. The schools are listed alphabetically by State, by career curricula, special programs, and sports.

EVALUATION:

This guidebook is a valuable resource for students with LDs and their parents. The author's experiences show in the compassionate tone of the opening sections of this book; written in the first person, they will help make parents and students feel comfortable immediately. It is nice to see a specialized guidebook that assumes that all students, regardless of their particular disability, are interested in knowing what academic programs are available and what sports the college participates in, as well as the services they provide. The profiles themselves contain more information than we have seen in other guidebooks for LD students. The information about admissions and services for LD students are listed at the beginning of each profile and is followed by useful information on campus life and housing; graduate/enrollment statistics are included. Type in this section is quite small, making it a little difficult to read. Some of the information may be dated, since this edition was published in 1993, but the contact information and the sections on what to expect and how to prepare should be current. This resource should help the LD student determine which of those institutions offer the level of support required.

WHERE TO FIND/BUY:

Bookstores and libraries.

50 College Admission Directors Speak To Parents

Author/Editor: Sandra F. MacGowan and Sarah M. McGinty
Publisher: Books for Professionals, Inc.
Edition Reviewed: 1st (1988)
Internet URL:

Media Type: Print
Price: $8.95
ISBN: 0-15-601595-1

RATINGS (1-4 STARS):

Overall:	★★★★	Excellent general reference on admissions process
Breadth Of Content:	★★★★	Covers all elements, with emotional support for students and parents
Value Added:	★★★★	50 responses to questions posed to nationwide admissions directors
Ease Of Use:	★★★★	Very organized and easy to read; narratives are short and to the point

---

DESCRIPTION:

The authors compiled this book based upon questions from parents. These questions were then posed to 50 admission directors of colleges across the country. Each chapter of this 267 page book includes a 1 to 3 page overview by the authors on the subject matter and then several responses from the admissions directors to these questions. The first 2 chapters give a basic overview of what is included in the rest of the book. Chapters 3 and 4 deal primarily with selecting colleges and narrowing down the choices. Chapter 5 discusses what happens in the admission committees. Chapters 6, 7 and 8 discuss elements of the application, namely, the importances of test scores, the high school record, and the college essay. Chapter 9 then offers suggestions on how to make the most of interviews, campus visits and independent college consultants such as counselors. Chapter 10 relates financial aid advice and financing options. Chapter 11 highlights special schools and programs for special students, such as minorities, learning disabled, etc. Chapters 12, 13 and 14 then discuss acceptance and rejection offers, transfer possibilities, and how to ease the transition from high school to college.

EVALUATION:

This book should ease the minds of many parents. Many questions that arise during the arduous process of selecting and applying to colleges are answered here by authorities who make that all-important decision - the admissions directors. Responses to typical concerns are presented here in a non-condescending style; these admission directors genuinely want to help make a good match between their colleges and students. Too often, other books present check-off calendars and offer suggestions to parents without keeping in mind that students play an important role too. Throughout this book, both sides are given credibility and support. In particular, chapters 5 through 8 serve to make the application process a bonding opportunity between parents and student. Students are encouraged to take on more responsibility with the parent as a guide and model. Most books also neglect the impact on students and parents after the student enrolls at a given college. Chapter 13 is a must-read for all students and parents as it details how to make the college transition easier for all. In particular, the authors list for students certain routines and habits that will help start the school year right. The authors also help parents understand how to allow students to develop meaningful new adult relationships and life skills.

WHERE TO FIND/BUY:

Bookstores and libraries.

Scaling The Ivy Wall In The '90's

★★★★

Author/Editor: Howard Greene and Robert Minton
Publisher: Little, Brown and Company
Edition Reviewed: 2nd (1994)
Internet URL:

Media Type: Print
Price: $12.95
ISBN: 0-316-32736-0

RATINGS (1-4 STARS):

Overall:	★★★★	Comprehensive overview of the admissions process
Breadth Of Content:	★★★★	Hits all areas of the college process; places student in a proactive role
Value Added:	★★★	Sections on marketing yourself, financial aid, chances of admission
Ease Of Use:	★★★★	Well-organized and easy to read; good student examples

DESCRIPTION:

The authors, a veteran admissions counselor and university administrator, have rewritten their book to include current trends in the college world, up-to-date statistics, and comments from students, admission directors, and counselors. The book begins with an introductory chapter that gives an overview of the book's purpose and defines selective colleges. The remainder of the book consists of 12+ chapters that detail the authors' 12-step method of gaining admission into these selective colleges. These 12 steps include the following areas: the admissions process, a self-analytical study, high school prep, testing, extracurricular activities, getting acquainted with the colleges, determining your chances of gaining admission, writing the essay, financial aid, marketing yourself to these colleges, and enrolling. Also included in the book are a 20- month calendar of the admissions process, a section explaining the importance of the liberal arts, a chapter focusing on how to apply from abroad, an appendix containing sample worksheets, a bibliography and an index. Within each of the 12-step chapters, you will find anecdotes from accepted students, statistics, questionnaires, etc. At the end of each chapter is a summary/checklist.

EVALUATION:

It's often misleading to believe that anything can be reduced to a simple process. At first glance, this book seems no exception. However, upon closer investigation the authors give many atypical suggestions throughout their book. One underlying theme running through this book is that students can take the initiative, determine their strengths, and market themselves to selective colleges such as Harvard, Yale, Stanford, etc. In particular, we liked the steps entitled "Determining Your Strengths", "Excel Outside Class", "Find Your Place in the Class Pie Charts", and "Market Your Strengths". These chapters help students find their own potential and future possibilities aside from their GPA, high school rank, or testing scores. Additionally, the chapter entitled "Plan Your Selective College Finances" highlights information and statistics (number of scholarships funded by given institutions, etc.) not usually encountered in other guide books. Finally, the worksheets explained throughout and provided at the back of the book (college requirements, college visits, financial aid, self-analysis, etc.) are also an asset. This book may not be for everyone but it certainly has much to offer to the student who is driven, organized and adventurous.

WHERE TO FIND/BUY:

Bookstores and libraries.

Multicultural Student's Guide To Colleges

★★★★

Author/Editor: Robert Mitchell
Publisher: The Noonday Press
Edition Reviewed: 2nd (1996)
Internet URL:

Media Type: Print
Price: $25.00
ISBN: 0374524769

RATINGS (1-4 STARS):

Overall:	★★★★	Extensive review of colleges by multicultural demographics and issues
Breadth Of Content:	★★★	Profiles 200+ colleges with pertinent details on social and academic life
Value Added:	★★★★	Narrative information takes into account student opinion
Ease Of Use:	★★★★	Very well laid out and explained; format is easy to read

DESCRIPTION:

In its 839 pages, this book takes a critical look at 200+ prominent colleges around the country. The book includes an introduction, 4 brief sections, and then the body of colleges profiled. Within these 4 sections, you will find information about how to use the contents of this book, the application process (9 pages), avenues for financial aid (7 pages), and a section citing pros and cons of selecting a predominately black college. The remainder of the book then lists college and university information alphabetically by state. Within each profile, you will find the following information: tuition, room and board, freshman characteristics, history of non-white enrollment, geographic distribution, top majors, retention rate of non-white students, scholarships available for non-white students, remediation programs, academic support services, ethnic studies programs, courses, and organizations, notable non-white alumni, faculty information, and recent non-white speakers. Following this statistical information is a narrative that discusses the social, academic life along with the geographic setting of the college. Information for the narratives was obtained from students through phone, mail surveys and in-person interviews.

EVALUATION:

Any student looking for a college to support their ethnic identity will find this useful book of great interest. Statistics such as the history of non-white students enrolled, the breakdown of the current student population by ethnic group (African, Hispanic, Asian, Native American), the ethnic make-up of the administration, and the retention rate of non-white students (those who return a second year, and graduate) help protray the underlying philosophy and climate of these colleges. Additionally, the presence or absence of organizations, programs, support services, and recent speakers that administer to the needs of these groups is enlightening. It is also refreshing to have students' opinions taken into account when discussing these colleges; other guidebooks often omit this. The narratives are upbeat, yet critical when needed. The author also states that colleges are not ranked because such rankings can be misleading and are usually subjective based upon input from college presidents, admissions deans, etc. We like this approach because it emphasizes the need for students to develop their own rating system given their individual situation. Although this book is written primarily for the non-white student, any student interested in attending a culturally diverse college will find helpful information here.

WHERE TO FIND/BUY:

Bookstores and libraries.

College Finder

Author/Editor: Steven Antonoff, Ph.D.

Publisher: Ballantine Books

Edition Reviewed: 1993

Internet URL:

Media Type: Print

Price: $12.95

ISBN: 0-449-90772-4

RATINGS (1-4 STARS):

Overall:	★★★	An "alternative" resource for building an initial list for further research
Breadth Of Content:	★★★	There's a suggested list of colleges for virtually every interest or question
Value Added:	★★★	They're just lists, but a lot of thought and experience has built them
Ease Of Use:	★★★★	Well-organized, with helpful indexes

DESCRIPTION:

This 500 page guidebook contains 475 lists, principally rankings of colleges across the country against a huge variety of criteria. The lists are organized into 10 categories relevant to the student doing a preliminary search for colleges; the categories are admission, academics, quality, social, internationalism, careers, athletics, enrollment, cost, and "morsels." Lists provided range from "Great State Schools for the Student with Average Grades and Drive for College Success" to "Colleges That Own Their Own Golf Courses." The book's author is a 25-year veteran of the college selection & admission process, both as an Admissions Director and as a independent consultant; his stated goal for the book is "to expand the pool of schools that you should consider." The largely subjective lists were generated from a variety of sources: a survey of college counselors and consultants, college visits, previous students, college personnel, guidebooks, and his own experiences. A subject index which includes all specific topics covered is provided, as is an index of all colleges listed, with page references.

EVALUATION:

One of the big challenges facing students trying to generate their initial list of college alternatives, is that few resources exist to provide suggestions when certain criteria are of interest. This book can help solve that dilemma. The author's experience is extensive; many of these lists were developed while answering questions about prospective colleges posed by students and parents. While keeping in mind that the author's lists are highly subjective and therefore subject to debate, nonetheless his suggestions can be a helpful starting point for further research on college choices. The breadth of the topics covered by various lists should satisfy most inquiries. There are lists and more lists: "Best Colleges for Aspiring Artists" to "Hidden Treasures" ("..provide an excellent education and student experience but are not well known..") to "Colleges for the Shy Person" to "Colleges for the Fashion-Conscious Student" to "Top-Notch Low-Cost Colleges." There seems to be a list of suggested colleges satisfying virtually every question and interest, from campus safety to playing golf. We think this book, while now 3+ years old, is nonetheless a helpful resource for students facing the initially overwhelming variety of college choices.

WHERE TO FIND/BUY:

Bookstores and libraries. Amazon.com notice as of 8/96: "Though not officially "out of print," this item is "out of stock indefinitely" at the publisher."

National Review College Guide

Author/Editor: Charles Sykes & Brad Miner (Editors)
Publisher: Simon & Schuster (A Fireside Book)
Edition Reviewed: 2nd (1993)
Internet URL:

Media Type: Print
Price: $13
ISBN: 0-671-79801-4

RATINGS (1-4 STARS):

Overall:	★★★	A excellent resource, provided your focus is a liberal arts education
Breadth Of Content:	★★	Only 58 schools meet the editors' criteria
Value Added:	★★★★	The focus of the book, and the writing style, is original and evaluative
Ease Of Use:	★★★★	Listed alphabetically, with an index by state

DESCRIPTION:

In its second edition, the National Review guide takes a unique approach to the question of deciding where to go to college: it applies a narrow set of criteria to the universe of college alternatives, and comes up with a short list of just 58 schools it recommends for a quality liberal arts education. The criteria used are: faculty quality (they must actually teach undergraduates), quality of the core curriculum (courses focused on traditional language arts and sciences), and the quality of the intellectual environment (freedom from trendy, restrictive, or "politically correct" administrations or faculty). The profiles of schools recommended, each 3-4 pages, are focused on explaining how each school meets these criteria, giving frequent examples of their successes (such as acceptance rates in graduate programs averaging over 90%!). Also included is a explanation of why some 12 "famous" schools did not make the cut (they call it the "Academic Gulag"). Some essential statistics for each school are also included.

EVALUATION:

This guidebook is unique. It is focused solely on recommending only the very best schools for getting an liberal arts education. The editors are straightforward and precise about their criteria for selection, and stick to those criteria while rejecting such alternatives as Harvard and Yale. The 10 page preface is worth reading if for no other reason than to understand why a liberal arts education is an important alternative in this age of specialization, and why we should focus on schools where the faculty actually does the undergraduate teaching (as opposed to graduate student teaching assistants). The writing style is sophisticated and focused solely on how each school meets their criteria; no insight into student life or campus "feel" is offered. The schools selected are, for the most part, both private and expensive (the editors point out how far these schools will go with financial aid to attract the best students). If a liberal arts education is your priority, you can't go wrong using this as a resource; if not, its tight focus may not be particularly useful.

WHERE TO FIND/BUY:

Bookstores and libraries.

Barron's Top 50   ★★★

Author/Editor: Tom Fischgrund (Editor)   **Media Type:** Print
Publisher: Barron's   **Price:** $14.95
Edition Reviewed: Third   **ISBN:** 0-8120-9053-5
Internet URL:

RATINGS (1-4 STARS):

Overall:	★★★	A useful resource, if you're targeting any of these schools.
Breadth Of Content:	★★	Covers only 50 schools.
Value Added:	★★★★	Comprehensive (10+ pages each) profiles based on standard format.
Ease Of Use:	★★★★	Listed alphabetically; easy to use.

DESCRIPTION:

This guidebook takes a highly focused approach and provides comprehensive essays on the "Top 50" schools in the nation. Essays (10-15 pages each) are written by recent graduates of the school. The schools reviewed are selected based on SAT I scores, % of applications accepted, and % of those accepted who enrolled, cut off after the top 50 are calculated. The profiles follow a standard format, which includes sections on: the education program (educational philosophy, strongest majors, defining characteristics), getting in/financial aid, the academic environment (requirements, atmosphere, teaching methods, class size), social life, extracurricular activities (what's available, what's popular, what's the housing like), graduates (what do students do after graduation), and a summary overview (summary, strengths and weaknesses). Short essays ("tips") are also provided on: selecting top colleges, getting in, filling out applications, financing, and succeeding while enrolled. "Insider's Perspectives" on the applications process, written by three admissions directors from these schools, are also included.

EVALUATION:

This guidebook takes a straightforward approach to selecting its "Top 50" -- simply ranking colleges based on SAT scores, % of applications accepted, and % enrolled of those accepted. Some would argue that other criteria are more appropriate, but at least these are straightforward and completely objective. Given this list, the approach taken by this resource is to have a recent graduate (recommended by the school) write a comprehensive essay about the school, following a standard format which includes short "chapters" on most issues of importance to the college selection process. The essays are long (10-15 pages) and well written; they provide some useful insights not generally available from other guides. One comes away from reading these essays with a genuine feeling that one knows the school a lot better -- that's good. That the writing is uniformly promotive in nature (somewhat like the smiling guides that you tour campuses with), and that it reflects the particular experience of a single student -- that's probably a little too subjective, so look for other opinions, too. The "Tips" essays are OK -- good summaries but no extraordinary insights. The 3 essays written by admissions directors are useful.

WHERE TO FIND/BUY:

Bookstores and libraries.

Profiles Of American Colleges

Author/Editor:
Publisher: Barron's
Edition Reviewed: 1995
Internet URL:

Media Type: Print
Price: $19.95
ISBN: 0-8120-1752-8

RATINGS (1-4 STARS):

Overall:	★★★	As good as any of the big indexes for basic info on college choices
Breadth Of Content:	★★★★	It's got information on all the four-year colleges
Value Added:	★★	Descriptions are provided by the colleges
Ease Of Use:	★★★	It's a monster, but well-organized

DESCRIPTION:

Baron's Profiles has over 1,600 pages. Most of this bulk is from 1 page descriptions of 1.650 colleges ("all accredited four-year colleges"), provided by the colleges themselves. These descriptions, organized by state, follow a standard format and are heavy with statistics; the typical summary statistics are found at the beginning of each profile. The guide includes 200+ pages of additional information as well, including essays on "Knowing Yourself," "Finding The Right College," "Getting In," and other topics. A major section is devoted to describing the various majors that colleges offer, then providing an index by major (every college offering each major is listed). Summary tables, organized by state, provide statistics on costs, test scores, etc. A final directory lists the colleges from least expensive to most expensive, in $2,000 increments. College descriptions include a note on the "selectivity" of each college, from Most Competitive to Less Competitive, based on average high school rank and GPA, and median SAT/ACT scores for admitted freshmen.

EVALUATION:

Most students will use one of the large, all-inclusive indexes early in their college search; Barron's is as good as any of the several that are out there. The trick is to recognize that the value contained in these listings is limited to their comprehensiveness, and their organization, not in original or evaluative data. Thus, while you can find information on virtually any college in the U.S., and make some preliminary choices based on location and major, you will have to do considerable additional research to gather more information. Remember in reading the information presented that it is provided by the colleges themselves. Other guides that are more selective and more evaluative will prove most useful in narrowing down your preliminary choices.

WHERE TO FIND/BUY:

Most libraries and bookstores.

Cass & Birnbaum's Guide To American Colleges   ★★★

Author/Editor: Julia Cass-Liepmann
Publisher: HarperCollins Publishers
Edition Reviewed: 17th
Internet URL:

Media Type: Print
Price: $19.95
ISBN: 0062734040

RATINGS (1-4 STARS):

Overall:	★★★	Among the better of the large, all-inclusive guides
Breadth Of Content:	★★★★	Typically strong, with 1,500 colleges profiled
Value Added:	★★★	Largely based on input from the colleges themselves; some innovations
Ease Of Use:	★★★	Well-organized, with useful indexes

DESCRIPTION:

This guidebook is a large one, with 1/2 page descriptions of some 1,500 colleges. Information included in these brief descriptions is similar to that typically supplied by colleges to all-encompassing guidebooks of this nature, including the usual summary statistics. Unique to this guide, and new to this edition, is a "College Selection Index." This index, organized by state, compares the colleges using a number of factors relating to four key questions: "What kind of education will I receive?" -- liberal arts, business, etc. "Can I get in?" -- "non-selective" to "most selective." "Can I afford it?" -- average annual cost, % of students receiving aid. "What will it be like when I get there?" -- comparisons shown for campus setting, undergrad enrollment, male/female mix, and campus life. Indexes are also supplied for religious orientation and for college majors, the latter including the unique feature of showing how many students recently received degrees.

EVALUATION:

This guidebook is one among roughly a half-dozen that are useful in generating that initial list of college alternatives. The descriptions of colleges are typical, based on material provided by the colleges themselves. But this guide has several wrinkles which set it apart somewhat from its crowd. First is an index based on religious orientation, with additional comments in the profiles on intensity of religious focus. They also include the typical index organized by college major, but add the very useful useful element of showing how many students received degrees in each major; this can help indicate the relative strength of major departments. Their "College Selection Index," listing colleges by state, is a useful way to compare some of the statistics (in this case roughly a dozen) that can be relevant to initial college selection -- it's easier to use this index than flip back and forth between pages of the profiles. The authors also provide a well-written introduction that explains why these particular statistics may be important to prospective college students as they create their initial list of alternatives.

WHERE TO FIND/BUY:

Libraries and bookstores.

Four-Year Colleges

★★★

Author/Editor: Peterson's Guides
Publisher: Peterson's Guides
Edition Reviewed: 1995
Internet URL: http://www.petersons.com

Media Type: Print
Price: $19.95
ISBN: 1-56079-364-3

RATINGS (1-4 STARS):

Overall:	★★★	Among the better of the all-inclusive tomes, but no subjective assessments
Breadth Of Content:	★★★★	Contains basic profiles on 2,000+ colleges and supplements on 800+
Value Added:	★★★	They've got more goodies and indexes than most, but nothing evaluative
Ease Of Use:	★★★	If you can carry it, you can use it easily

DESCRIPTION:

Peterson's Four-Year Colleges is one of a half-dozen all-inclusive guidebooks, in this case covering 2,000 four year colleges. At the core of the guidebook are roughly 1/2 page (VERY small type) profiles of each college, supplied by the colleges, which contain basic information and statistics. Supplements to these profiles are also included, for some 800+ colleges. These supplements provide 1-2 pages of additional descriptive information, also supplied by the schools, containing descriptive information about each school, its location, majors and degrees, academic facilities, faculty, and a number of other topics. Peterson's also includes four indexes: a state-by state summary table (enrollment, SAT/ACT scores, etc.), the colleges' self-ranking (from Most Difficult to Non-Competitive), a listing of the colleges by cost (from <$2,000 to >$20,000), and a listing of all colleges offering each of 450+ majors). Inside the covers, Peterson has also bound a 12-page color magazine ("Inside College") and a 3-1/4" DOS disk (the "college application planner") which includes the basic college profiles.

EVALUATION:

There are roughly a half-dozen large, all-inclusive printed college guides out there, each of which contains basic information and stats about the four-year colleges, in every case supplied by the colleges themselves and in no case providing any evaluative input. They're all useful for constructing a first cut at possibilities for colleges, and Peterson's, in our opinion, is one of the better from this group. Why? Because it does provide some supplemental information on some 800+ colleges, and it has most of the indexes that can prove useful in comparing colleges to your academic interests and profiles. Just recognize that when it comes down to paring your list down to those schools meriting further research, you'll need to go elsewhere to find someone willing to state an opinion about a school or provide some original insight.

WHERE TO FIND/BUY:

Bookstores and libraries, or direct from the publisher at 800-338-3282.

College Handbook

Author/Editor: The College Entrance Examination Board
Publisher: College Board
Edition Reviewed: 1996
Internet URL:

Media Type: Print
Price: $20
ISBN: 0-87447-506-6

RATINGS (1-4 STARS):

Overall:	★★★	One of the better of the all-inclusive guides, particularly for its indexes
Breadth Of Content:	★★★★	It's got all accredited two and four year colleges listed
Value Added:	★★	Not much; the usual basic facts provided by the schools themselves
Ease Of Use:	★★★	Very large, but well organized; many useful indexes

DESCRIPTION:

The College Handbook is one of the half-dozen or so all-inclusive guidebooks; this one contains all the accredited two and four year colleges in the country (3,215!), as well as the largest number of indexes of any in this class of guidebook. The information shown for each college, listed by state, is typical to this kind of guidebook, a half page or so of basic descriptive text and the usual statistics. This guide includes 20+ pages of essays on choosing a college and paying for college; the essays are supplemented with short profiles written by students about their recent experiences in selecting their college. 30+ indexes are included in the guidebook: 6 focused on general colleges (two year vs. four year, men/women only, etc.), 9 focused on specialized colleges (agricultural, art/music, business, engineering, etc.), 8 organized by campus environment (small, medium, large, etc.), ROTC indexes, Hispanic/black indexes, and more. A glossary and a "How to use The College Handbook" section are included as well.

EVALUATION:

This is one of the more useful of the all-inclusive guides, which as a group are helpful early in the college selection process. The many indexes are useful in creating an initial list of college selections, provided you have some strong feelings about a factor addressed by one of the indexes (small or large, men/women only, those specializing in certain degrees, ROTC, etc.). The "Choosing A College" essay, 15 pages long, is particularly useful in helping get the initial search process organized. A number of helpful checklists/questionaire's are included in this essay, as are a number of insightful profiles written by students about their own reasons for picking the college they selected. This is one of the better of the large guides; just remember that you'll need to consult with other resources to find original insight into what life might really be like at the schools you're interested in.

WHERE TO FIND/BUY:

Bookstores and libraries, direct from the publisher by calling 800-323-7155, or on the World Wide Web at http://www.collegeboard.org.

Choosing A College

★★★

Author/Editor: Gordon Porter Miller
Publisher: College Board Publications
Edition Reviewed: 1990
Internet URL:

Media Type: Print
Price: $9.95
ISBN: 0-87447-333-0

RATINGS (1-4 STARS):

Overall:	★★★	Helpful to those overwhelmed by the college decision process
Breadth Of Content:		Not applicable
Value Added:	★★★	The author knows decision-making science, perhaps too well
Ease Of Use:	★★	Clear explanations, but many, perhaps too many exercises to complete

DESCRIPTION:

This 160 page book, published in 1990, provides a process to help prospective college students answer two important questions: 1) Which colleges are best suited for the student, and 2) Which college, of those that have offered admission, should the student attend. The thirteen short chapters each use the same approach; namely, lots of questions to be answered and lists to be completed, all carefully explained, and all intended to help students get in touch with how they make decisions, and to help them work through this important decision in a disciplined way. The chapters are focused on how decision-making works, defining what the student's priorities and expectations are, identifying and deciding among alternatives, applying for admission, and deciding among those colleges that offer admission.

EVALUATION:

The principal benefit of using the process outlined in this book is to make rational a decision-making process which all too often is driven by emotion and frequently suffers from poor preparation. The commentary between exercises is useful and reads easily. The exercises, when taken seriously, should throw some light on key factors in making the college selection decision, particularly for those high schoolers who are really unfocused. The book could be improved through simplification of process and design -- there are a LOT of checklists, questions, and matrices to fill out. Some high schoolers may not have the interest or discipline to stick to it; they'll probably require a lot of parental involvement to get through the exercises. In addition, some of these exercises may be perceived as too far removed from the specific issue at hand to hold interest. Nonetheless, this book may prove useful to those who might be overwhelmed by the college decision (and it's inexpensive as well).

WHERE TO FIND/BUY:

Bookstores and libraries, direct from the publisher by calling 800-323-7155, or on the World Wide Web at http://www.collegeboard.org.

Kaplan's The Road To College

Author/Editor: Steven Frank, Fred Zuker, Bart Astor
Publisher: Bantam Doubleday Dell Publishing Group, Inc.
Edition Reviewed: 1996
Internet URL:

Media Type: Print
Price: $19.95
ISBN: 0-385-31536-8

RATINGS (1-4 STARS):

Overall:	★★★	A useful and well-written resource; stronger in admissions than selection
Breadth Of Content:	★★★	This resource covers all the bases, at times at the risk of needed depth
Value Added:	★★★	There's a lot here; the college insights are original, if short
Ease Of Use:	★★★★	Very nicely designed book; easy to read and use

DESCRIPTION:

This sizable (500+ pages) resource attacks all three aspects of the college decision: selection, admissions, and financial aid. Each subject is addressed by a different author, in multiple chapters. The largest section covers "College Selection" -- here, the student is guided through an overview of 8 major decision factors, then through a workbook exercise which results in a prioritized list of ten personal college selection statements ("I want my professors to know me by name.", etc.). Students then match their priorities to 400+ schools, grouped in 17 categories ("Think Tanks","Value Marts", etc.); schools within selected categories should match their interests. The descriptions for each college cover 1-2 pages, and provide sketches which address the campus, student makeup, academic environment, social life, etc. In the "Admissions" section, chapters cover when to apply, how to apply, essays, recommendations, interviews, and making the final decision. The "Financial Aid" section provides overviews of the financial aid process and programs available; details are provided on completing the PROFILE and FAFSA applications. Suggestions are provided for negotiation following initial financial aid offers.

EVALUATION:

There is a great deal of information contained in this new resource; it portrays itself as "everything you need". It's scope is admirable, and there is much to recommend it. Some factors weigh against it, however, particularly in the college selection section. The process which prioritizes student interests is not very deep. Limiting initial possibilities to just 400+ schools may not be wise; classifying those schools within 17 categories may be too simplistic an approach. In addition, no information is provided on the author's background, and no rationale/methodology is offered for how schools were assigned to each category, so approach these recommendations with eyes wide open and some additional resources at hand. The admissions section contains a great deal of useful information, well organized and written in an understandable style; this material could serve as much of the resources needed to get the applications job done well. The financial aid section deals with the ins and outs of the financial aid game in an overview fashion -- it's a good read, and understandable. Details about specific elements of the financial aid process are lacking, however.

WHERE TO FIND/BUY:

Bookstores and libraries, direct from the publisher at 800-527-4836, or on the Web at http://www.kaplan.com.

College Guide For Parents

Author/Editor: Charles J. Shields
Publisher: College Board Publications
Edition Reviewed: 3rd (1995)
Internet URL:

Media Type: Print
Price: $14
ISBN: 0-87447-474-4

RATINGS (1-4 STARS):

Overall:	★★★	A very helpful resource to parents of college-bound students
Breadth Of Content:	★★★★	Very broad in its treatment of the whole spectrum of issues
Value Added:	★★★	Some chapters stronger than others, but all have value
Ease Of Use:	★★★	Style and tone targeted at parents; lots of short chapters a helpful tool

DESCRIPTION:

This 180+ page book, written by an experienced high school counselor, provides a thorough overview of virtually the entire spectrum of issues involved in the decision to go to college: the high school years, the process of self-assessment and discovery involved in finding the right group of colleges to apply to, the application process itself, and other issues. The book is addressed to parents of students making these decisions, and reflects this perspective. After a chapter which offers methods to help crystallize reasons why college may or may not be the right next step after high school, the book offers two chapters focused on a college preparation calendar and on high school coursework. Several chapters are provided on the college choice process, including a chapter focused on athletes, minorities, and the disabled. The admissions process is given several chapters, including perspectives on admissions tests, applications, and how Admissions Committees work. A chapter is focused on a thorough treatment of the world of college financial aid. Finally, the book goes past getting admitted, with chapters discussing college housing issues, separation anxiety, and the first year at college.

EVALUATION:

This resource is addressed to parents of students considering going to college. It's writing style and reassuring tone reflects this point of view, and as such can be very helpful to "first-time" parents of college-bound students. Some chapters are more helpful than others, but all can be useful to parents intimidated by the process, the terminology, and the myths of the college search and admissions process. For example, the first chapter provides some useful aids to help parents and students decide why college might (or might not be) be the right step after high school. The chapter on making the right college choice is focused on issues the author believes are important in focusing the college search, including distance from home and admissions selectivity; particularly helpful to the parent is the reassurance that most students can get into most colleges, with only 200 or so brutally competitive. Chapters on applications, admissions, and financial aid are thin relative to more specialized books, but nonetheless provide a helpful overview. Most helpful are the final chapters which focus on such potentially troubling issues as college housing alternatives, and preparing for and dealing with separation anxiety. This book can be a reassuring companion to parents throughout this time of transition and decision-making for their sons and daughters.

WHERE TO FIND/BUY:

Bookstores and libraries, direct from the publisher by calling 800-323-7155, or on the World Wide Web at http://www.collegeboard.org.

College Planning For Dummies

Author/Editor: Pat Ordovensky
Publisher: IDG Books
Edition Reviewed: 1995
Internet URL:

Media Type: Print
Price: $16.99
ISBN: 1-56884-382-8

RATINGS (1-4 STARS):

Overall:	★★★	An exhaustive, and sometimes exhausting, college planning reference
Breadth Of Content:	★★★★	Very broad treatment of most of the issues, sometimes with little depth
Value Added:	★★★	The author's experience shows; there's lot of information here
Ease Of Use:	★★	The "Dummies" model helps readability; too much detail hinders it

DESCRIPTION:

The IDG "Dummies" books are well known. Designed as a "light" read on serious subjects, they use a uniform model of multiple chapters, short, titled subject sections and paragraphs, lists, and icons. This 300+ page book follows this model, including the use of "College Myths" and "College Reality" icons (plus 6 others) to highlight important points. The book is organized into six parts, with a total of 25 chapters. "Getting Ready" consists of chapters on kinds of colleges, information sources, etc. "Finding The Right College" has 6 chapters on what you should be doing during the 10th-12th grades to develop, and pare down, a list of colleges, as well as hints on campus visits and interviews. "Getting In" focuses on all aspects of the college application. "Paying For It" has 5 chapters (75+ pages) on financial aid, including a thorough overview of the process and discussion of the various sources of aid. "The Rest Of The Story" provides advice on decision-making once the acceptances come. The book closes with a series of lists, from bad essay topics to questions you should ask during interviews, and an appendix with 20 questions to ask before picking a college.

EVALUATION:

The value in the IDG books comes from their light-hearted, but thorough treatment of serious subjects; here, we get some comic relief for what can become an all-too-serious process (the obligatory icons are overdone, though). In addition, the book is organized like a reference work; thus, jumping in and out of various chapters to read about today's hot topic is easy. The author has been an education writer for USA Today, and his prose reflects that training: short, concise sentences, light in tone. The description (Chapters 4&5) of how a high school student should work though the preliminary college selection process is a helpful introduction to an intimidating task. Good value is provided by spending the pages necessary to walk through a sample calculation of Expected Family Contribution (what the government expects you to pay towards the cost of college), filling out the FAFSA (the government's form for determining EFC), and evaluating aid offers from different schools. A chapter addressing the alternative of two-year colleges is useful as well. The book's pervasive (overdone?) light-hearted tone may not, in the end, be altogether appropriate to this subject; endless details, some irrelevant, make it harder to read than it should be.

WHERE TO FIND/BUY:

Bookstores and libraries.

Handbook For College Admissions

Author/Editor: Thomas C. Hayden

Publisher: Peterson's Guides

Edition Reviewed: 4th (1995)

Internet URL: http://www.petersons.com

Media Type: Print

Price: $14.95

ISBN: 1-56079-428-3

RATINGS (1-4 STARS):

Overall:	★★★	A useful overview resource, particularly for parents
Breadth Of Content:	★★★★	One resource that tries (and largely succeeds) to cover it all
Value Added:	★★★	Valuable perspectives and advice from this veteran of the process
Ease Of Use:	★★	Lots of small text, lots of topics, lots of reading

DESCRIPTION:

The author has extensive experience in admissions and counseling, on both the college side and the high school side. This 270+ page guidebook is made up of 10 chapters, covering the entire spectrum from college selection and admissions, to financial aid, to acceptance and freshman year adjustments. The book opens with some self-assessment exercises, then moves into the process of choosing colleges, including college visits. After a chapter explaining test (ACT/SAT) timing and test-taking strategy, the author focuses on college applications (including tips on creating a differentiating edge and constructing a powerful, integrated application). Financial aid gets a chapter, with the usual terminology explained and some aid evaluation tips included. The eighth chapter is for parents, offering some perspectives and advice on college choice and how/when to help and/or stay out of the process. The book closes with chapters devoted to the spectrum of outcomes and actions that can occur with acceptance and rejection by colleges; a final chapter offer perspectives and advice for the freshman year.

EVALUATION:

With breadth as a primary objective, most guidebooks have to trade off in-depth coverage; so it is with this book. The corollary questions which then pop up are: when can the book be valuable, and where should lack of depth be covered by other resources? We like this book's tone, which is serious, supportive, and addressed to parents as much as students; it could serve particularly well as a reference for parents to use to educate themselves broadly on the college search and admissions process. Strengths? The chapter on college visits gives two really helpful examples of effective and ineffective interviews. Chapters on test-taking and "developing an edge" in college applications are particularly strong. The chapter addressed to parents ("The Myth Of College & Success") provides some useful and frank opinions on parents' roles. Weaknesses? We've found other resources that do a better job of guiding students through the process of evaluating college decision factors; financing the costs of college is covered more thoroughly in books focused solely on that subject. All things considered, we'd recommend this resource to parents and students wanting a good overview and reference to go back to as the process unfolds.

WHERE TO FIND/BUY:

Bookstores and libraries, or direct from the publisher at 800-338-3282.

K&W Guide To Colleges For The Learning Disabled

★★★

Author/Editor: Marybeth Kravets & Imy F. Wax
Publisher: Educators Publishing Service, Inc.
Edition Reviewed: 3rd (1995)
Internet URL:

Media Type: Print
Price: $28.00
ISBN: 0838822495

RATINGS (1-4 STARS):

Overall:	★★★	Specific information of interest to students with learning disabilities
Breadth Of Content:	★★	Profiles just 265 colleges and universities
Value Added:	★★★★	Brings together information not readily available elsewhere
Ease Of Use:	★★★	Easy to use; well organized visually

DESCRIPTION:

This guidebook profiles 265 colleges and universities in the United States with reference to the services and programs available to students with learning disabilities (LDs). The profiles are listed alphabetically by State. The colleges and universities have been grouped into three categories: Structured Programs, those campuses which offer the most comprehensive services for students with LDs and have special admission requirements, Coordinated Services, those campuses which offer services which are not as comprehensive and which may not offer help in the admissions process, and Services, those campuses which provide the least amount of services and may require documentation of the disability in order for the students to receive accommodations. Each profile is two pages long and includes information on: LD programs and services (special centers for students with LDs, etc.), LD admissions information, LD services (such as, note takers and the # of LD specialists on campus), general admissions information, college graduation requirements, and additional information. A contacts list and an alphabetical list of colleges by degree of level of support is included as well.

EVALUATION:

This resource starts with "thoughts from. . . ", a series of essays written by various people on what it means to be a college student with an LD. While self-congratulatory in tone, this section of the book provides useful and positive perspectives on the issues surrounding higher education for LD students. The information provided in the profiles comes from a survey conducted by the authors and contains valuable information not likely to be readily available elsewhere. The profiles are accessible by State, level of services, and by school name. Since the information provided in these profiles is so specific, this listing can be used to determine which schools you want to contact for further information. If you are more interested in pursuing a particular course of study or living in a particular geographic area, than you may want to use this book to see which of the campuses you are already considering offer the types of services needed for LD students.

WHERE TO FIND/BUY:

Find in libraries and bookstores or call the publisher at 800-225-5750.

Writing A Successful College Application Essay ★★★

Author/Editor: George Ehrenhaft
Publisher: Barron's
Edition Reviewed: 2nd (1993)
Internet URL:

Media Type: Print
Price: $8.95
ISBN: 0-8120-1415-4

RATINGS (1-4 STARS):

Overall:	★★★	150 pages of helpful essay-writing information
Breadth Of Content:		Not applicable
Value Added:	★★★	Wholly original writing style; the author's experience is evident
Ease Of Use:	★★★★	Easy to read; use of examples a plus

DESCRIPTION:

This book provides step-by-step instructions on how to write a college application essay. The author is head of the English department at Mamaroneck High School and has 20+ experience as an educator. Excerpts from college application essays written by a wide variety of students are used throughout the book to illustrate the author's points. In the first chapter, the author explains the purpose behind application essays and the role they play in the admissions process. Chapter 2, entitled "Essays that Work," elaborates on essays that will get noticed and why. The author discusses problem areas, such as boasting and the "Last summer I went to..." essay . The rest of the book outlines the steps you need to take in order to write the application essay (choosing your topic, followed by composing the essay, rewriting and editing and the final presentation of the essay). The author discusses details such as "hooking" the reader and the role active verbs play in creating a well-thought out essay. Sample essay topics from fifty popular colleges and samples of essays in progress and completed essays are located at the back of the book, along with an index.

EVALUATION:

The author took much of his own advice while writing this book. He has written about something that is important to him, that he knows something about, and he has written it in his own words. His frequent use of examples make this book fascinating to read as well as informative. In the second chapter where the author discusses common mistakes students have made, he also points out that no subject is off-limits; if you must write an essay about your trip to Germany last summer, find a way to make it unique. He then provides you with examples of students who have done just that. Chapters three through six contain very specific writing tips on such aspects as sentence structure and the difference between being verbs and active verbs, using examples to illustrate points. This book was easy to read, thought provoking and fun. It will be useful to students who are not comfortable with the writing process as well as to those who are.

WHERE TO FIND/BUY:

Find in libraries and bookstores.

Women's Colleges ★★★

Author/Editor: Joe Anne Adler
Publisher: ARCO/Prentice Hall, Inc.
Edition Reviewed: 1994
Internet URL:

Media Type: Print
Price: $15.00
ISBN: 0-671-86706-7

RATINGS (1-4 STARS):

Overall:	★★★	An excellent resource for those seeking a women's college
Breadth Of Content:	★★★★	Profiles virtually all women's colleges in the United States
Value Added:	★★★★	Descriptions are wholly original and informative
Ease Of Use:	★★★	Needs to be properly indexed

DESCRIPTION:

This guidebook provides profiles of 76 women's colleges in the United States. The author visited all 76 campuses and conducted interviews with the students, faculty and administration. The book begins with a foreword by Linda Koch Lorimer, the Secretary of Yale University, followed by a brief history of women's colleges in the United States. In a "Note from the Author" it is explained that Radcliffe, Sophie Newcomb College and West Hampton were omitted from this book because they are considered undergraduate schools within Harvard, Tulane, and University of Richmond and not separate colleges. The rest of the book is taken up by the profiles which are listed alphabetically. Each college is given three and a half pages and the following points are covered: school history, academics (including core requirements and majors offered), students and student life (demographics, sports, clubs, sororities and campus traditions), campus and community, an admissions note, and a list of academic programs. A chart, listing the colleges alphabetically , lists tests required, application deadlines, expenses, and percentage of students receiving financial aid.

EVALUATION:

The lack of indexing is the only significant shortcoming for this book. The profiles are listed alphabetically, as is the "Guide to Women's Colleges" chart at the back of the book;, but the book's utility would be improved with indexes by State or academic program. It is not the author's intent for anyone to use this book as their sole guide to getting into college; the reader should find information on financial aid and the application process elsewhere. The point of this book is to give an overview of women's colleges and this is accomplished with excellence. The profiles written by the author contain a good deal of useful information for women who wish to continue their education in a same sex environment and are interested in evaluating their alternatives. The author provides some compelling rationale in the introduction as to why women should attend women's colleges. Several of the colleges listed have close relationships with all-male campuses in their community and it is noted when classes are coed. The colleges profiled are not ranked. This book is recommended for the college bound student interested in women-only institutions.

WHERE TO FIND/BUY:

Find at bookstores and libraries.

America's Black and Tribal Colleges

Author/Editor: J. Wilson Bowman, Ph.D.

Publisher: Sandcastle Publishing

Edition Reviewed: 1994

Internet URL:

Media Type: Print

Price: $19.95

ISBN: 1-883995-02-7

RATINGS (1-4 STARS):

Overall:	★★★	A fairly good starting place for Black and Native American students
Breadth Of Content:	★★★	Profiles 27 Tribal and 101 Black colleges
Value Added:	★★	Profiles contain only information provided by the colleges
Ease Of Use:	★★★★	Lists colleges by several criteria for quick access

DESCRIPTION:

This guidebook profiles 128 black and tribal colleges and universities in the United States. The book begins with two forewords, "Why Black Colleges" and "Why Tribal Colleges", followed by short chapters on financial aid and admissions. The profiles are listed alphabetically by State, range in length from one to three pages, and contain a short history of the college, information on geographic settings, contact information, enrollment, campus layout, student/faculty ratios , housing , academic programs , fees, and distinguished alumni. The profiles are followed by several appendices which list the colleges by different criteria: tribal colleges alphabetically, black colleges alphabetically, tribal colleges by State, black colleges by State and athletic Association affiliation, black colleges supported by the United Negro College Fund, and church related black colleges. An eight page list of scholarship providers listed by subject is included. The bibliography lists further reading on financial aid, the admissions process, and minority issues.

EVALUATION:

The information on admissions and financial aid given in this book provide no more than the most minimal overview of these very important topics. What makes this book unique is the number of different ways the information can be accessed: by State, alphabetically, by church affiliation, etc. . We would have liked to see a listing by academic programs and more information about the ratio of minority to non minority students at these campuses. Most of the schools are exclusively for Blacks or Native Americans, but those that are not are not clearly identified. Since this book is written for Blacks and Native Americans who wish to study in a predominantly black or Native American environment those statistics are needed. Compared to other books written for minorities, this guidebook gives comprehensive and balanced information which will help students write their initial list. It should be used in conjunction with other guidebooks and additional resources on financial aid and the application process.

WHERE TO FIND/BUY:

Find in libraries and bookstores or call the publisher at 800-891-4204.

Making A Difference College Guide

★★★

Author/Editor: Miriam Weinstein
Publisher: Sageworks Press
Edition Reviewed: 4th (1995)
Internet URL:

Media Type: Print
Price: $16.00
ISBN: 0963461834

RATINGS (1-4 STARS):

Overall:	★★★	A good resource that targets students seeking alternative programs
Breadth Of Content:	★★	Only 100 schools meet the editor's criteria
Value Added:	★★★	Essays a useful perspective; profiles provided by colleges
Ease Of Use:	★	Listed alphabetically by school, state index; some material incomplete

DESCRIPTION:

Weinstein, an environmental and social activist, compiled this resource guide highlighting colleges with innovative programs. These programs offer hands-on experiences for students who are concerned with social and environmental responsibility. The first section consists of several essays written by students, graduates, professors, and environmentalists, outlining serious questions facing today's students. Two of the essays address concerns a worried parent may have regarding their child's choice of these programs. Two other essays discuss college choices for a quality education. In particular the chapter entitled "What is education for?" sums up Weinstein's premise to rethink education. The second section lists, in alphabetical order, colleges and field programs that offer "relevant, values-based education." Within each college's description, an individual will find the following: the number of students attending, the degree of selectivity of applicants, a description of the educational atmosphere and of the community, and finally the college's philosophy. Also included is a list of "making a difference studies." Finally there are statistics included which list the profiles of the student and faculty populations, tuition costs, and a condensed version of the school's attributes. An index of all of the colleges and programs listed alphabetically by state is also provided.

EVALUATION:

Weinstein's book is of particular use to students and parents seeking an alternative education. The colleges described within her book place emphasis on meaningful career-oriented studies and hands-on training for future jobs. Weinstein successfully captures the questions many students have in this time of social and environmental awareness. The programs of the nearly 100 colleges outlined in the guide attempt to address these questions. The essays in the first half of the book are useful for those parents and students who have not quite decided if an innovative college program will suit their needs; these narratives serve to convince one of the need to offer alternatives to traditional college courses. What remains unclear in the guide is whether or not the lists of studies are one-time courses or entire programs; are there degree options if an individual wishes later on to pursue more study? Weinstein mentions that the schools categorized their own degree of selectivity, and asks the reader to be aware that selectivity is based upon rather faulty premises. This guidebook will be useful for students who are seeking choices different than those offered by the traditional college institutions.

WHERE TO FIND/BUY:

Bookstores and libraries.

Complete Guide To American Film Schools   ★★★

Author/Editor: Ernest Pintoff
Publisher: Penguin Books
Edition Reviewed: 1994
Internet URL:

Media Type: Print
Price: $16.95
ISBN: 0140172262

RATINGS (1-4 STARS):

Overall:	★★★	An excellent initial resource for this area of focus
Breadth Of Content:	★★★	Variety of listings, both two year schools and four year institutions
Value Added:	★★★	Guide POV, listing of alumni, and anecdotes all add interest
Ease Of Use:	★★★	Organized alphabetically by state

DESCRIPTION:

In this 510 page resource, Pintoff has compiled a state-by-state listing of American schools for those seeking a career in television, the cinema, or video. The author himself has been involved in animation, television and film directing, and writing; he currently is a professor of film at the University of Southern California. Each school listing includes the location of the school (rural, suburban, urban), the number of students, the academic calendar (quarter, semester), entrance requirements, degrees offered, curricular emphasis, special activities, facilities and equipment that are available to students, names of well-known alumni, and a "Guide POV" (point of view). The POV is a subjective overview of each program and is based upon input from departments, catalogs, and students. At the end of each state section is an anecdote from students, graduates and professionals who reflect upon their own experiences in school and offer advice to someone embarking upon a career in these fields. At the end of the book are two glossaries outlining academic and technical terms.

EVALUATION:

This guide addresses many of the important points important to making an initial decision as to which schools to consider for a future career in the cinema and television media. Each school's important features are highlighted, enabling the reader to make cross-comparisons of schools (missing is the cost of tuition). Pintoff does a fine job presenting various types of schools, both two and four-year institutions. Although the "Guide POV" may read as an advertisement for a particular school, the POV and the listing of recognized alumni add interest and personalization to the book. Pintoff and many of the anecdotal authors reflect upon the importance of gaining "a broad-based background"; they advise that the humanities should not be overlooked. Therefore, a student might consider institutions that not only offer general education courses but also offer specialized fields of study in the television and film industry. While this guide will be helpful in selecting alternatives, students should seek information from professionals in the field and others to find out how these schools are perceived in the industry.

WHERE TO FIND/BUY:

Bookstores and libraries.

Campus Opportunities For Students With Learning Differences

★★★

Author/Editor: Judith M. Crooker
Publisher: Octameron Associates
Edition Reviewed: 4th (1994)
Internet URL:

Media Type: Print
Price: $5.00
ISBN: 0-945981-93-7

RATINGS (1-4 STARS):

Overall:	★★★	Well-written specifically for the student with learning differences (LD)
Breadth Of Content:	★★★	Covers all the bases for an LD student deciding to go to college
Value Added:	★★★	Personal comments from an LD college students are included
Ease Of Use:	★★★	Short chapters and sections which don't waste words or confuse

DESCRIPTION:

In its fourth edition, this 41 page pamphlet sets out to reassure the student with a learning difference (LD) that there are opportunities for them at a post-secondary level. The book addresses the LD student with supportive information for parents. The book is organized into nine chapters, the first three of which explain what learning differences are, and how parents can help their LD child maximize their potential by possibly setting their sights on college. Chapters 4 and 6 focus on basic personal and study skills that are necessary to survive and succeed in college. Chapter 5 discusses the process used in choosing a college or an alternative school. Advice is given on how to obtain information about schools, questions to ask of admissions personnel, a self-assessment inventory to see if the LD student is ready, and finally how to apply to the school. Chapter 7 lists some LD "success stories" while Chapter 9 provides an annotated list of resources which include books, hardware/software, and organizations that can help to inspire and support the LD student. Chapter 8 highlights some summer programs for LD students to ease their transition from high school into a post-secondary situation.

EVALUATION:

This book fulfills a need for both parents and LD students alike. It reads comfortably and with a great deal of emphaty for the student with learning differences. Each chapter is short, to the point, and well-organized in format. In particular Chapters 4 and 6 are helpful for an LD student in making the decision whether or not college is right for them. Chapter 4 gives pointers on how to prepare for college while in high school in terms of academic skills , practical skills and personal skills. This chapter also gives the LD student a checklist to help them get ready during high school - a "year by year plan." Chapter 6 gives many suggestions on taking notes, preparing for class, taking tests, writing papers, organizing yourself and your time, and how to find supportive services on campus. Throughout the book are boxed-in comments from a student with learning differences who "survived his college years." In general, any parents of an LD child will find the information in this book useful in helping their child succeed during their college experience. In particular, this book is helpful in encouraging and supporting the LD student's decision to pursue a college education.

WHERE TO FIND/BUY:

Bookstores and libraries or directly from the publisher at 703-836-5480.

Admissions Essay: How To Stop Worrying & Start Writing!

Author/Editor: Helen W. Power, Ph.D. & Robert DiAntonio, Ph.D.
Publisher: Carol Publishing Group
Edition Reviewed: 1st (1987)
Internet URL:

Media Type: Print
Price: $9.95
ISBN: 0-8184-0436-1

RATINGS (1-4 STARS):

Overall:	★★★	Useful step-by-step hints on writing the admissions essay
Breadth Of Content:	★★	Explains all the steps with emphasis on why the essay is important
Value Added:	★★★	Provides 50 original student essays on various topics
Ease Of Use:	★★★	Follows logically through brainstorming, revising, and editing

DESCRIPTION:

This 220-page book offers guidelines on writing a college entrance essay. Input was taken from college admissions officers, high school college counselors and senior English teachers in the preparation of this book. The Admissions Essay is divided into two parts. The first part consists of six chapters. Two chapters outline the purpose of the application essay and explain what the admissions committee really is looking for. Another set of chapters provide step-by-step hints on writing the essay. Finally, the last two chapters discuss common problems students face, how to solve those problems, and remedies for the common mistakes that admissions officers find in student essays. Each chapter presents a problem a student may face while drafting their admissions essay. The second part of the book includes more than fifty essays written by students who were admitted to renowned universities, with subchapters for essays that address different topics from "writing about job experiences" to "writing about political and social involvement." Also included are questions and comments that an admissions officer might ask when reading a particular essay.

EVALUATION:

This book does a good job of stressing to prospective college students the importance of the college admissions essay. With its tone of familiarity and its supportive nature, the book offers a fresh approach as it directs young people in their writing. Although the entire book offers valuable information and hints, the chapters in particular that would be useful to students are Chapters 3 and 4 on "Getting Started" and "Getting It On Paper." These two chapters offer much in terms of getting students to brainstorm ideas, organize their thoughts, and get their ideas down in their own "voice" while keeping the audience -- the admissions officer -- in mind. Too many times students write their essays in formal language which does not give colleges a true picture of the student. Often student essays tend to drift away from the topic being addressed. This book strives to keep students on the "write" track and to offer them constructive criticism to give them the best chances for getting into the colleges of their choice. The second half of the book consists of student essays which offer insights into students' minds and efforts. It reads very clearly, provides positive inspiration, and the comments from admissions officers are useful as an evaluative tool.

WHERE TO FIND/BUY:

Bookstores and libraries.

Complete Idiot's Guide To Getting Into College ★★★

Author/Editor: Dr. O'Neal Turner
Publisher: Alpha Books
Edition Reviewed: 1995
Internet URL:

Media Type: Print
Price: $14.95
ISBN: 1-56761-508-2

RATINGS (1-4 STARS):

Overall:	★★★	A good resource for an overview; you'll need other resources for college info
Breadth Of Content:	★★★	Broad coverage of most of the issues encountered
Value Added:	★★★	Author's experience at both high school and collegiate levels shows
Ease Of Use:	★★★★	Easy to read, humorous

DESCRIPTION:

The author of this 350+ page guidebook has worked at the high school level as a teacher and college counselor, on the collegiate in admissions; he's currently the Director of College Advising at Culver Academies. This guidebook provides step-by-step instructions on everything from deciding to go to college to handling letters of rejection. Each chapter starts with a summary and ends with a review. Cartoons and "college trivia" bubbles are used throughout the book to illustrate each topic. The book is broken down into six parts, starting with "Beginning at the Beginning" -- deciding to go to college, coming up with an initial list, and getting information. It continues in a chronological fashion, moving from campus visits to completing the application, finding financial aid and waiting to hear from the schools. Part six includes a complete timetable of activities starting with ninth grade, an overview, and the author's recommended lists of colleges by major program and "special categories", including his favorites by Region.

EVALUATION:

While the book is meant to be used as a manual, the author uses cartoons, trivia bubbles and lots of bullet points to get his message across. This layout may make the book appear less than serious, but it contains a wealth of useful information, and its quality is consistently excellent. The author assumes that the college application process is a new experience for every student and tries to have an answer for every question (including answers to questions that will help students feel comfortable with the experience). The chronological layout lets students read one chapter at a time or read ahead to know what to expect next. This book is directed to high school students, and incorporates a style they'll understand without feeling talked down to. The section at the end of the book, a list of the author's college picks listed by program and "special categories", may contribute some ideas for colleges to look at. This book is recommended, particularly for its value in providing an overview of the college selection and admissions process; its strongest section is on college visits. Other resources will have to be used to create and refine lists of colleges of interest.

WHERE TO FIND/BUY:

Find at bookstores and libraries.

How To Write A Winning College Application Essay

★★★

Author/Editor: Michael James Mason
Publisher: Prima Publishing
Edition Reviewed: 2nd (1994)
Internet URL:

Media Type: Print
Price: $11.95
ISBN: 1-55958-345-2

RATINGS (1-4 STARS):

Overall:	★★★	A useful and well-written resource
Breadth Of Content:		Not Applicable
Value Added:	★★★	Author has incorporated the suggestions of students to improve this edition
Ease Of Use:	★★★★	Easy to read and use

DESCRIPTION:

This book is the result of several years of conducting writing workshops for students. Chapter 1 explains how to use this book and outlines the steps students will go through to write the essay. In Chapter 2 the author includes the answers he received from college admissions officers to several questions, such as, "How important is the application essay?". The author then proceeds to show students how to advertise themselves to the colleges and universities they wish to attend. The application essay is presented as the best way for students to present the unique qualities they have to offer. Chapters 3 through 7 take students through a step-by-step process of writing a successful college application essay; sample essays are included. There is a brief checklist in Chapter 11 of small details that shouldn't be forgotten. The new materials in this edition are a chapter on how to write a good SAT essay and a chapter on writing essays for scholarships. These additions stem from letters and comments from students who used the first edition.

EVALUATION:

The straightforward writing and easy-to-read layout of this book are appealing. The author presents a basic no-frills essay writing process which gives students a way to present themselves in the best possible light. The focus is on proper grammar, sentence and paragraph structure and on writing what the application asks for and not on showy, slick gimmicks. An entire chapter is devoted to "Do's" and "Don'ts". The chapters on SAT essays and essays for scholarships are particularly useful additions. The author explains the differences between the types of essays concisely, in language that will help students stay focused on the intent of the essay. The sample essays provided are a mix of good and bad, followed by the author's evaluation. These evaluations could have been more specific, perhaps quoting the essay to clarify which section he is discussing, but overall they provide adequate guidance. This will be a useful resource helpful to those struggling with their essays.

WHERE TO FIND/BUY:

Bookstores and libraries, or call the publisher direct at 916-632-4400.

Guide To Nursing Programs

Author/Editor:
Publisher: Peterson's Guides
Edition Reviewed: 2nd (1996)
Internet URL: http://www.petersons.com

Media Type: Print
Price: $24.95
ISBN: 1-56079-565-4

RATINGS (1-4 STARS):

Overall:	★★★	Lots of information; take the in-depth profiles with a grain of salt
Breadth Of Content:	★★★★	Lists all accredited and chartered nursing programs in the U.S. and Canada
Value Added:	★★	No evaluative information provided
Ease Of Use:	★★★★	Very well organized and easy to use

DESCRIPTION:

This is one of Peterson's specialized guides, listing more than 2,000 nursing programs at over 625 schools in the United States and Canada. All of the programs profiled in this guide are four-year and graduate level programs; no comparative or evaluative information is provided. The programs are all accredited or have candidate-for-accreditation status in the U.S., and Canadian programs are all chartered or accredited. The first section includes articles on nursing careers today, how to finance your education, and tips for returning students. Section two contains the profiles, organized alphabetically by State and Province. The profiles range in length from 1/4 of a page to a page and a half and contain information on enrollment, academic facilities, student life, contact information, expenses and programs offered. In-depth descriptions of the nursing programs, written by the schools are provided in section three. These essays are approximately two pages long and Peterson's does not take responsibility for their content (not all of the schools chose to be included in this section). The final section is a series of indexes by institution name, type of program, masters level programs, area of study and concentration.

EVALUATION:

Peterson's has written several very good guidebooks and this is no exception. This is an impressive tome, at 688 pages, and it contains a lot of information focused on college nursing programs. Peterson's does not evaluate the colleges they profile; information included is provided by the colleges and universities and consists largely of statistics on enrollment and basic information on the programs, expenses and student life. The information is helpful in deciding which schools to contact for further information and it will give you a good idea of what to expect in course load and expenses. One the strengths Peterson's provides is a variety of indexes that make it possible to find exactly the information you are looking for. The in-depth profiles of the programs were provided by the schools and should be read with the same caution used when reading official school publications; it's important to look elsewhere for an evaluative opinion or original insight into the relative quality these programs.

WHERE TO FIND/BUY:

Bookstores and libraries, or see Peterson's website at the URL: http://www.petersons.com.

Colleges With Programs For Students With Learning Disabilities

Author/Editor: Charles T. Mangrum II, Ed.D.
  & Stephen S. Strighart, Ph.D.

Publisher: Peterson's Guides

Edition Reviewed: 4th (1994)

Internet URL: http://www.petersons.com

Media Type: Print

Price: $32.95

ISBN: 1-56079-400-3

RATINGS (1-4 STARS):

Overall:	★★★	An all-inclusive specialized guide; focus is on LD programs & services
Breadth Of Content:	★★★	800+ programs, including those in Canada
Value Added:	★★★	Good section on "College Opportunities" but little else that is novel
Ease Of Use:	★★	Small type and amount of information presented makes it difficult to read

DESCRIPTION:

In its fourth edition, this 674 page guide profiles 800+ programs that focus on the needs of students with learning differences (LD). The list was compiled by mailing questionnaires to all accredited two-year and four-year U.S./Canadian colleges and universities (3,300+) to identify programs or services for LD students. This edition consists of 6 parts. One part describes learning disabilities and characteristics of LD students, and explains assistance colleges can provide for these students. Two sections deal with selecting a college (visits, creating a comparative checklist of LD programs, etc.). The 5th part includes testing accommodations and highlights organizations for LD students. The last two sections focus on specific college programs that are available. One of these sections is a quick-reference chart listing colleges and includes a column which ranks entrance difficulties (based upon both entering freshmen's high school rank and SAT/ACT scores); the other profiles each of the 800+ programs. These profiles have two parts; the first describes colleges that offer "programs" for students with LD, the other, colleges that have "services" for LD students. Within each profile, specific information on the LD program (fees, admission requirements, staffing, LD student population, support services,etc.), general college information (student/faculty population, expenses, financial aid, housing, college life, majors, etc.), etc., are provided.

EVALUATION:

This edition offers some value for parents of LD students in their search to find the right college program. The editors, who have worked in special education programs and with students of learning disabilities, attempt here to present an "end-all" guide to colleges for students with LD. The book is often difficult to wade through because of small type and the variety of information presented. Most of the schools seem to have close to the same opportunities available, and no attempt is to rank LD programs. The method used to rank schools in the chapter entitled "Quick-Reference Chart of Colleges", as with many other college guides, is suspect. Simply ranking schools based upon entering freshmen's high school ranking and test scores provides only a hint of relative "quality" and no evidence of "fit". The section entitled "College Opportunities for Students with Learning Disabilities" can be valuable because it highlights special needs that may arise in college, such as counseling, tutoring, special courses, auxiliary aids and services, and so on.

WHERE TO FIND/BUY:

Bookstores and libraries.

I Am Somebody: College Knowledge
For The First-Generation Campus Bound

★★★

Author/Editor: Anna Leider

Publisher: Octameron Associates

Edition Reviewed: 6th (1994)

Internet URL:

Media Type: Print

Price: $6.00

ISBN: 0-945981-94-5

RATINGS (1-4 STARS):

Overall:	★★★	A positive approach for first generation college-bound students
Breadth Of Content:		Not applicable
Value Added:	★★★	Provides clear answers to tough questions
Ease Of Use:	★★★	Worksheets require commitment but are worth it

DESCRIPTION:

This book outlines the process of getting into college for the first generation college-bound student. A foreword to parents asks them to encourage their children to go to college and is provided in English and Spanish. Several education counselors, high school counselors , college admission offices, and financial aid officers cooperated in the production of this book. Chapter one tells the stories of several famous minorities and explains how their stories should inspire students to pursue a college education. Chapter two lists composite descriptions of first generation college students written by HS counselors and based on students they have helped in the past. These profiles illustrate the different financial, academic, and social standing of these students; it's the author's intent that students reading this book will see themselves and be encouraged. Chapters three and four list reasons a student should go to college and refute myths that keep students from going to college. A brief overview of the selection and admissions process is followed by information about financial aid (what financial aid is, how to get it,several sources of aid described). The last third of the book includes a senior year timetable, several worksheets and a glossary .

EVALUATION:

Although addressed to all first generation students going to college, this book focuses on first generation minority students -- the listing of scholarship providers lists only those who provide scholarships to minorities, such as the American Indian College Fund, and the profiles of first generation college students are all of minorities. Nonetheless, the positive message of this book help ensure its value to all first generation college bound students. The strongest section of this book is Chapter 6: Financial Aid. It includes several mathematical examples that are easy to follow and understand. The emphasis is on applying correctly and on time, with several easy-to-use worksheets are included to help students gather information to get the aid they need. The senior year timetable in Chapter 7 contains references back to other chapters to help students complete the right step at the right time. The author encourages students to continue their education in a way that is positive and tries to help students see the rewards and not the obstacles. This book is recommended for all first generation college bound students.

WHERE TO FIND/BUY:

Find in Libraries or Bookstores, or call the publisher direct at 703-836-5480.

Behind The Scenes: An Inside Look At The Selective College Admission Process ★★★

Author/Editor: Edward B. Wall   **Media Type:** Print
Publisher: Octameron Associates   **Price:** $4.00
Edition Reviewed: 10th (1994)   **ISBN:** 0-945981-89-9
Internet URL:

RATINGS (1-4 STARS):

Overall:	★★★	Great suggestions and examples from a veteran admissions director
Breadth Of Content:	★★	Narrow focus on admissions process, using Liberal Arts examples
Value Added:	★★★	Profiles provided of students who were accepted and rationale as to why
Ease Of Use:	★★★	Chapter headings, Q&A format make it an easy read

DESCRIPTION:

This 7-chapter, 36 page book, written by a 30+ year veteran in student admissions and counseling, outlines the admissions process. Chapter 1, dedicated to dean of admissions at Amherst, gives you a history of admissions' policies. Chapter 2 answers the most common questions about selective admission. Chapter 3 outlines strategies for the student when interviewing with prospective colleges. Information is also given about choosing schools, contacting and applying to schools, facing a personal interview, financial aid, and summer programs. Chapter 4 outlines the "mechanics of selection" and Chapter 5 answers the questions of "what are you looking for? what kinds of applicants are accepted?" by presenting profiles of 18 students who were admitted and enrolled at Amherst. Chapter 6 lists several arguments in support of a liberal arts education. Finally, chapter 7 is a one-page statistical profile of a class from the "most competitive year at Amherst". Information is listed such as: the volume of applicants ("accepted", "early decision matriculated", etc.), college board aptitude scores from those who applied, were accepted, were matriculated, rankings of students (public schools, private schools), etc.

EVALUATION:

This little book covers the important aspects of the admissions process. Within its cover you will find pertinent advice concerning contact with a college, how to prepare in your high school years, the worthiness of test scores, and how to supply useful information that gives colleges a true picture of yourself. In particular, chapter 1 gives a dean of admissions' point of view to exemplify what decisions are used to accept or reject applicants. Chapter 2 at first glance seems to have a hodgepodge of questions, but there are several suggestions here which should be taken seriously as students prepare for their college years. Chapter 3 also offers great advice on how to conduct yourself with the college of choice, including interview questions that might be asked of any applicant. Additionally, specific advice on the application process, from when to apply to what to include, is also supplied. Of particular interest are chapters 4 and 5 which give you an inside look into the admissions officers' thought processes. Chapter 4 outlines what actually goes on as the finalist list is narrowed down and chapter 5 profiles a variety of students and explains why they were accepted to Amherst. In all, this book does a great job of summing up the important points of the admissions process in a neat little package.

WHERE TO FIND/BUY:

Bookstores and libraries or through the publisher at 703-836-5480.

College Admissions: A Crash Course For Panicked Parents

Author/Editor: Sally Rubenstone & Sidonia Dalby
Publisher: Macmillan
Edition Reviewed: 1st (1994)
Internet URL:

Media Type: Print
Price: $12.00
ISBN: 0-671-87056-4

RATINGS (1-4 STARS):

Overall:	★★★	Great resource and support for parents beginning the admissions process
Breadth Of Content:	★★★	Includes all information necessary to get through the process
Value Added:	★★★★	Useful generalized checklist for parents for 9th grade - 12th grade
Ease Of Use:	★★★★	Well-organized, question-answer approach

DESCRIPTION:

The authors, admissions counselors/directors, offer this 200 page book for parents as they prepare their child for the admissions process. The first two chapters deal with the decisions involved with finding the right match between student and college. A self-assessment survey for parents and students focuses on the student's strengths and desired college outcomes. Chapter 3 targets testing, including a section that discusses preparing for college entrance tests. Chapter 4 deals with campus visits, interviews, college fairs and reps. Chapter 5 focuses on financial planning and financial aid. The next 3 chapters concern the application process from how to fill out an application, to how admissions decisions are made, to specific concerns such as wait lists, transferring, etc. Chapter 9 deals with special situations such as advanced standing, early entrance, students with disabilities and special needs, etc. Finally, chapter 10 offers "words of wisdom: advice from educators and once-panicked parents." Two appendices are supplied, the first explains terminology a parent or student may encounter through this process, the second is a checklist/calendar for parents to stay abreast of the admissions process from 9th grade through the 12th grade.

EVALUATION:

This is a no-nonsense book that helps give parents a quick overview of the admissions process. The book's question-answer format makes it easy for "panicked parents" to find information. The emphasis in chapter 1 on making college choices a family decision coupled with the self-assessment surveys provided for parents and students is a nice touch. Additionally, the checklist and calendar in the appendix also give parents an easy step-by-step path toward helping their child through the admissions process (use this as a starting point and not as an end-all in case something is not included that is pertinent to your situation). Also noteworthy are chapters 5 and 6 which are respectively "money matters: financial planning and financial aid" and "pushing papers: the application itself." Within these chapters are helpful tips that will ease any parent's mind on these two subjects. Tips for applying for financial aid, budget worksheets, and information about educational loan programs are included within chapter 5. Chapter 6 includes great advice about writing the essay and also what to include and what not to include on the college application. Overall, this book is recommended for parents who need some reassurance and an overview.

WHERE TO FIND/BUY:

Bookstores or libraries.

Essays That Worked

Author/Editor: Boykin Curry and Brian Kasbar
Publisher: Ballantine Books
Edition Reviewed: 2nd (1990)
Internet URL:

Media Type: Print
Price: $10.00
ISBN: 0-449-90517-9

RATINGS (1-4 STARS):

Overall:	★★★	Positive and upbeat book
Breadth Of Content:	★★★	Provides 50 positive essays written on a variety of subjects
Value Added:	★★★	Overall comments from admissions officers helpful
Ease Of Use:	★★★★	Well-organized and easily read; not overwhelming

DESCRIPTION:

This 145 page book, consisting of 4 parts, includes 50 essays accepted from college applications. The first two parts include a rationale as to why this revised edition was written and an introduction explaining the purpose of the essay. The third part, "An Interview with an Admissions Officer", presents a narrative discussion between a possible admissions officer and a possible applicant. The quotes in this section were compiled from the comments of all the admissions officers that the authors interviewed. The final section encompasses the majority of the book. It subdivides fifty essays based on subject matter such as relationships, obstacles, offbeat subjects, etc. These essays were selected by the authors in conjunction with admissions officers from some of "the nation's top colleges" (Yale, Harvard, etc.). The authors reviewed essays from hundreds of thousands applications. At the beginning of each essay sub-division is a 1 to 2 page recap of the essays that follow. Within this recap, admissions officers explain the high points of each essay and offer suggestions about writing on that particular subject matter. At the beginning, middle, and end of the book are 3 blocked-off paragraphs that offer 5 suggestions each to help the writer.

EVALUATION:

It's always interesting and enlightening to read great college application essays. Although this book does not offer any specific help for students as they try to figure out what to write about, often good models themselves will present brainstorming possibilities. As with other books, the authors justifiably stress the importance of expressing the "real" you when writing the all-important essay. To that end, the preface should be read carefully before any student reads further. The quote from the dean of admissions at Bates College helps in keeping one's perspective on reading the enclosed essays. As he states, any book that includes essays should not freeze students up and make them feel that they can not offer anything as brilliant. Instead students should feel encouraged to search their own experiences for something unique. The preface to each essay subdivision and the comments from admissions officers allow students that opportunity in quick little snippets. The book is positively written and provides ample opportunity for students to see some good examples of essays written by students who were accepted at well-respected universities. Missing from this book are prompts that might directly give students some ideas for their writing and some pointers on the revising and editing processes.

WHERE TO FIND/BUY:

Bookstores and libraries.

Guide To Architecture Schools

★★★

Author/Editor: Richard E. McCommons
Publisher: Association of Collegiate Schools of Architecture
Edition Reviewed: 5th (1994)
Internet URL:

Media Type: Print
Price: $19.95
ISBN: 0-935502-06-8

RATINGS (1-4 STARS):

Overall:	★★★	Brief descriptions of ACSA architecture programs and worldwide programs
Breadth Of Content:	★★★	118 U.S. and Canadian schools described
Value Added:	★★★	Charts in each profile listing degrees, admission requirements,etc. helpful
Ease Of Use:	★★	Alphabetically by school; map at beginning needed to find schools by state

DESCRIPTION:

This 297+ page resource guide was developed for prospective architecture students and professionals in the field. There are 7 sections at the very beginning of the book. The first section gives a brief overview of the history of architecture education. The second and third sections outline ways a student may prepare in high school before they select an appropriate school. Section 4 details the practice of architecture. Sections 5 - 7 explain accreditation methods, locations of architecture schools (a U.S. map is illustrated), and a list of affiliate members of the Association of Collegiate Schools of Architecture (ACSA). There is an appendix that lists degree types, specializations within the architecture degree, related degree programs, scholarships, organizations, and a list of abbreviations. The remainder of the book includes profiles of 118 schools arranged alphabetically by school. Within each profile, you will find: tuition and fees, degrees offered, number of years to complete the degrees, school population demographics, special activities, opportunities, resources and programs, description of the facilities, scholarships available, philosophy statements from the undergraduate and graduate programs, etc.

EVALUATION:

The author's purpose in this book is to describe the opportunities available in the field of architecture so that students can match their potential and interests with an appropriate program. This book does conveniently provide students and professionals with information that can be used to compare one school with another. However, since the information contained within profiles is supplied by the schools themselves, there is little feel for the actual school and the climate of learning within. The philosophy statements read as a marketing brochure would - too vague, without any specific goals. Additionally, there is no real idea of how the schools are perceived by students in attendance or architecture professionals. Although specific programs of study are shown to be accredited or not, some comments about the programs from professionals in the field would be helpful. The author does, however, make some useful suggestions in the beginning sections of his book concerning architecture education. Any prospective architecture student should in particular read sections 2 - 4 that describe the "real" picture of what is involved with becoming an architect and what the field of architecture is really like. This book can give you a start on deciding which schools of architecture might serve your needs, but further research will be also needed.

WHERE TO FIND/BUY:

Bookstores and libraries.

Help Yourself: Handbook For College-Bound Students With Learning Disabilities

Author/Editor: Erica-Lee Lewis
Publisher: Random House Inc.
Edition Reviewed: 1st (1996)
Internet URL: http://www.randomhouse.com

Media Type: Print
Price: $20.00
ISBN: 0-679-76461-5

RATINGS (1-4 STARS):

Overall:	★★★	Concisely written and user-friendly for students with LD
Breadth Of Content:	★★	Good overview of the important aspects; few details
Value Added:	★★	Appendices of words commonly used in SAT and ACT tests
Ease Of Use:	★★★★	Highlighted notes in margin useful are summaries

DESCRIPTION:

The publishers of this book have written others that focus on test preparation for colleges, grad schools and professional licenses. In this 236 page book, their focus is for students who have learning disabilities (LD) who wish to pursue college. The first of the seven chapters defines learning disabilities. Chapter 2 concentrates on test taking tips while chapters 3 and 4 concentrate on the admissions process and selecting the right school. Chapter 5 gives pointers on dealing with college and financial aid applications. Specific tips are offered on tackling the college essay, an outline is provided to help you focus and present yourself on the application positively, and various financial aid programs are explained. Chapter 6 - "Showtime" - offers advice on how to survive and enjoy the college experience. Advice is offered on budgeting, getting along with a roommate, organizing time and money, using study techniques, preparing for class, etc. Chapter 7 lists addresses of organizations a student with LD can turn to for help and support. Two appendices are also provided that offer vocabulary words a student with LD might study in conjunction with preparing for the SAT and ACT and for use while writing the college essay.

EVALUATION:

If you are a student with learning disabilities and looking for a book that explains the college application process in an easy to read manner, then this book will initially suit your purposes. All the major aspects are explained and summaries are highlighted in the margins of the book. The book reads well, headings make information easy to find, and there is not much fluff to detract from the information provided. The best information and advice are provided in chapters 1 (defining LD), 2 (testing tips), and 6 (surviving and enjoying college). This book also provides many supportive features including the list of resources in chapter 7 and the appendices of vocabulary words. However, some features are lacking or some aspects are presented too briefly. For example, other books provide several essay examples and critiques; only one example is presented here. Also, students with LD might benefit from books that provide completed sample college applications; none were provided in this book. Although the appendices can be useful for students with LD, they may also intimidate students. Overall, this book provides a gentle and reassuring start for students as they decide whether or not college is the right path for them, but a student would also need to read other sources to gain a full measure of advice.

WHERE TO FIND/BUY:

Bookstores and libraries or through the publisher at 1-800-REVIEW-6.

Visiting College Campuses

★★

Author/Editor: Janet Spencer & Sandra Maleson
Publisher: Villard Books (Princeton Review - Student Access)
Edition Reviewed: 1995
Internet URL:

Media Type: Print
Price: $19.95
ISBN: 0-679-75910-7

RATINGS (1-4 STARS):

Overall:	★★	Helpful if you need planning aids; otherwise just call the admissions office.
Breadth Of Content:	★★	Information is included for roughly 250+ schools.
Value Added:	★★	Recommendations on lodging and attractions are helpful.
Ease Of Use:	★★★★	Organized by state, and very easy to use.

DESCRIPTION:

The full title of this guide, in its second edition, is "The Princeton Review - Student Access Guide To Visiting College Campuses." Its focus is to help those students and families planning their trips to visit college campuses, by providing the information necessary to plan and manage the travel logistics involved. For example, the 250+ colleges and universities included are organized by state; at the beginning of each state section is a map showing where colleges are located within the state, and their road mileage from each other and central transportation hubs. For each college, details are provided to help plan the day of the visit, such as when campus tours and admissions interviews are available and how long they last, and where the admissions office is located on campus. For each college, the guide also includes details and suggestions for transportation to the campus, driving directions, overnight accommodations, and local attractions.

EVALUATION:

The information contained in this guide is essential to making a stress-free trip to visit a number of colleges. Particularly useful are the descriptions and recommendations made for overnight accommodations, and the state charts showing where colleges are located within each state, with mileage between the various colleges also shown. However, most of this information is available by telephone from the admissions staff; in many cases, they'll have this information already in printed form and are happy to mail it to you.

WHERE TO FIND/BUY:

Bookstores and libraries, or order direct by calling 800-793-BOOK.

Right College

★★

Author/Editor: College Research Group
Publisher: Macmillan/Arco Publishing
Edition Reviewed: 7th
Internet URL:

Media Type: Print
Price: $22
ISBN: 0-671-89030-1

RATINGS (1-4 STARS):

Overall:	★★	Another of the big guides, offering nothing unique
Breadth Of Content:	★★★★	It's got 'em all
Value Added:	★★	Very little added value; the usual short profiles and stats
Ease Of Use:	★★★	Organized by state

DESCRIPTION:

This guidebook is one of a half-dozen all-inclusive guidebooks to four-year colleges offering degrees, in this case 1,500+ schools. As an all-inclusive guide, it relies primarily on information provided by the schools, resulting in a page of information profiling each college and providing the usual statistics. Topics addressed in every profile (usually in just several sentences) include the Student Body, Programs Of Study, Student Life, Athletics, Admissions, Financial Aid, Student Employment, Computer Facilities, and Graduate Career Data. The guide also includes an index organized by state which assigns a point value to Selectivity, SAT/ACT scores, Tuition, Size, etc. Preceding the profiles are several useful essays on Choosing a College, Completing the Application, Financial Aid, and other topics.

EVALUATION:

Breadth but not depth, is the keyword to this and other guides. Since they include virtually ALL the possible college choices, this and other all-inclusive guides are useful to the high school student's initial survey of possibilities, but none offer any real methodology to help the student arrive at the right initial choices. Thus, this guidebook and its brethren are useful IF you know generally what you're looking for, less useful if you haven't got a clue. A quick read of the basic information provided for each school will give you a feeling for whether or not a school may fit your criteria.

WHERE TO FIND/BUY:

Bookstores and libraries.

Competitive Colleges 1995-1996

★★

Author/Editor:
Publisher: Peterson's Guides
Edition Reviewed: 1995
Internet URL: http://www.petersons.com

Media Type: Print
Price: $16.95
ISBN: 1-56079-480-1

RATINGS (1-4 STARS):

Overall:	★★	Not much here to help winnow down that initial list of colleges
Breadth Of Content:	★★	375+ colleges profiled, based on freshman academic credentials
Value Added:	★★	No evaluative input; just summaries of stats and facts commonly available
Ease Of Use:	★★★	Easy-to-use, listed alphabetically

DESCRIPTION:

This guidebook represents Peterson's approach to providing some insight into colleges generally considered competitive. The 375+ colleges are included based on "competitiveness of the admission environment..as evidenced by the quality of students applying..."; no specifics are disclosed. The profiles provided for each college, one page apiece, include short paragraphs covering: academics, computers on campus, campus life, and admissions details. A paragraph provided by the college is usually included. Statistics are provided as well, under the headings of: getting in last year (academic profile of freshman admitted), the student body (geographic and ethnic distribution), how many students return after the freshman year, when they graduate, what they do after graduation, and what you will pay. Short essays are provided on the admissions and financial processes. Fourteen indexes are provided, covering everything from majors offered, to colleges specializing in the arts, to those deemed predominately African-American, to listings of colleges organized by religious emphasis, and so on.

EVALUATION:

Many of the publishers of the all-enclusive guidebooks seem compelled to also publish "selective" guidebooks. This is Peterson's version. They make the case in their introduction that statistically-based college rankings are NOT the way to go; instead, they've used the academic profile of admitted freshmen to provide their listing of 375+ competitive colleges. What this guidebook does NOT provide is student input, or original essays, or any evaluative input of any kind. Instead, each college profile is limited to highly summarized statistics and text, no doubt extracted from Peterson's huge database of information compiled for each college in the country. This doesn't give students working to pare down their initial lists very much to work with that they haven't already found in the larger, all-enclusive guides. Many of the other selective guides available provide most of the statistics included here, and usually express an evaluative opinion about colleges reviewed, frequently based on student input; we'd recommend some of them instead of this work.

WHERE TO FIND/BUY:

Bookstores and libraries, or direct from the publisher at 800-338-3282.

Index Of Majors & Graduate Degrees   ★★

Author/Editor:
Publisher: The College Board
Edition Reviewed: 1996 (18th)
Internet URL:

Media Type: Print
Price: $17
ISBN: 0-87447-507-4

RATINGS (1-4 STARS):

Overall:	★★	Don't bother with this if you can get help from a more focused guidebook
Breadth Of Content:	★★★★	Every major, at every level, at every institution
Value Added:	★	It got all the data organized by state and major, period
Ease Of Use:	★★★	Nicely organized

DESCRIPTION:

This tome provides a very comprehensive reference to virtually all majors at virtually all levels of study at virtually all institutions in the U.S., from two-year colleges to graduate schools. It thus serves an audience made up of not only prospective college students, but students at all levels. The book first lists major fields of study (majors) by general discipline, then provides a brief description of each field of study (1-2 sentences), all 600 of them. It then provides a listing, roughly 550 pages long, by state, of every institution offering each major; each listing also indicates at what level the major is offered (bachelor's, master's, etc.). The book then provides additional listings of institutions offering special academic programs, ranging from a "semester at sea" to "weekend college". An alphabetical listing of majors closes out the book.

EVALUATION:

The College Board also publishes a much more focused guidebook, called the "Guide To 150 Popular College Majors"; we'd recommend that choice over this book. This guidebook can be useful if your major of interest is not included in the more focused study, or if you're seeking an associate degree or a masters degree, for example. Their "College Majors" guidebook provides some really helpful insights into each major; this guidebook simply gives a listing of institutions offering each major, organized by state. Nothing more -- no indication of the quality of their program, or the size of their program, nothing. Treat this as the reference work it is, and don't spend the money unless the local library or your college counseling office doesn't have a copy.

WHERE TO FIND/BUY:

Bookstores and libraries, direct from the publisher by calling 800-323-7155, or on the World Wide Web at http://www.collegeboard.org.

College Admissions

Author/Editor: Adam Robinson & John Katzman
Publisher: Princeton Review/Random House
Edition Reviewed: 1994 (2nd)
Internet URL:

Media Type: Print
Price: $12
ISBN: 0-679-74590-4

RATINGS (1-4 STARS):

Overall:	★★	This is at best an overview of the obvious issues
Breadth Of Content:	★★	Tries to cover all the bases in a short 160 pages
Value Added:	★★	Just an OK effort; not much depth given its premise
Ease Of Use:	★★★	Well organized; flows well between chapters

DESCRIPTION:

This 160 page book is offers assistance to high school students interested in attending a selective college. The first chapter, "Picking Colleges", is focused on the factors (the authors discuss seventeen) involved in deciding where to apply. The remainder of the book is "devoted to helping you maximize your chances of being accepted". The "Test Scores" chapter provides details on the SAT's background, its importance, and preparation for the test. "Grades & Extracurricular Activities" provides advice on which high school courses and activities will be received more favorably by college admissions staff. Dos and Don'ts for filling out applications are provided in "Your Applications"; similarly, advice is included for "Essay, Recommendations, & Interviews" as well. The chapter on "Financial Aid" is a quick overview of the financial aid process and terminology.

EVALUATION:

There are some style issues in this book that put us off a bit. The book never misses an opportunity to promote the Princeton Review, its books, its SAT prep courses, etc., to the point of being intrusive. The writing, in an attempt to relate to the high school student, is just too darn cute; this makes the advice given seem less credible. These issues aside, our principle criticism of this book is that it seems content to provide advice that is largely obvious; we're not convinced that the strategies described would make a substantial difference in how an applicant to a selective college is perceived by its admission staff. The advice and strategies provided, while basic, would provide the average high school student with an overview of the obvious mistakes to avoid in preparing for, and completing, the college application process.

WHERE TO FIND/BUY:

Bookstores and libraries, or order direct by calling 800-793-BOOK.

Best Buys In College Education

Author/Editor: Lucia Solorzano
Publisher: Barron's
Edition Reviewed: 3rd (1994)
Internet URL:

Media Type: Print
Price: $14.95
ISBN: 0-8120-1857-5

RATINGS (1-4 STARS):

Overall:	★★	Methodology for picking these 300 neither clear nor convincing
Breadth Of Content:	★★	Just 300 schools profiled
Value Added:	★★★	Profiles are well-written, but not real deep
Ease Of Use:	★★★	Profiles organized by state; some indexes provided

DESCRIPTION:

This is an "evaluative" guidebook that uses as its basis for selection a combination of factors. First, it focuses on tuition rates "as compared not only with the national average for schools of the same type but also..similar schools in that region or schools of comparative selectivity or academic emphasis." Then, it factors in percentages of Ph.D.s, freshmen who graduate, and graduates seeking advanced degrees. The final list was selected based on these statistics plus student feedback via surveys, which was also used as the basis for much of the narrative profiles of each college. For each college profiled, a "Data Capsule" provides a quick reference for choosing or rejecting choices based on such factors as college setting, enrollment, freshman academic profile (SAT/ACT scores, etc.), tuition and fees, percentage receiving financial aid, and average aid given, and on campus job opportunities for students. The written profiles include descriptions of the student body, academics, facilities, and campus life. A "Cost Cutters" section includes financial aid statistics and details on types of awards, job earnings, average indebtedness of graduates, and special scholarships available. Data is based on surveys taken in late 1993.

EVALUATION:

The stated intent of this guidebook is to identify schools that "breach the supposed link between college price and college quality." However, the methodology described to make these selections doesn't really convince. Percentages of freshmen who graduate, or those seeking advanced degrees, don't seem clearly linked to whether or not the money spent was a "best buy." Colleges selected run the gamut from small to large, private to public, with total costs ranging from less than $5,000 to more than $20,000. We suppose this guidebook could be used as a list of suggestions to take a look at, but doubt it's the best way to get to a best buy in college education; better, it seems, to pick a list of colleges based on factors other than cost, then narrow that list with an eye to costs. This issue aside, the statistics chosen for highlighting are a useful way to eliminate or add colleges to your initial list. The profiles are better than those of the all-inclusive guidebooks, and include evaluative narrative based on student surveys. Still, the narrative profiles are heavy with statistics, and aren't really deep enough to create a strong image of what it would be like to attend each particular college.

WHERE TO FIND/BUY:

Most libraries and bookstores.

Getting Into College

★★

Author/Editor: Pat Ordovensky
Publisher: Peterson's Guides
Edition Reviewed: 1995
Internet URL: http://www.petersons.com

Media Type: Print
Price: $8.95
ISBN: 1-56079-463-1

RATINGS (1-4 STARS):

Overall:	★★	A reasonably thorough overview, but only that
Breadth Of Content:	★★★	Virtually every base is touched, but only briefly as a rule
Value Added:	★★	Reads somewhat like a compilation of newspaper columns
Ease Of Use:	★★★	Nicely organized and laid out

DESCRIPTION:

This book provides an overview of the college selection, admissions, and financing process, written by an experienced education writer for Gannett New Service and USA Today. This 150 page book includes eleven chapters, including an introductory chapter, a chapter on the Community College (2 year) option, and a closing chapter consisting of questions and answers on various topics. The "meat" of the book focuses on identifying college choices, college visits and interviews, choosing colleges to apply to, completing the application and helping yourself stand out from the crowd, and working through the financial aid process.

EVALUATION:

The writing style of this book makes it an "easy read" -- it's crisp and concise. The breadth of the book's ambitions reflect the author's experience writing on these topics for newspapers. The flip side of this approach, unfortunately, is that many topics addressed by the book are given fairly shallow treatment. While the number of topics covered within chapters is large, each topic is given what is basically an overview treatment. Thus, the book can be useful as a good overview of the process (the chapter on financial aid is particularly effective in this regard), but shouldn't be viewed as exhaustive treatment on any one topic; other, more detailed resources should be used.

WHERE TO FIND/BUY:

Bookstores and libraries, or direct from the publisher at 800-338-3282.

Lovejoy's College Guide

Author/Editor: Charles Straughn & Barbara Sue Straughn
Publisher: Macmillian General Reference
Edition Reviewed: 23rd (1995)
Internet URL:

Media Type: Print
Price: $21.95
ISBN: 0-02-860304-4

RATINGS (1-4 STARS):

Overall:	★★	Another of the large, all-inclusive guidebooks, with little that's special
Breadth Of Content:	★★★★	Includes short profiles for every 4-year college
Value Added:	★★	Little information added to the basic stats and facts
Ease Of Use:	★★	Nothing to distinguish itself, just lists and lists

DESCRIPTION:

This large, all-inclusive guidebook's been around longer than most; this is the 23rd edition. The guidebook is divided into four sections. Section One provides brief overviews of financial aid, veterans benefits, and the college admissions process. Section Two is designed to provide various majors of interest and the colleges which offer them; it provides a short listing of "Accrediting Bodies & Recognized Associations" which can be good sources of career information, lists 500 majors and the colleges offering them, and closes with a listing of colleges offering special programs. Section Three lists 2,500 schools, including two-year and graduate schools; four-year institutions include 1/2 page profiles. The profiles include an indication of selectivity, the usual statistics, and short paragraphs on academics, special programs, financial aid, admissions, student life, athletics, etc. Section Four is a sports index which shows colleges offering various sports for men and women; it indicates which programs offer scholarships.

EVALUATION:

Data for this guide, and most of the all-inclusive guides, comes from the colleges themselves, typically organized and dispersed by Wintergreen/Orchard House, a database publishing company specializing in this area. Since the profiles contained in this guidebook are based largely on this data, they read pretty much the same as the other large guidebooks. Choosing between these kinds of guides thus pretty much depends on their indexes and special presentations of basic statistics. This guide includes helpful listings of majors and sports programs, without any indication of the relative quality of these programs. Their college selection and financial aid overviews are quite abbreviated compared to other guidebooks. Keeping in mind that this genre of guidebooks is best used only for quick reference, this particular version is probably OK. But you'll have to look elsewhere for more subjective information.

WHERE TO FIND/BUY:

Bookstores and libraries.

Your College Application

Author/Editor: Scott Gelband, Catherine Kubale, Eric Schorr
Publisher: College Board Publications
Edition Reviewed: 1991
Internet URL:

Media Type: Print
Price: $9.95
ISBN: 0-87447-428-0

RATINGS (1-4 STARS):

Overall:	★★	An exhaustive (and exhausting) treatment of college applications
Breadth Of Content:		Not applicable
Value Added:	★★★	The authors know their stuff, almost too well
Ease Of Use:	★★	This is a hard read; too much detail, some irrelevant

---

DESCRIPTION:

The authors are former admissions officers at Yale; this 140+ page book reflects their cumulative experience in evaluating thousands of applications. As the title implies, the book focuses in considerable detail on various components making up the typical college application. The authors discuss those components within three main chapters: "Academic Evaluations" (high school transcript, class rank, and test scores), "Personal Statements" (essays, extracurricular activities, and campus interviews), and "Supporting Documents" (teacher recommendations, guidance counselor's report, and supplementary materials). Additional chapters are devoted to debunking college admission myths ("Is is true that geography is a consideration?"), and "Special Situations" typically encountered by transfer students, foreign students, etc.

EVALUATION:

There's a good deal of useful material in this book that students would find helpful in completing their college applications. Unfortunately, much of it is hidden behind too much detail, some not particularly necessary or relevant (explaining different methods schools use to calculate class rankings, for example). At times, paragraphs are spent explaining the obvious (defining the difference between "breadth" and "depth" in high school course selection, for example). In contrast, the section on teacher recommendations is very good, with tips on which subjects to choose and which teachers to ask; also helpful are suggestions for materials which can be used to supplement the standard application, and the chapter debunking typical admissions "myths." This is not an expensive resource (less than $10), and probably worth the money, but it's not an easy read.

WHERE TO FIND/BUY:

Bookstores and libraries, direct from the publisher by calling 800-323-7155, or on the World Wide Web at http://www.collegeboard.org.

Playing The Selective College Admissions Game   ★★

Author/Editor: Richard Moll	**Media Type:** Print
Publisher: Penguin Books	**Price:** $9.95
Edition Reviewed: 2nd (1994)	**ISBN:** 0-14-051303-5
Internet URL:	

RATINGS (1-4 STARS):

Overall:	★★	If you're DETERMINED to go to a selective school, you'll find this useful
Breadth Of Content:	★★	This book is only for those who want to REALLY work the details
Value Added:	★★★★	The author's experience is obvious; very deep analysis of most subjects
Ease Of Use:	★★	You'll find 200+ pages of small type and dense prose herein

DESCRIPTION:

The author is an experienced college admissions director; he's written several books and many articles on the subject of college admissions; this revised edition updates a book first published 15+ years ago. The introduction states: "This book is an attempt to share insider talk on selective college admissions... And this is, essentially, a how-to book." The book begins with a "mock" admissions committee session at a fictitious, selective college; this device allows the author to provide explanations of key variables in the admissions process, as well as some insights into what factors come into play as the committee decides to admit or reject various candidates. The 2nd chapter focuses on myths of college selection, while the 3rd chapter provides insights into exactly how selective colleges make decisions on who will be admitted (grades, tests, activities, essays, etc.). A shorter chapter follows on why both colleges and students must sell themselves. Several appendices are provided, including how to evaluate an independent counselor and a reprint of Caltech's Financial Aid Guide (a typical overview).

EVALUATION:

This is a useful reference for those targeting the highly selective colleges. The 85+ page "mock" admissions committee deliberation makes for informative reading, but it's very dense prose -- almost as if the author wanted us to experience firsthand the agonies experienced in admitting one student over another. The chapter on myths typically encountered during the college selection process is excellent, with lots of valuable insights to help high school students objectively pick target colleges. The following chapter, an exposition on how various factors are weighted by admissions committees, offers many insights not found elsewhere, but is generally so steeped with detail it could serve as a seminar text for new admissions staff. The depth of the author's experience in admissions with selective colleges shines through on nearly every page; his writing is professional, well organized, and on target. However, what emerges from this expertise is, in the end, a highly specialized and highly detailed analysis that will be of interest only to those students and parents obsessed with the goal of admission to one of the highly selective colleges. Such a high level of interest will be required to wade through these pages.

WHERE TO FIND/BUY:

Libraries and bookstores.

How To Get Into And Graduate From College In 4 Years...   ★★

Author/Editor: Martin J. Spethman
Publisher: Westgate Publishing & Entertainment Inc.
Edition Reviewed: 1992
Internet URL:

Media Type: Print
Price: $10.95
ISBN: 0-9633598-0-0

RATINGS (1-4 STARS):

Overall:	★★	More focused on college life than on getting in
Breadth Of Content:	★★	Covers a lot of topics, but without much depth
Value Added:	★★	Unique style, directed at high school students
Ease Of Use:	★★★★	Easy to read, humorous, with helpful worksheets

DESCRIPTION:

This book is written in a workbook format. Each chapter contains sections for students to fill in with addresses, telephone numbers, and other information. At the end of each chapter there is a page for students to write down notes and questions they still have and a space to note answers (from counselors), make suggestions for further reading, and add additional information. The book is laid out in a chronological fashion, starting with making sure you are taking the correct classes in order to get into the college of your choice (a worksheet is provided to write down the preadmissions requirements of your top six college choices). It moves through the application process, getting financing and choosing where to live on campus. The second half of the book deals with campus life -- from understanding your professors, learning how to study and how to cultivate proper study habits to how to get the most out of your leisure time. Four cartoon characters: Steve & Celeste Super Perfect and Kelmar & Kippy Couch Potato show up throughout the book for illustration and comic relief.

EVALUATION:

This book 's approach and style is targeted directly at high school students; it's easy to read and full of straight-forward information. The author maintains that he made every mistake possible when it came to college and wants to help students avoid the problems he faced. The extremely long title and the cartoons contribute to this book's "cool" appearance masking the solid advice and information it contains. Some parts of this book contain simple maxims, such as "eat right" and "save money", but other focus on specifics; the author includes information taken from the College Entrance Examination Board Booklets in Chapter 5: Tests You Must Take to Get In, for example. The chapters on leisure activities are very balanced. Parents don't have to worry about this book encouraging their child to "party hardy"; the author's emphasis is on doing well in school first and then relaxing in a fun and healthy environment.

WHERE TO FIND/BUY:

Find at bookstores and libraries.

100 Best Colleges For African-American Students

Author/Editor: Erlene B. Wilson

Publisher: Plume

Edition Reviewed: 1993

Internet URL:

Media Type: Print

Price: $12.00

ISBN: 0-452-27020-0

RATINGS (1-4 STARS):

Overall:	★★	Fails to provide a real rationale for picking this group of colleges
Breadth Of Content:	★★	Profiles just 100 colleges
Value Added:	★★	Additional statistics of interest to Black students
Ease Of Use:	★★	Colleges are listed alphabetically by State; no indexes provided

DESCRIPTION:

This guidebook provides profiles of 100 colleges in the United States, with a stated emphasis on opportunities for African-American students. The book , 325+ pages long, includes 2-3 pages for each profile, including statistics. Colleges are listed by State with information on SAT/ACT scores, enrollment, number of African-American students, number of African-American faculty, prominent African-American graduates, ROTC, and financial aid. Profiles include excerpts from student input.   The colleges profiled here responded to a survey mailed out by the author. Preceding the profiles is an introduction and a chapter, "Your College and Your Future". The introduction explains how the colleges and universities were chosen for this book and discusses why African-American students pick predominantly white or black campuses. "Your College and Your Future" discusses the application process and options for financing your education. The author lists scholarship providers with information on how to contact them, deadlines, and requirements. There is also a section on financing your education through the military.

EVALUATION:

There is no effort made to rank the colleges in this guidebook; indeed, the author states that those profiled are simply those that responded to her survey. The focus provided here is unique and some of the statistics are not readily available elsewhere, but without indexes useability suffers. If you are interested in going to a predominantly African-American college, for example, you will have to go through this book profile by profile to see which ones have the highest ratio of African-American students. It would have been more useful if the author had listed the colleges from highest to lowest ratio of African-American students instead of by State. The chapter "Your College and Your Future" provides useful information on financing a college education. If you are concerned about the ratio of African-American students at the school you attend, then this book may be useful after your initial list is complete. It's not recommended as a preferred source of information because of its dense writing style, poor layout, and unconvincing case that it has, in fact, picked the best colleges for Afican-Americans to consider.

WHERE TO FIND/BUY:

Find at bookstores and libraries.

Guide To Jewish Life On Campus

Author/Editor: Ruth Fredman Cernea, Ph.D
Publisher: Princeton Review Publishing
Edition Reviewed: 1996 (1995)
Internet URL:

Media Type: Print
Price: $17.00
ISBN: 0-679-76914-5

RATINGS (1-4 STARS):

Overall:	★★	Sparse information provided not particularly useful
Breadth Of Content:	★★	Profiles 500 colleges and universities worldwide
Value Added:	★	Very little useful information is provided
Ease Of Use:	★★★	Profiles organized by State and country

DESCRIPTION:

This guidebook profiles Jewish life on over 500 college and university campuses around the world. The book has three main sections; Part one explains the Hillel Foundation, provides contact information for Hillel Foundation centers, and lists the various kinds of fellowship and service activities available to Jewish students on many campuses. The college and university profiles in part two are organized alphabetically by State and country; the colleges and universities are not ranked. Each profile includes information on enrollment (including estimated number of Jewish students), availability of kosher food, religious services, Jewish studies, study in Israel, and a brief description of Jewish life on campus. Many of the profiles also contain comments by Jewish students on those campuses. Part three is focused on Resources; lists of short term and summer programs for Jewish students, National agencies and institutions with resources and programs for college students, and Jewish books on campus: "what they're reading." An aplhabetical index is provided at the back of the book.

EVALUATION:

The amount of information provided in this guidebook is disappointing. Most of the profiles are only a half a page long. In part one, the editor admits that you can not expect an active program for Jewish students on all of the campuses profiled. In some cases, the only connection is a local community member who has agreed to provide information for prospective students; one wonders why these institutions were included. The availability of Kosher food on campus also seems to be in doubt; the book tells the reader that it is up to them to find out who supervises kashrut and if a Rabbi is present in the kitchen. For a book that is supposed to be about Jewish life on campus there seems to be very little concrete information in this book aside from the address and contact information for the local Hillel Foundation Center. The directory of foundations and organizations are somewhat useful, but you can find that information elsewhere.

WHERE TO FIND/BUY:

Find in libraries and bookstores.

Student Guide to College Admissions

★★

Author/Editor: Harlow G. Unger
Publisher: Facts on File
Edition Reviewed: 1990
Internet URL:

Media Type: Print
Price: $10.95
ISBN: 0-8160-2306-9

RATINGS (1-4 STARS):

Overall:	★★	Other, similar resources will be easier to read and more up-to-date
Breadth Of Content:	★★★	Covers the spectrum of the process
Value Added:	★★★	Author's experience shows
Ease Of Use:	★	Extremely dense writing style; not a quick reference guide

DESCRIPTION:

This book covers the entire selection and admissions spectrum: deciding to go to college, selecting the right college, college admission requirements, the application process, and financing your college education. There is a summary at the end of each chapter for quick reference and an index at the back of the book. The first chapter discusses how every student can get into college even if they aren't class president or captain of the football team. There are tips on how to get into college without depending on your high school counselor for everything, and tips on understanding what the college guidebooks are really saying about entrance requirements. In Chapter 2: How to Pick the Right College - For You, the author goes into more detail on how to use college guidebooks and provides an example entry from the College Admissions Data Handbook. Chapter 3 explains how to put together the perfect college admissions "package" and chapter 4 explains what happens with your application once it reaches the admissions office. A timetable for college admissions and an explanation of college entrance examinations is included.

EVALUATION:

This book is not for anyone who doesn't enjoy reading. There are no bullet-points, summaries, or visual relief to be found, just paragraph after paragraph of densely packed information. This makes the chapter on financial aid almost impossible to follow (it's somewhat outdated as well, given the book's pubication date). This section in particular would have benefited from the use of charts and columns as well as a worksheet or two. The author takes the subject very seriously but the dense writing style will not appeal to most students. The presentation is better suited to educating parents on the process of helping their child get into the college of their choice. The chapter on developing the college admissions package is particularly useful. It discusses not only grades and extracurricular activities, but class ranking and character as well.

WHERE TO FIND/BUY:

Find in libraries and bookstores or call the publisher at 1 -800-322-8755.

Compact Guide To Colleges

★★

Author/Editor:
Publisher: Barron's Educational Series, Inc.
Edition Reviewed: 9th (1994)
Internet URL:

Media Type: Print
Price: $8.95
ISBN: 0-8120-1886-9

RATINGS (1-4 STARS):

Overall:	★★	Basic all-inclusive guidebook
Breadth Of Content:	★★	400 schools profiled that are considered "competitive" to some degree
Value Added:	★	Little information added to the basic statistics,
Ease Of Use:	★★★	Organized alphabetically, with an index listing colleges by state

DESCRIPTION:

This edition of Barron's college guide is a 776 page abridged version of Barron's Profiles of American Colleges. It presents only those colleges that are ranked most competitive, highly competitive, and very competitive. Also included are schools with special art/music programs; institutions with the largest undergraduate enrollments have also been included. The book consists of an introductory section which explains how to read the college profiles, a section on finding the right college and how to go about finding funding, and an explanation of collegiate terms. The remainder of the book is devoted to college descriptions which are organized alphabetically. There is also an index which lists colleges alphabetically by state at the end of the book. All of the information was obtained from Barron's Profiles of American Colleges (20th edition); college admissions offices supplied the data. Each college profile includes a beginning "capsule" -- enrollment, statistics on the faculty, expenses, information on entering freshmen, and an overall ranking. Following the capsule is a general description of the school including types of study programs offered (special programs are included), student life, housing, sports, admissions and financial aid data, and computer facilities.

EVALUATION:

Barron's Compact Guide can be a useful tool for a parent trying to form an initial list of competitive colleges for their child. A multitude of information is available in each college's profile. A word of caution: the statistics in the capsules try to do too much. While it is valuable to find some information at a glance (freshman applicants that applied, were accepted, and were enrolled), the statistics profiling a faculty's desirability can be misleading (some statistics are based upon the salary earned). Although the guide states that faculty-student ratios can be misleading (due to the fact that those who don't teach can also be included in the ratios), Barron's nonetheless lists those statistics. Also deceiving can be the ranking of the colleges themselves. Ratings are based not on academic standards or on quantity of educational programs. The categories of competitiveness in this guide are based upon averaging several different test scores, class rankings, grade point averages, and the percentage of freshman who were accepted to the school. In summary, this guide does contain valuable information that, if used judiciously, can be helpful in an initial investigation.

WHERE TO FIND/BUY:

Bookstores and libraries.

Do It Write: How To Prepare
A Great College Application

★★

Author/Editor: G. Gary Ripple, Ph.D.
Publisher: Octameron Associates
Edition Reviewed: 6th (1995)
Internet URL:

Media Type: Print
Price: $5.00
ISBN: 1-57509-002-3

RATINGS (1-4 STARS):

Overall:	★★	Fairly thorough but not the only resource you'll need
Breadth Of Content:	★	Some advice on the application; mostly focused on essay questions
Value Added:	★★★	Offers the perspective of an admissions officer
Ease Of Use:	★	Small text, lack of headings make it difficult to find information

---

DESCRIPTION:

Ripple, a director of admissions at various universities and colleges for the past 16 years, wrote this 40 page book on successfully completing a college application. The first chapter touches on parts of the application including the following: the importance of high school transcripts, how test scores are viewed, which recommendations to get, how to approach application deadlines, which extracurricular activities should be noted, why you should research colleges, waiving application fees, and how technology can be used in the application process. Chapters 2, 4, 5, and 6 deal with essay questions asked on college applications. Topics that are covered include what admissions officers are looking for, general guidelines for writing the essay, sample questions, and sample essays. Chapter 3 includes a "conversation with the dean" which is a scripted dialogue that answers questions a student may ask when filling out an application; most of its emphasis is again on the essay question. The last chapter is a one-page list of do's and don'ts that reiterates much of what was written earlier in the book.

EVALUATION:

At first glance, the organizational style of Ripple's book can be a hindrance. The small print and lack of discernible organizational elements such as major headings might not invite another look. However, the first chapter of Ripple's book is useful if for no other reason than to grant them an insider's view of what admissions committees are looking for. Not only does it explain why these forms are the way they are - they have not been created to "ruin your senior year of high school" - but it also explains how to approach the application so that you achieve what you set out to do, to be accepted. The other valuable chapter is Chapter 6 which begins with ten examples of what not to do when writing an essay and then follows up with fifteen positive examples. Each example contains an evaluation based upon how the admissions committee would view that essay and how the essay reflects on the applicant. The other chapters cover the essay process but not to the same extent as other books on the same subject. Overall, this book contains elements of interest if you sift through it but other resources on the same topic will give you more in-depth advice on actually completing college applications.

WHERE TO FIND/BUY:

Bookstores and libraries or direct from the publisher at 703-836-5480.

How To Get To The College Of Your Choice: SE States ★★

Author/Editor: L. Meredith Phillips
Publisher: Kraus International Publications
Edition Reviewed: 1993
Internet URL:

Media Type: Print
Price: $17.95
ISBN: 0-527-42649-0

RATINGS (1-4 STARS):

Overall:	★★	Nearly all this information is available from your colleges of choice
Breadth Of Content:		Not applicable
Value Added:	★	More current information is available free from admissions offices
Ease Of Use:	★★★	Large, easy to read maps

DESCRIPTION:

This book is an atlas to 155 colleges and universities in the Southeastern United States; the series provides similar volumes for the Northeast, West, and Central. The information provided maps, directions, and other resources intended to help out-of-State visitors find their way to and around these campuses (selected based on the percentage of out-of-State freshman enrolled). The book contains toll-free reference numbers for airlines, car rental agencies, buses, trains and hotel/motel chains. There is a State map for each State included in the front of the book. The colleges and universities are listed by State, and each profile contains a localized area map, a city map, and a detailed campus map (provided by the college). Campus information includes: average yearly temperatures, contact information, office hours, information about tours, exact directions to the campus by car, visitor parking, directions via public transportation, airlines, buses, and trains, and contact information for a variety of hotel/motel accommodations.

EVALUATION:

Since virtually all the information provided in this book is available from the campuses themselves or their local chambers of commerce free of charge, why would someone pay for this information? The maps are already three years old; it's possible that changes have taken place. In its defense, map reproductions are high quality, information is presented in a handy, large-size paperback, and useful area maps, showing campus locations in a common geographical area, are provided. Nonetheless, if you've pared your list down to four or five colleges before going on campus visits, you'll have already been in contact with these schools and will have received this material from them. Campus maps are usually printed in at least one brochure, and if you are out-of-State you will probably have received the rest of the information provided in this book as well. You'll be better off contacting the few schools you intend to visit for the most current maps and information on campus visits.

WHERE TO FIND/BUY:

Bookstores and libraries.

Looking Beyond The Ivy League

Author/Editor: Loren Pope
Publisher: Penguin Books
Edition Reviewed: 1995
Internet URL:

Media Type: Print
Price: $11.95
ISBN: 0-14-023952-9

RATINGS (1-4 STARS):

Overall:	★★	Other resources will probably be more useful
Breadth Of Content:	★★	Brief comments on 200+ colleges
Value Added:	★★	Strong on opinion; adds little of value to selection process
Ease Of Use:	★	Dense prose in an unremitting march; not a handy reference

DESCRIPTION:

Published originally in 1990, this 267 page revised edition encourages parents and students to look beyond the name and reputation of the Ivy League schools to find the college that will meet all their needs. The author (now an independent college counselor) explains in the introduction how he has seen many people choose their college or university based on their perceptions of that institution, not on concrete information and an assessment of how that college will help them achieve their goals. Chapter 1 refutes "20 Myths that can jinx your college choice". The chapters which follow (16 in all) cover a variety of topics, including taking a year off and campus visits. Chapter 10 contains the short profiles of over 200+ colleges. They are listed under categories, such as, "For the self-sufficient Self-starter" and "The Best Buys for a Wide Range of Abilities". The majority of the profiles are listed under "Nearly 200 More Worth Going to" and consist of one or two sentences about each institution. Chapters 11 through 15 cover the bases from what to do while in high school, how to go through the application process and the interview, and what to do if you've "made a mistake." The final two chapters discuss the options of working with a private counselor instead of a high school counselor and "some truths about financial aid."

EVALUATION:

The author feels very strongly that people generally do not choose their college or university for the right reasons, and maintains that "name recognition" usually doesn't guarantee a solid education . While the book contains useful perspectives on many topics ("Twenty Myths" is pretty much on target, for example), it reads like 17 separate monographs without a clear theme or thread. The book is long on opinion, strongly stated and sprinkled with anecdotal references, but short on actionable plans for students and parents. The author strongly encourages the reader to investigate colleges without strong name recognition, but then provides very little data on each of the colleges recommended (for the University of Chicago, just: "Better than most Ivy universities"). This is not enough information for anyone to make an informed decision on which schools to investigate for themselves. While many of the author's opinions are commonly held among professionals in the field,there is little unique information contained in this book. Those who believe that an Ivy League education will change their life aren't likely to pick this up, those who don't won't need to.

WHERE TO FIND/BUY:

Bookstores and Libraries, or call the publisher directly at 1-800-253-6467.

Getting Your Child Into College: What Parents Must Know   ★★

Author/Editor: Susan Newman with Janet Spencer King
Publisher: St. Martin's Press
Edition Reviewed: 1st (1996)
Internet URL:

Media Type: Print
Price: $10.95
ISBN: 0-312-14107-6

RATINGS (1-4 STARS):

Overall:	★★	General guide to the application process
Breadth Of Content:	★★	Includes a brief snippet on most of the elements of the application process
Value Added:	★★★	Targets the emotional turmoil that can arise for parents and students
Ease Of Use:	★★★	Chapter headings and sub-headings are useful

DESCRIPTION:

This 8 chapter 146 page book addresses concerns that parents of college bound students may have. The first 2 chapters discuss feelings students and parents might have. Chapter 3 focuses on how to find the right college match for your student. Chapter 4 outlines tips for visiting colleges and interviewing administrators and college personnel. Chapter 5 highlights the steps involved in the application process. Chapter 6 discusses the range of outside consultants, advisers, and prep courses that are also available to help parents and students in this process. Chapter 7 presents, in its 15 pages, some ideas of the financial aid options that parents might wish to pursue. Chapter 8 refocuses on the emotional side of the application process. Subjects are discussed such as how to cope with rejection, how to determine which college option to take, and how to prepare parents and students for departure. An additional section is given at the back of the book which includes resources for additional materials (electronic search aids, financial aid, etc.) and three sample applications. The reader is invited to read these applications and then to perform the duties of an admissions director and decide who is accepted, wait-listed or rejected.

EVALUATION:

Although this book resembles other books at first glance, it also presents some of the human elements involved in the application process. The authors do a good job of summing up some of the emotional issues that may evolve during this big event in students' and parents' lives. In particular, the first two chapters coupled with the last chapter discuss the pressure and stress that both students and parents go through. Recognizing some of these problems may help alleviate stress typically encountered and work toward solutions. Subjects such as students' fear of failure and fear of disappointing parents are discussed; in turn, parents' wish to protect their child and their view of their child as an extension of themselves are also discussed. The remainder of the book gives pretty much a basic overview of the application process from visiting and selecting colleges, to writing the application essay, to deciding upon your final choice. However, none of these subjects is considered in as much depth as other books on the same subject. Although the inclusion of the sample applications is novel, it would be more beneficial to see a critique of these applications as seen through the eyes of an admissions officer.

WHERE TO FIND/BUY:

Bookstores and libraries.

Getting Into College: A Guide For Students And Parents ★★

Author/Editor: Frank C. Leana
Publisher: The Noonday Press
Edition Reviewed: 2nd (1990)
Internet URL:

Media Type: Print
Price: $9.95
ISBN: 0-374-52242-1

RATINGS (1-4 STARS):

Overall:	★★	Good overview; includes little that's different from the rest
Breadth Of Content:	★★	Includes the usual elements involved in the application process
Value Added:	★★★	Brief sections on needs of learning disabled, transfer, and foreign students
Ease Of Use:	★★★	Organized, easy to find information at a glance

DESCRIPTION:

The author, an admissions counselor, wrote this second version to address the changes that have taken place since the 1980's in terms of the college application process. There are 2 parts to this 162 page book. The first part is entitled "Getting Ready" and includes discussions of many of the elements of the application process. Topics discussed include: the advantage of early planning for college during the high school years, extracurricular interests, standardized testing, types of colleges, alternatives to college, and how to use available resources (guidebooks, counselors, etc.) to help you in the process. Part 2 - "Getting There" - focuses on the college application, the admissions office, campus visits, interviews, and the essay. Also included in this section is a brief case study of an applicant, a section on financial aid (10+ pages), and information for special need situations (students with learning disabilities, transfer applicants, foreign country applicants). At the back of the book is a check-list calendar for application procedures from a student's junior year of high school through their senior year. Finally, a selected bibliography is provided for further reading on colleges, financial aid, the application process, etc.

EVALUATION:

There are many books written on the subject of how to survive the application process. There is nothing really novel within this book that cannot be found in other books on the same subject. If you are just looking for a quick overview of the general process with no real specifics, then this book will serve your needs. The section on writing the personal essay is, however, well-done and includes 10 topics that are offered as sample questions. Useful tips are given on how to write the essay. The author also provides 7 positive examples of essays written by students and gives a brief critique of why the essay serves as a good model. Another chapter - "Alternatives to College" - can be useful for students and parents who choose not to go the usual route of college after high school. Although the chapter is brief (4 pages), it does present the flip side of the typical college application process. Topics included here are studying abroad, early college entry, work experience, or "taking the year off". In a nutshell, this book presents short snippets on many subjects, but you would need to use another resource to get more comprehensive, usable information on the details of the application process.

WHERE TO FIND/BUY:

Bookstores and libraries.

Professional Degree Programs In The Visual And Performing Arts

★★

Author/Editor: Peterson's
Publisher: Peterson's
Edition Reviewed: 1st (1996)
Internet URL:

Media Type: Print
Price: $21.95
ISBN: 1-56079-536-0

RATINGS (1-4 STARS):

Overall:	★★	An all-inclusive general book based upon submissions from schools
Breadth Of Content:	★★★★	900+ professional programs detailed
Value Added:	★★	Nothing noteworthy or exceptional added
Ease Of Use:	★★★	Schools arranged alphabetically within each program type

DESCRIPTION:

Peterson's 618 page edition consists of four main parts: a quick-reference chart of programs, program descriptions, an appendix, and an index of schools. The quick-reference chart (about 25 pages) is organized geographically and provides basic information about schools described in the book (name of school and location, degrees offered, enrollment, tuition and fees). The program descriptions comprise the majority of the book (about 490 pages) and are subdivided into four sections: art, dance, music and theater. Within each section schools are listed alphabetically. Information is given at the beginning of each section about the programs available, the admissions process, suggestions as to how to determine your goals and needs, and what to look for in a program. Within the schools' descriptions you will find the following information: school type and enrollment, degrees offered and majors within each degree, profiles of students and faculty, student life, expenses including financial aid information, application information, and who to contact. The appendix lists all U.S. and Canadian four-year colleges and universities that offer the B.A. or B.S. degree in the visual and performing arts. The index is organized alphabetically by school.

EVALUATION:

Peterson's book is exactly what it claims to be: "a first step when identifying potential programs." Although the book profiles many school programs (900+), valuable information is missing. The information detailed was supplied by the schools themselves but no philosophy or mission statements were provided. This is an important piece students need when determining each school's future direction especially in the changing and volatile art fields. No opinions are offered either from current students or graduate students as to the quality of the programs. Also lacking is some mention of how the schools' programs are perceived in the professional visual and performing arts fields. No mention is made as to the quality or availability of facilities that art students need during their course of study. Finally, a listing of professional alumni who have graduated from the various programs would also be useful for students. Some useful information that is provided include the following: whether or not graduate students are used as instructors, awards/financial aid available for specific programs, applicable student groups and performance opportunities, etc. The book does offer students a breadth of programs that are available, but students will need to look further to find more in-depth and pertinent information.

WHERE TO FIND/BUY:

Bookstores and libraries.

How To Write Your College Application Essay

Author/Editor: Kenneth A. Nourse
Publisher: VGM Career Horizons
Edition Reviewed: 1994
Internet URL:

Media Type: Print
Price: $12.95
ISBN: 0-8442-4169-5

RATINGS (1-4 STARS):

Overall:	★	Other resources on this topic are far better
Breadth Of Content:		Not applicable
Value Added:	★	Very little content for the price
Ease Of Use:	★★	Wide margins make this book a very quick read

DESCRIPTION:

This books provides an overview of how to write a college application essay. In the first section of this book (Chapters 1 -4) the author defines the college application essay and explains the importance of the application essay and its role in the admissions process. Chapters 5 -8 cover the writing process. Sample essays are included in every chapter, and chapter nine consists of several more. Chapter eleven contains essays on the importance of the application essay in the admissions process, written by eighteen counselors and admissions officers from around the country.   The book is published in a large paperback format with extra large margins.

EVALUATION:

Compared to other books on writing college application essays, this resource has little to offer. At 95 pages it's a slim volume, and that includes three-inch margins. Without the fifteen or more sample essays and the comments from counselors and admissions officers from around the country, original content is less still. If the author had provided some sort of analytical criticism of the sample essays, at least students would know if they were comparing their writings to something well-written or not. The comments by the "pros", counselors and directors of admissions, for the most part, consist of commentary on the college application essays role in the admissions process and not on writing essays. There are several better resources available on this topic; use them instead.

WHERE TO FIND/BUY:

Find in libraries and bookstores.

Gourman Report: A Rating Of Undergraduate Programs

Author/Editor: Dr. Jack Gourman
Publisher: National Education Standards
Edition Reviewed: 9th (1996)
Internet URL:

Media Type: Print
Price: $19.95
ISBN: 0-918192-16-1

RATINGS (1-4 STARS):

Overall:	★	Does not present a credible case for its rankings
Breadth Of Content:	★★	140+ programs are listed and ranked
Value Added:	★	Rankings are of interest but criteria are not specified for each program
Ease Of Use:	★★	Hierarchical tables of statistics make the rankings easy to read

DESCRIPTION:

Gourman, a former professor of political science and CEO, presents this report to parents and students as a qualitative guide to American and international institutions. This 300 page book consists of fourteen parts in which schools have been given numerical scores assessing the strengths and weaknesses of various programs. The primary part involves undergraduate programs and is listed alphabetically by areas of study. Another part ranks prelegal and premedical education in the U.S. The next two parts discuss the ranking of university administrative areas (such as alumni associations, athletic-academic balance, libraries, etc.) and a ranking of administrations, regents and trustees. Part 7 ranks the top fifty undergraduate programs in the U.S. while Part 8 rates international universities. Other parts list criminal justice, forensic science programs, and education programs that are NOT on Gourman's approved list. Finally, there are several appendixes which contain tables of itemized statistics to show how information was taken from the university samples.

EVALUATION:

Gourman's intent in compiling and ranking these programs is notable, but the results fall short. The principal deficiency of this work is the absence of any objective rationale for the ratings presented. In a brief preface, the author lists a number of "shortcomings" that may have caused schools to perform poorly -- most measures listed can't in fact be measured objectively, if at all; some are just bizarre (lack of secretarial help?). As stated in his introduction, Gourman wants to simplify the task of comparing one program against another, and he does rank schools. This is usually not the case with many college guidebooks which simply use profile information from applicants and accepted freshman in determining rankings. However, it is impossible to detect which criteria were used for each program since, as Gourman states, "the significance given each criteria will vary from one rating of one discipline to the next." He claims, however, that his evaluation was consistent for all schools listed within a given field of study. Given the failure of the author to provide a credible rationale for his rankings, we can't recommend that they be used to form even a preliminary opinion about schools or their programs.

WHERE TO FIND/BUY:

Bookstores and libraries.

Common Sense Guide To American Colleges 1993-1994

Author/Editor: Charles Horner	**Media Type:** Print
Publisher: Madison Books	**Price:** $14.95
Edition Reviewed: 1992	**ISBN:** 0-8191-8734-8
Internet URL:	

RATINGS (1-4 STARS):

Overall:	★	Inflammatory, not constructive; politically biased
Breadth Of Content:	★	Profiles for just 110 colleges
Value Added:	★★	Narratives contain unsubstantiated claims on the climate of the campuses
Ease Of Use:	★★	Colleges listed alphabetically

DESCRIPTION:

This guidebook, with profiles on 110 colleges and universities in the United States, focuses on the quality of liberal arts programs at these schools. The profiles are written with a focus on "the general social and ethical climate that [the schools] foster". The authors chose colleges and universities that they felt "people would like to know more about", and interviewed students and faculty on each campus. Each profiles range in length from 4 to 7 pages and contain information on enrollment, application requirements, expenses, size of library holdings, ROTC and a lengthy narrative on the atmosphere of the campus. Particular attention is focused on each school's curriculum (for example, does the campus offer courses in multiculturalism?), and on the actions of minorities and gays on campus, with any instances of refuted racism or enforced "political correctness" analyzed in detail. The profiles are listed alphabetically by name; there is no index to this 653 page book.

EVALUATION:

This publication is quite conservative and the compilers have gone to great lengths to ferret out any small incident or class that they can use to brand many of the campuses profiled here as "liberal". For example, some incidents of refuted racism and injustices to whites are reported without corroborating evidence and in language that suggests that minority groups and the campus administration deliberately persecute white, (mainly) male, students. Many profiles highlight one or two courses from the 1991-92 course catalogs as examples of the slant of the liberal arts programs at these colleges and universities. Whenever possible, courses dealing with homosexuality, multiculturalism and diversity are singled out. For Stanford University for example, the courses highlighted are "Black Hair As Culture And History" and "Gender-specific Perspectives Of Birth Control" -- but clearly, these are not representative of the overall liberal arts program at Stanford. In the second paragraph of the introduction, the authors state that so many changes take place on any given campus in four years that it is virtually impossible to produce a book that will not be out-of-date as soon as it is printed, then state they took over two years to gather the information for this book.

WHERE TO FIND/BUY:

Bookstores and libraries.

College Board Online

★★★★

Author/Editor:
Publisher: The College Board
Edition Reviewed:
Internet URL: http://www.collegeboard.org

Media Type: Internet
Price:
ISBN:

RATINGS (1-4 STARS):

Overall:	★★★★	A "must-see" site for their ExPAN college database
Breadth Of Content:	★★★★	The ExPAN database includes all 2 and 4 year colleges
Value Added:	★★★	Value concentrated in ExPAN and college information therein
Ease Of Use:	★★★★	A well-designed website; nice graphics, well organized

DESCRIPTION:

This is a large website, second only in breadth to Peterson's site. The site has been developed with the Educational Testing Service, and thus emphasizes services like SAT preparation and registration. As for offerings related to the process of selecting colleges, the site provides a page of services for students and parents (largely services related to SAT preparation and financial aid); a comprehensive college search facility, using their "ExPAN" system, is included. Multiple criteria are available for searches: geographic, majors, general (size, setting), student life (housing, etc.), admissions/aid, special programs, advanced placement, and sports. An exhaustive list of choices is available for each criteria, and all can be combined in a search. Information provided for each college is generous, roughly a dozen pages of stats and basic information, some reprinted from their guidebook, "The College Handbook." The site provides an extensive online store, which contains thumbnail descriptions of the complete line of College Board publications (including software and video titles); these books can be ordered online with a credit card (secure if a Netscape browser is used), or by calling an 800 number.

EVALUATION:

The best feature of this site is the The College Board's ExPAN database (ExPAN is one of the better commercial systems sold to high school career/counseling centers). It's been implemented recently, and the site notes that its career-planning module will be added in the future. In a word, the ExPAN database as implemented here is the most comprehensive college search facility available online. That comprehensiveness extends to the number of colleges in the database (all 2/4 year schools), the number of search variables and values available, and the amount of information provided for each school. This said, users of this facility have to be careful in using the power of their search engine: specify too many variables, and it eliminates all the colleges. But, if used with care, this site can be used to generate a pretty good initial list of colleges of interest (with the caveat, of course, to do lots more research using evaluative guidebooks, campus visits, talks with counselors and others, etc.). Additional value on the site is concentrated in services related to SAT preparation. The comprehensive online store offers the broad line of College Board books, videos, and software, which can be valuable if one can't find their resources elsewhere. They use Netscape's SSL protocol for encryption of credit card information; for other browsers, an 800 number is offered. This site really shows the value of the Internet realized in practical, time and money saving terms.

WHERE TO FIND/BUY:

Find on the WorldWideWeb using the URL: http://www.collegeboard.org. Orders from the online bookstore can be placed online (securely, with Netscape browsers), or are available direct at 800-323-7155.

CollegeXpress

★★★

Author/Editor:
Publisher: Carnegie Communications, Inc.
Edition Reviewed:
Internet URL: http://www.collegexpress.com

Media Type: Internet
Price: $
ISBN:

RATINGS (1-4 STARS):

Overall:	★★★	A good source for basic information about 400+ private institutions
Breadth Of Content:	★★★	400+ private college/university profiles and data offered
Value Added:	★★★	Useful essays, helpful information provided
Ease Of Use:	★★★	Nicely designed website, with good tools to get to lots of information

DESCRIPTION:

This is a large website that is the online counterpart of the magazine, Private Colleges & Universities (various editions of this magazine profile some 400+ institutions; it's distributed to 1.3 million college-bound high school students each spring). The site includes a comprehensive (but optional) registration form that is used to fulfill requests for college information made on the site. The principal feature of the site is a database of the college profiles included in their magazine, searchable by region, alphabetically, or keyword, or with a "profile search" (uses major, region, size, tuition, sports, and religious affiliation as variables). For each college found, a two page narrative (provided by the college) is provided, with pictures of campus scenes. Complete statistical information (from the College Board database) for each college is also available (degrees and majors offered, data on admissions, athletics, expenses, financial aid, etc.). A number of essays are offered on admissions topics, as are threaded discussion forums with counselors. Several books, and the magazines themselves, are featured as well, with ordering information included.

EVALUATION:

If you're interested in attending a private college or university, you'll want to visit this website. On this site you'll find profiles (written by the colleges themselves, and thereby promotive in tone) and data (from the College Board database) on some 400+ private colleges and universities across the country. The search facilities to find colleges of interest works well. Registration, while comprehensive, is optional; it's used by the company to forward requests for more information to colleges of interest to the student. The numerous essays, on a variety of topics relevant to the college search and admissions process, are useful and well written (even those that promote private institutions over the public school alternatives). Additional information from schools can be requested easily. The negatives? Well, the universe of institutions covered is limited, and to private colleges and universities at that, excluding the very worthwhile universe of public school alternatives. The college profiles provided are, of course, universally flattering. And there are some gaps in coverage, too. Nonetheless, we're recommending this resource because it's free and easy to use. Treat it as just one source of information to generate an initial list of colleges that interest you, however.

WHERE TO FIND/BUY:

On the World Wide Web, using the URL: http://www.collegexpress.com.

Collegiate Choice Walking Tours ★★★

Author/Editor:

Publisher:

Edition Reviewed:

Internet URL: http://www.register.com/collegiate/

Media Type: Internet

Price:

ISBN:

RATINGS (1-4 STARS):

Overall:	★★★	A pretty good idea, one that may help families save some time and $
Breadth Of Content:	★★	Just 400+ college videos are available, concentrated in the East
Value Added:	★★★	The advisors ask the questions and provide an "informal" look at colleges
Ease Of Use:		Not applicable

DESCRIPTION:

This is a service set up by several independent college advisors "who work with families in Bergen County, New Jersey." Since 1988, these advisors have taken amateur videos of the tours offered by some 400+ colleges throughout the country. Their intent in doing so has been to provide those families they work with an opportunity to "visit" colleges of interest that they aren't able to visit in person. They charge $15 per video plus a $6 handling/shipping fee per order (videos are ordered via mail or toll phone call; the website does not support online purchases). The website includes information explaining the service; these pages make it clear that these videos have been made by amateurs using hand-held video cameras, and that they are not intended to replace viewbooks and catalogs available from the colleges. Their value, the site explains, is found in the experience of the advisors taking the college tours -- in the questions asked, and the "feel" for the school created by an informal, unbiased approach. The videos vary in length from 20-100 minutes in length (average roughly 60+ minutes). A brief essay on making a college visit is included on the site, as are simple lists of "best colleges" from U.S. News, Money Magazine, etc.

EVALUATION:

This is a useful service. We've ordered and viewed several sample tapes. Each tape provides a "real" tour of the college, lasting roughly 60 minutes. You get to see lots of buildings and classrooms, students in informal, unrehearsed settings, and hear the Q&A of the tour participants and the guide. The questions asked by these college advisors are useful (and consistent from tour to tour); no subjective commentary is added (judgments are left to the viewers). The video quality is quite good, the audio quality less so. Guides can be good (enthusiastic, well-informed) or bad (dull, ill-informed). One video we saw on a college we know well was 4 years out-of-date and the answers given by the guide in some cases were inaccurate. The price of $15/video may seem steep, but value added, measured by an unbiased view of the schools toured, should be higher than the standard "canned" college viewbook. When each video was taken is not revealed in their listing, but an email inquiry brought a response that they try to update each video at least every 5 years. There are a healthy number of colleges from each state listed (albeit with an East Coast concentration), and these videos could serve as a practical alternative to a college visit for those families whose budgets or schedules prohibit a visit to all colleges of interest.

WHERE TO FIND/BUY:

Find on the Web at the URL: http://www.register.com/collegiate/; order videos by calling 201-871-0098.

CollegeAssist

★★★

Author/Editor:	**Media Type:** Internet
Publisher: edworks, inc.	**Price:**
Edition Reviewed:	**ISBN:**
Internet URL: http://www.edworks.com	

RATINGS (1-4 STARS):

Overall:	★★★	Definitely worth a visit; an ambitious site focused on college admissions
Breadth Of Content:	★★★	Very broad subject coverage, sometimes not deep without paying the fee
Value Added:	★★★	The searchable database is as useful as we've seen; no evaluative comments
Ease Of Use:	★★★	Quick navigation, well designed and useful

DESCRIPTION:

This is a large website, focused almost exclusively on the process of selecting and applying to colleges. As such, it's practically unique. Its Home Page has six principle areas: College Research, Personal Organizer, Financial Aid, Personal Profile, Admission Test, and Application Essays. Each area has features available to "guests," and each page has additional services available for a single $39 fee (good for 12 months). The "free" features for the College Research area are substantial: guests can search a database (supplied by College Research Group) of 3,000 colleges using a number of criteria "sets" (admissions, sports, costs, majors, etc.), with results available by region. The facts provided for each college by CRG are comprehensive. Links to college home pages are provided (and organized by state). The free areas for the remainder of the site consist largely of lists of tips and short essays (tips on writing essays, descriptions of types of financial aid, etc.); taking advantage of the full complement of features in these areas requires payment of the fee. Several features profiled (essay evaluation, scholarship search) require additional fees. Some links to related websites are provided.

EVALUATION:

This comprehensive website is worth a visit for sure, simply because such a large percentage of its content is focused on selecting and getting into colleges. The college database output (statistics) is quite comprehensive, well formatted, and easy to navigate, equal to alternatives we've found anywhere else; the trick is that the search engine is much less flexible (and results can't be saved) in the "free" area. After payment of the fee, search "sets" can be retained, refined, and compared. The Personal Organizer is virtually unavailable without payment of the fee, but when paid for provides a comprehensive integrated planning and reminder calendar. The Personal Profile area, after payment of the fee, provides a very useful tool for building a documented profile of the student, all retained by the CollegeAssist database for later use (an online common application form is planned, for example). The principal value-added feature of the paid portion of the "Essays" section is a $49 service of essay evaluation. The Financial Aid section's principal feature is material provided by the National Scholarship Research Service (which costs $75). Too commercial? Sometimes. Do we recommend paying the fee? It's too close to call -- the database facilities and the personal organizer would be worth it to some, while other features may lack practical application for others. But, visit this fine site and decide for yourself!

WHERE TO FIND/BUY:

On the Internet at the URL: http://www.edworks.com.

CollegeNet

Author/Editor:

Publisher: Universal Algorithms, Inc.

Edition Reviewed:

Internet URL: http://www.collegenet.com

Media Type: Internet

Price:

ISBN:

RATINGS (1-4 STARS):

Overall:	★★★	A site worth visiting for its search capabilities and specialized lists
Breadth Of Content:	★★★	Comprehensive database, limited information on non-linked colleges
Value Added:	★★	Additional value provided by search engine and supplemental college data
Ease Of Use:	★★	Well-organized; response time OK

DESCRIPTION:

Much is included in this website; the publishers have a database of about 3,000 colleges. With this as a foundation, the site supports searches, with up to four variables: state, enrollment size, tuition range, and majors; you can also search for a college by name. The search pulls up a listing of schools with basic contact information; links are provided to college home pages if available. "Featured" schools (currently 8) provide additional admissions-oriented information; schools with home pages are linked as well. An online application to selected schools is being developed, but is still noted as being for "demonstration purposes only." The site offers listings of specialized schools (Catholic, Ivy League, Women's, Historically Black, etc.). Listings of academic resource links and information about financial aid are included also. Users of the site can also complete a request form which will bring more information from selected colleges and advertisers. Recent additions to the site include a planetarium, a notice about impending college-oriented magazines, a search capability for schools in Canada/New Zealand/Australia, and a $5,000 scholarship.

EVALUATION:

This is a useful site, particularly for its ability to search its database, for example, for all undergraduate colleges in Oregon that have less than 5,000 students and cost no more than $10,000/year. The listing returned from such a search is a useful beginning but provides just basic contact information. The links to colleges' home pages are helpful as well, with the usual variations in quality and relevance found in those home pages (some colleges provide additional information focused solely on admissions). The listings of specialized schools and graduate programs are helpful (although just a list of colleges names by state), too, as are hypertext links to financial aid information resident on the Internet. The site is managed as a commercial site by Universal Algorithms, a provider of scheduling software to colleges; the site is supported by colleges' purchases of additional listings and services. The value of this site is concentrated in its database, search engine, and specialized listings -- the information gleaned from time spend "on site" is just a starting point for college research.

WHERE TO FIND/BUY:

Find on the WorldWideWeb using the URL: http://www.collegenet.com

Peterson's Education Center

Author/Editor: Peterson's Guides, Inc.
Publisher: Peterson's
Edition Reviewed:
Internet URL: http://www.petersons.com

Media Type: Internet
Price:
ISBN:

RATINGS (1-4 STARS):

Overall:	★★★	Definitely worth a visit, but not yet a big help to college-bound students
Breadth Of Content:	★★★	Comprehensive catalog of their print offerings; other content will grow
Value Added:	★★★	Ambitious concepts; will have more value as more colleges participate
Ease Of Use:	★★★★	The site, though large and multi-purposed, is well designed

DESCRIPTION:

This is Peterson's corporate web site. They have set very ambitious objectives for themselves: "give individuals the ability to make inquiries, apply, send transcripts... Every private school, camp, college, and university will have its own site... ..communicating with admissions officers, registrars, and faculty members, taking..tests..will all be part of everyday life in The Center." The site provides a wide range of information on colleges, graduate schools, and more. For the college-bound, a search among colleges is possible, using an alpha or geographic path; a search by religious affiliation or majors offered are also options. Standard information on colleges selected is limited; however, some schools have viewbooks online, and some have online applications available for downloading. The online Peterson's Catalog is comprehensive, and includes an ordering form; the college admissions section of the catalog includes 2 dozen+ Peterson's publications in print. Their recent upgrade features a new interface/graphics, a keyword search engine, online viewbooks, campus tours, direct email to college admission offices, and much improved speed.

EVALUATION:

If Peterson's can achieve its stated objectives for this site, then it will become among the best resources available on the web. If we limit our focus to the challenge of selecting a college, then this site is worth visiting, but is currently of limited value. You can do an initial screen of colleges, but only by geographic region or religious affiliation. The information available for colleges selected is very limited; you'll have to use other resources to help construct your initial short list. Online viewbooks and campus tours are great ideas, but are currently available for just a few colleges. Currently, 200+ college have direct email links and online applications set up (many use the Common Application). Their online catalog is useful, if you are focused on print resources and want to see the full spectrum of their offerings (Peterson's also publishes guides to Christian Colleges, Colleges with programs for students with Learning Disabilities, etc.). If they are successful over time building all the links and database depth necessary to support the kind of "one-stop shopping" experience they aspire to, then Peterson's will have contributed to a revolution in how high school students complete the college selection and admission process; they've taken some excellent first steps.

WHERE TO FIND/BUY:

Find on the WorldWideWeb using the URL: http://www.petersons.com.

FishNet

Author/Editor:	**Media Type:** Internet
Publisher: Journalistic, Inc.	**Price:**
Edition Reviewed:	**ISBN:**
Internet URL: http://www.jayi.com/Open.html	

RATINGS (1-4 STARS):

Overall:	★★★	A useful site for teenagers; limited resources on colleges
Breadth Of Content:	★★	The database of colleges is too small to support extensive searches
Value Added:	★★★	Original Q&A section, as well as useful articles about admissions process
Ease Of Use:	★★★	A well-designed and interesting web site

DESCRIPTION:

This is a substantial web site, with a number of resources directed at the teenage audience of the company's magazine, "Edge" ("the high performance magazine for students"). The site's features include a database of articles of interest to teenagers, the electronic version of "Edge" magazine, and a forum to exchange questions and ideas. Relevant to our purposes is their "College Guide", which has a number of features. There is a college search capability, using up to 5 criteria (and an optional keyword): region, cost, freshman class size, community size, and public/private. Students can build a profile to send to colleges resident on the site, and request information from those colleges. A question and answer section contains a series of college admissions and selection questions, being added to regularly (25+ in the last three months). Finally, a number of articles about the college admission process are included.

EVALUATION:

This is an interesting site, and worth a visit from high school juniors and seniors. Their "College Guide" has some useful features not found elsewhere, including a helpful list of admissions-oriented questions and answers, and a collection of articles about college and the admissions process, some irreverent but all interesting. The database of colleges to search is so small as to be pretty useless in conducting a screen/search of colleges for purposes of building an initial list of interest. Only 15 colleges are currently listed in the "West" region, for example. The list can be searched alphabetically for information on selected colleges. The target market for the site seems to be academically gifted students (they publish a college guide with this focus), but the information provided by the site, taken as a whole, will be useful to any high school student.

WHERE TO FIND/BUY:

Find on the WorldWideWeb using the URL: http://www.jayi.com/Open.html.

CollegeView

★★★

Author/Editor:	**Media Type:** Internet
Publisher: CollegeView	**Price:**
Edition Reviewed:	**ISBN:**
Internet URL: http://www.collegeview.com	

RATINGS (1-4 STARS):

Overall:	★★★	Broad stats on colleges; hard to get to through their search engine
Breadth Of Content:	★★★★	Data for 3,300 two and four year institutions included
Value Added:	★★★	Complete stats on colleges, with some pictures/graphics/links available
Ease Of Use:	★★	A well-designed site, but an ineffective search engine

---

DESCRIPTION:

CollegeView is one of the leading multimedia college search programs available in high schools, containing information of 3,300 two and four year colleges and universities; this website is a limited version of that program. The website's main feature is "College Search," a search engine offering 11 criteria for selection of colleges from their database (fields of study, state, size, coed & ethnic mix, religious affiliation, public/private, athletics, city size, special programs, and services for the disabled). For colleges selected, 4+ pages of statistics and basic facts are provided. For the 100+ colleges that have paid for a "WebView" presentation, nine additional pages of information are available; these pages consist of campus pictures and graphics, downloadable audio clips, and electronic mail and college home page links. Registration is optional, but is used to support electronic mail messages. "News" areas are available for students, counselors, and colleges -- these include some articles of interest and promotional material about the company's products.

EVALUATION:

This is a well-designed and easy-to-navigate website. It serves multiple purposes, providing both a vehicle to promote the company's products and a facility to search their college database and comprehensive stats about selected colleges. Registration for use of the database is optional (but required for if sending email to colleges). The biggest drawback we encountered on the site was the search engine; while the number of criteria for selection is adequate, only one choice/criteria can be made (ie: one state, one major, one size). These searches generate too narrow a universe of college alternatives; stating "no preference" for criteria generates too large a return -- this weakness cripples the utility of the search engine. Information returned on colleges selected, while just statistics, is generous. Additional "multimedia" information is available for a limited number of colleges (100+ when we visited), and is of limited value in providing further helpful information (in most cases, just campus pictures and graphic representations of statistical facts already provided). When they fix the search engine, this will be a helpful site; until then, other alternatives will probably be more helpful.

WHERE TO FIND/BUY:

Find on the WorldWideWeb using the URL: http://www.collegeview.com.

Princeton Review

★★★

Author/Editor:

Publisher:

Edition Reviewed:

Internet URL: http://www.review.com

Media Type: Internet

Price:

ISBN:

RATINGS (1-4 STARS):

Overall:	★★★	You can search their "Best 309 Colleges" guidebook for free
Breadth Of Content:	★★	Pretty limited for the college-bound, with the great exception noted above
Value Added:	★★★	Lots of information about Princeton products; two useful databases as well
Ease Of Use:	★★	A recent redesign made it a WORSE site!

DESCRIPTION:

The is The Princeton Review's large corporate website. It includes pages which reflect their wide range of products and services, covering not only college testing and admissions but also testing and admissions to Business, Law, and other graduate school programs. Princeton is known, of course, as one of the leading test preparation companies, with scads of books, software, and courses to help students prepare for admissions tests (this site includes a searchable database of course locations, for example). Focusing on the college arena, the site concentrates, of course, on SAT preparation. For the student trying to choose a college, the principal feature is a searchable database of their book "The Best 309 Colleges"; the database is searchable by name, region, or state. The information returned is virtually the same found in their $18 guidebook. The site includes a listing of their print resources and a threaded discussion forum on the topic "SAT & College Admissions." The site also includes a section on career advice, which includes a searchable database of comprehensive career descriptions.

EVALUATION:

This website will no doubt see lots of traffic. Its focus on selling Princeton's products and services is done in a relatively unobtrusive manner; there is much of value for free available on the site. The breadth of information and services for students seeking information to help select, or get admitted to a college is limited. Apart from SAT preparation, the site promotes Princeton's college guidebooks and provides a discussion forum. The two principal attributes of value to the college-bound student are the searchable databases of career descriptions (you have to know which career you want to learn about to do a search; there's no interest/profile matching available), and the searchable guidebook "The Best 309 Colleges." We like this print resource as a very useful tool for learning more about a short list of colleges being considered -- it's largely based on student input, and contains subjective opinions on a variety of topics for each college. The whole book is searchable on this site, for free. The only drawback is the limited criteria for a search; however, if a student has narrowed his list to a dozen or so "finalists," then this book may provide some evaluative input useful to making up a final list. A recent redesign of the site (using frames) backfired -- the site is more difficult to use now in every respect -- use the "Text Only" option instead!

WHERE TO FIND/BUY:

On the Web at the URL: http://www.review.com.

College Edge   ★★★

Author/Editor: **Media Type:** Internet
Publisher: SNAP Technologies, Inc.   **Price:**
Edition Reviewed: **ISBN:**
Internet URL: http://www.CollegeEdge.com

RATINGS (1-4 STARS):

Overall:	★★★	Nice breadth and good overview articles; come back to see their progress
Breadth Of Content:	★★★	Includes wide variety of short articles on majors and college choice
Value Added:	★★★	Listing of summer programs; feedback on majors and careers
Ease Of Use:	★★★★	Nicely designed site; useful graphics/icons, fast, easy navigation

DESCRIPTION:

The home page links to information on colleges & admissions, financial aid, careers/majors, and fun/games. Following the college info branch, 9 options are available, 3 under construction. One option matches you with a college based upon criteria that you provide (college type, public/private, location, setting, size, major). The generated list is then linked with colleges' home pages. Another option gives you articles about researching, applying to, and getting accepted into colleges. Information can be found here about touring campuses, essays, applications, admissions, interviews, and more. Two other options link you up with college home pages based upon alphabetical or geographical listings. A fifth option provides you with a list of summer programs (study abroad, internships, etc.) offered through various colleges. The last option links you with a company that, for a fee (up to $250), will help you with the personal statements and essays on your college application. Three other options under construction include: feedback you can give and get about a particular college, and a third section which involves applying to colleges online.

EVALUATION:

While the primary purpose of this website is to promote their CD-ROM product, the company has provided a useful amount of information on a well-designed site. The search engine simply leads to college websites. A number of short articles are available on college choice and admissions topics, financial aid, and majors; they provide a useful overview. The listing of summer programs available for students is quite comprehensive and will be a useful value for some. The "mini-interviews" provided to show what a (limited) variety of careers and majors are like is an ambitious idea; these interviews come off so far as heavily edited and a bit shallow. They are gathering feedback direct from currently enrolled college students on their experiences to date; it will be interesting to see how/if this feedback is converted to useful information later. This site design is excellent; graphically interesting without being too slow; logical layouts and links, lots of useful information logically organized, very crisp response times -- a really great job. The company promotes their CD-ROM ($49.99) they say it provides you with an "expert matching system" along with an "analysis of the admissions criteria of particular colleges, on-line college applications, and more."

WHERE TO FIND/BUY:

On the Internet at the URL: http://www.CollegeEdge.com.

National Liberal Arts Colleges

Author/Editor: Richard Floyd
Publisher:
Edition Reviewed:
Internet URL: http://www.aavc.vassar.edu/libarts.colleges.html

Media Type: Internet
Price:
ISBN:

RATINGS (1-4 STARS):

Overall:	★★	Useful to varying degrees, depending on the quality of the linked sites
Breadth Of Content:	★★	Narrow; focused on "national liberal arts colleges" only
Value Added:	★	Just links to college home pages
Ease Of Use:	★★★★	Point & click on a single page

DESCRIPTION:

This is one of several World Wide Web sites that is a simple listing containing links to the home pages of colleges listed. The focus of this list is liberal arts colleges so classified by the Carnegie Foundation. The list is alphabetical, showing college names (also shows the city and state where the college is located).

EVALUATION:

This is a useful tool for getting to the home pages of most of the better-known liberal arts colleges in the country. The focus of the list is on "nationally-known" institutions, which will omit more schools than it will include. The home pages linked to vary widely in quality and focus, but are always useful to some degree when broadly sampling alternatives.

WHERE TO FIND/BUY:

Find on the WorldWideWeb using the URL: http://www.aavc.vassar.edu/libarts.colleges.html

College & University Home Pages

Author/Editor: Christina DeMello
Publisher:
Edition Reviewed:
Internet URL: http://www.mit.edu:8001/people/cdemello/univ.html

Media Type: Internet
Price:
ISBN:

RATINGS (1-4 STARS):

Overall:	★★	Useful links to college home pages; pages vary in quality & relevance
Breadth Of Content:	★★★★	It's got 'em all...
Value Added:	★	At this point, just a listing of links to college home pages
Ease Of Use:	★★★★	Point & click; useful to have both alpha and geographic listings

DESCRIPTION:

This is probably the best known web site (and certainly one of the first) that is a simple listing of links to virtually all the colleges' and universities' home pages, principally in the U.S. but also worldwide as sites are discovered and added. This one is maintained by Christina DeMello, who started the list when she was at MIT. The links can be accessed through an alphabetical listing or a geographical listing. Mirror sites, several outside the U.S., are listed to facilitate faster access. The author has also made a survey available, designed to solicit input on the best examples of homes pages; survey results are updated weekly. A list of FAQs about the site is available as well.

EVALUATION:

This is a useful tool for getting to the home pages of most of the college and universities in the country (most now have home pages). The home pages linked to vary widely in quality and focus, but are always useful to some degree when broadly sampling college alternatives. Christine says she's working on converting the listing to a searchable database; she's also trying to add information within the database that would allow selection on criteria like which degrees are offered. Check back to see what this work produces.

WHERE TO FIND/BUY:

Find on the WorldWideWeb using the URL: http://www.mit.edu:8001/people/cdemello/univ.html

American Universities

Author/Editor: Mike Conlon
Publisher:
Edition Reviewed:
Internet URL: http://www.clas.ufl.edu/CLAS/american-universities.html#2

Media Type: Internet
Price:
ISBN:

RATINGS (1-4 STARS):

Overall:	★★	Useful links to college home pages; pages vary in quality & relevance
Breadth Of Content:	★★★★	Virtually all the U.S. colleges with home pages are listed
Value Added:	★	At this point, just a listing of links to college home pages
Ease Of Use:	★★★	Point & click; takes time to load entire alphbetical listing

DESCRIPTION:

One of the web sites that is a simple listing of links to virtually all American colleges' and universities' home pages. This one is maintained by Mike Conlon. The links can be accessed through an alphabetical listing.

EVALUATION:

This is a useful tool for getting to the home pages of American college and universities. The home pages linked to vary widely in quality and focus, but are useful to some degree when broadly sampling college alternatives. The only appreciable negative to this list is that it loads the entire alphabetical listing on a single page, which takes more than a few moments. Thereafter, easy navigation is possible by selecting the first letter of the school desired.

WHERE TO FIND/BUY:

Find on the WorldWideWeb using the URL: http://www.clas.ufl.edu/CLAS/american-universities.html#2

Adventures In Education

★★

Author/Editor:

Publisher: Texas Guaranteed Student Loan Corporation

Edition Reviewed:

Internet URL: http://www.tgslc.org/

Media Type: Internet

Price:

ISBN:

RATINGS (1-4 STARS):

Overall:	★★	Not much here that can't be found elsewhere.
Breadth Of Content:	★	For college-bound students, just some notes on the selection process.
Value Added:	★	At this point, little information that isn't better stated elsewhere.
Ease Of Use:	★★	Adequate but not outstanding design

DESCRIPTION:

This is a web site supported by the nonprofit company that administers the Texas Federal Family Education Loan Program; they list their 800# for questions and assistance. The home page lists a variety of links targeted at high school and college students, to parents and counselors, to student loan borrowers and lenders. Other links have routes to information on careers, selecting schools, and paying for school. Focusing on college selection, for example, the site provides a "Guided Tour" consisting of short essays on 10 steps to selecting a school, from "Gathering Information" to "Applying For Admission." Much of the information contained in these pages can be accessed through multiple links; for example, "10 Steps To Planning For Your Future" contains pretty much the same information as the "Guided Tour", but organized by a high school timeline.

EVALUATION:

This site is certainly well-intentioned, and should be particularly useful for those students seeking information on financing a college education. Beyond that, focusing just on the college selection process, the site has little to recommend it. Information and short essays provided repeat information contained in most guidebooks and on other sites, don't provide much detail, and are too highly summarized to stand out from the alternatives.

WHERE TO FIND/BUY:

Find on the WorldWideWeb using the URL: http://www.tgslc.org/

America's Best Colleges

★★

Author/Editor:

Publisher: U.S. News & World Report, Inc.

Edition Reviewed: 1996

Internet URL: http://www.usnews.com/usnews/fair/home.htm

Media Type: Internet

Price:

ISBN:

RATINGS (1-4 STARS):

Overall:	★★	Statistically comprehensive, but not credible as a shortcut to real research
Breadth Of Content:	★★★	1,400+ schools are analyzed, profiled, and ranked
Value Added:	★★	Lots of computer time went into this, but in the end its just data
Ease Of Use:	★★	The type is tiny and the selectivity/regional tiers a bit confusing

---

DESCRIPTION:

The principal attribute of this website is the U.S. New's annual ranking of 1,400+ colleges. This universe of colleges is divided into four major groups, "National" universities and liberal arts colleges (more selective), and "Regional" universities and liberal arts colleges (less selective); selectivity is determined by a combination of freshmen accepted and enrolled, average scores on the SAT/ACT, and high school class standing of entering freshmen. The rankings, in quartiles, are derived from the weighted opinions of 2,700+ college presidents, deans, and admissions directors on "academic reputation", combined with statistical rankings of selectivity, faculty resources (5 factors), financial resources, retention (returning freshmen and % graduated in 4 years), and alumni satisfaction (% who contribute to fund drives). All these figures come together in the rankings. The "best" business schools and engineering programs are highlighted as well. Following the rankings comes a 130+ page directory of the schools, with basic stats for each school provided. Several articles from the magazine version are reprinted on the website. Ordering information for the magazine and their CD-ROM product are provided.

EVALUATION:

This magazine's annual ranking of colleges is well known and widely available. As such, it garners considerable interest and press, both pro and con. For many people, its convenience, low cost, and strict rankings present an alluring alternative to more exhaustive research. For many professionals in the field, the largely numbers-based rankings are exactly the wrong way to go about deciding which colleges to apply to. For each of the measures used to derive these rankings, it could be argued that there is a relationship between the variable and the quality of the school. It could also be argued that any ranking that is based on so FEW variables cannot possibly represent an accurate guideline for most prospective applicants. And therein lies the difficulty. Selecting a college is a process that has many steps, some introspective, some research-based, and some based simply on "look and feel." Thus, to imply that any ranking can be taken as conclusive, even one as statistically comprehensive as this, is fundamentally misleading. Where we come out on this research tool is this: Hey, it's cheap, buy one, have some fun looking at the rankings, maybe even take down some names of schools that you hadn't thought of before, but DON'T view this as anything more than just a starting point for your research.

WHERE TO FIND/BUY:

Find on the Internet at the URL: http://www.usnews.com/usnews/fair/home.html. Can also be ordered direct by calling 800-836-6397.

Search By Video

★ ★

Author/Editor:	**Media Type:** Internet
Publisher: Search By Video	**Price:**
Edition Reviewed:	**ISBN:**
Internet URL: http://www.searchbyvideo.com/	

RATINGS (1-4 STARS):

Overall:	★ ★	A useful service for getting a "feel" for a college on your short list
Breadth Of Content:	★ ★ ★	Videos for 300+ colleges are available
Value Added:	★ ★	The videos are prepared by colleges for recruitment purposes
Ease Of Use:		Not applicable

DESCRIPTION:

This company provides a service which compiles videos of colleges you select onto a single videotape (up to 8 videos). They charge $6/video selected, plus $2.95 for shipped/compiled videotape. The videos you select are those provided by whatever colleges are participating (currently over 300). "Superlinks" are available for selected colleges listed on their website; these contain links to college home pages and email links.

EVALUATION:

If you're down to a short list, and you'd like to see what your choices look like on videotape, this can be a very useful service and a cost-effective alternative to a college visit. Recognize, of course, that the videos are created for recruitment purposes, and will highlight each institution's strong points. Nonetheless, this visual tool can be useful in your initial selection process, in providing a first impression of the "look and feel" of a campus. You should also call the schools you're interested in, ask for their video and see if they'll mail it to you for free.

WHERE TO FIND/BUY:

Visit their website using the URL: http://www.searchbyvideo.com/. Obtain a brochure listing college videos available, and place an order, by calling 800-248-7177. Cost is $6/videotape plus $2.95/order.

Preparing Your Child For College ★★

Author/Editor:

Publisher: Department Of Education

Edition Reviewed:

Internet URL: http://www.ed.gov./pubs/Prepare/

Media Type: Internet

Price:

ISBN:

RATINGS (1-4 STARS):

Overall:	★★	Not a bad starting point for getting ready for college
Breadth Of Content:	★★★	Includes chapters and resources on both college and aid
Value Added:	★★	Includes supplemental charts and a listing of other sources of information
Ease Of Use:	★★★	Nicely organized for an online book, with helpful hypertext links

DESCRIPTION:

This is one of the Department Of Education's "books on the Web." This book consists of a number of chapters focused on the broad issue of preparing children for college. Chapter topics include general questions about college, preparing for college, choosing a college, financing a college education, and long-range planning. A long list of additional resources are provided in one appendix; other appendices include a variety of checklists (course planner, etc.) and charts (questions for guidance counselors, typical college costs, etc.). An ASCII version of the book is available for downloading, as is a PDF format version (280K).

EVALUATION:

This is a well-intentioned effort, and will be a useful resource for students and parents just beginning their research on the college search and admissions process. The book is well written, with an easy-to-read style. Many of the supplemental resources provided could be useful. The listing of additional resources is quite broad (covers a number of related topics) but provides just a few resources for each topic. There are other print resources which can cover this topic in more depth, but this resource provides a very helpful starting point, and it's free.

WHERE TO FIND/BUY:

Find on the Internet at the URL: http://www.ed.gov./pubs/Prepare/.

College Zine

Author/Editor:	**Media Type:** Internet
Publisher: Kaplan	**Price:**
Edition Reviewed:	**ISBN:**
Internet URL: http://www.kaplan.com	

RATINGS (1-4 STARS):

Overall:	★★	Interesting reading but not much depth; 1 page of advice on most areas
Breadth Of Content:	★★	420 schools profiled; nothing you can't get from a better source
Value Added:	★★	You can send away for admissions counseling information
Ease Of Use:	★★	Logical follow-through and easy to navigate

DESCRIPTION:

Kaplan Educational Centers consider themselves the "nation's premiere educational company specializing in test preparation, admissions, career services, and K-12 academic services." The company is affiliated with The Washington Post Company and has been around since January 1995. Their website offers advice in the following areas: the admissions process, choosing schools, application factors such as transcripts, test scores, interviews, recommendations, and financial aid. These areas are each covered in about one page of printed matter. Kaplan also offers "Kaplan Admissions Consulting" which states that their counselors know "what schools are looking for and how you can help provide it." Information is not given at this website but you can send away for it. Links are also provided to most of the 420 top schools featured in Kaplan's guide book, The Road to College. Information is provided by the colleges and the depth of coverage and speed of access varies. Kaplan's Site of the Week highlights a particular school in a brief paragraph.

EVALUATION:

Kaplan is foremost interested in their testing preparation materials and courses. This is evident here in their lack of detail in describing the areas involved in college admissions. At best, Kaplan's website offers students and parents a starting point in researching the many facets of selecting a college and applying for admission. The advice they give in their one-page summaries is well-intentioned but far too brief to be used alone. Other resources and websites can offer you much more extensive information. The information provided by the colleges in the "College Home Pages" is basic - admissions policies, degrees offered, campus activities, etc. - and doesn't really give you a feel for the actual campus even though touted as "Virtual Campus Tours." Again other websites give you a more personal feel for the schools and more extensive information. This website seems to be a teaser to entice you to apply for either more information about Kaplan's courses or to purchase their books. In either case, your search for real information to assist you in this important decision needs to be elsewhere.

WHERE TO FIND/BUY:

Find on the Internet at the URL: http://www.kaplan.com

EASI - Easy Access For Students And Institutions   ★★

Author/Editor:

Publisher: U.S. Department of Education

Edition Reviewed:

Internet URL: http:easi.ed.gov/

Media Type: Internet

Price:

ISBN:

RATINGS (1-4 STARS):

Overall:	★★	Don't waste your time unless you haven't access to any other source
Breadth Of Content:	★★	Weak treatment of most subject matter
Value Added:	★★	On-line book provided within (no real depth of any subject matter)
Ease Of Use:	★★	Some pages had nothing to do with topic highlighted

DESCRIPTION:

The U.S. Department of Education initiated this effort as a collaborative effort among a group of government, business, and education leaders. This website focuses on the following four areas: planning for your education, applying to schools, receiving financial aid, and repaying your loan. The first section primarily links you to various sites for testing information and for home pages on postsecondary, community/junior colleges, and technical/proprietary schools. An entire publication - Preparing Your Child for College - is also provided online. Within this on-line book, you will find such subjects as "Preparing for College," "Choosing a College," "Financing a College Education," "Long-Range Planning," and more. Charts and checklists are provided for students and parents for many of these areas. An extensive list (20 pages) is also provided that lists information sources on how to prepare for standardized tests, how to choose occupations/careers, how to choose a college and more. The other three sections provide similar information on financial aid.

EVALUATION:

This is a worthy idea, but there is not enough substance here to help you in preparing for or selecting a college. The links to educational institutions' home pages is not novel nor is their publication Preparing Your Child for College, which is the focus of the section on "planning for your education." Some of the advice provided within this book such as "continue to save for college" (under the heading of "Financial Preparation Checklist for Parents") leaves us wondering how much energy was devoted to this publication. The rest of this book offers suggestions that might be of value to those who have absolutely no idea and need a jumpstart on helping their child get ready for college. Much of the information instead can be readily available from the colleges themselves or through your high school guidance counselors. The charts provided in the book look appealing but are not easily used due to their limited graphics and space. The section on "applying to schools" is misleading and really involves applying for student aid from the U.S. government.

WHERE TO FIND/BUY:

On the Internet at the URL: http:easi.ed.gov/.

College Choice

Author/Editor:	**Media Type:** Internet
Publisher:	**Price:**
Edition Reviewed:	**ISBN:**

Internet URL: http://www.gseis.ucla.edu/mm/cc/home.html

RATINGS (1-4 STARS):

Overall:	★★	Good for a preview of topics; not much in-depth on any subject
Breadth Of Content:	★★★	Touches briefly on all areas of the selection and admission process
Value Added:	★★	Timeline (6th - 12th grades), section on how admissions decisions are made
Ease Of Use:	★★★	Well-organized; easily navigated

DESCRIPTION:

Within this website you will find information on: preparing for college, choosing a school, the college application, paying for college, your first year away, timeline, and links to other sites. The website is a "nonprofit information service for college bound students." "Preparing for college" outlines courses that should be taken, relevance of grades, class rank, standardized tests, extracurricular activities, and more. "Choosing a school" defines the different types of schools, along with items to consider when evaluating colleges. Ways to gather information about schools and how to develop an initial list are also included. The bulk of the website is devoted to the application process with information from start to finish. A section on how colleges make their admissions decisions is also included. The section entitled "timeline" lists personal and study habits for students to concentrate on from 6th grade through 12th grade; a month-by-month calendar is provided from 10th grade on. Finally, this website links you to other sources for information on specific subjects, such as other websites and databases, African American resources, Asian American resources, resources for women and more.

EVALUATION:

All of the basic topics are discussed here in this website but nothing in great depth. Primarily we find that this website would be of benefit if you want your college bound student to get an overview of what is involved in the college search process. It is well-written in that regard - brief snippets that reinforce the main ideas, but little help in any direct way. The most useful section is that regarding how admissions decisions are made. Five criteria are spelled out and explained (intellectual students, students with special talents, students of color, students of alumni, and the all-American student). Also provided in this section is a narrative from the director of admissions at U.C.L.A. detailing how freshmen will be selected for the fall of 1996. Although this website contains information on all of the elements involved with the admissions/application process, students will need other more exacting resources to help them through this process successfully. This site is merely a start.

WHERE TO FIND/BUY:

On the Internet at the URL: http://www.gseis.ucla.edu/mm/cc/home.html.

CollegeTown ★★

Author/Editor:
Publisher: CollegeTown
Edition Reviewed:
Internet URL: http://www.ctown.com

Media Type: Internet
Price:
ISBN:

RATINGS (1-4 STARS):

Overall:	★★	Incomplete directory; commercial flavor too strong
Breadth Of Content:	★★	Database of 10,000 schools (vocational, two year and four year institutions)
Value Added:	★	Nothing you couldn't get from more comprehensive sources
Ease Of Use:	★★	Straightforward; many flaws in way school searches are conducted

DESCRIPTION:

CollegeTown's website includes a database of over 10,000 institutions from "beauty schools to the Ivy League." Once you register in their guest book and establish your own "personal access key", you may do a college search of vocational/occupational schools, two year and four year institutions. Searches are conducted either by region (then narrowed alphabetically) or by keywords (name, city or state). Within the searches of two and four year institutions, you may also give "preferences" (region, school type, religious affiliation, and more). School data typically includes basic demographics (address, number of students, diversity. etc.), academic and admission information, student services (counseling, placement, remedial, etc.), and costs. You can create "personal notebooks" and store data received from these searches. Some schools have "expanded portfolios" that include a photo tour of campus. The website includes a list of related books about colleges available online (through a link to Amazon.com). You may read excerpts from the U.S. Dept. of Education's publication Preparing Your Child for College 1996-97. Future plans include an online campus store.

EVALUATION:

Registration is mandatory and requires name and address data. Sounds impressive but this website is little more than an incomplete directory of facts about schools and an avenue for organizations to market their services and products. It is difficult to locate information about schools primarily because of the way the college search engine is set up. If you wish to locate a school say in either the "Southwest" or the "Plains", you must do separate searches. However, even once you specify the region, you then narrow it down based upon the letter of the alphabet you specify. That's great if you are looking for a school in the Southwest that starts with the letter "M"; otherwise, it really isn't useful; you can also search by state, city, or school name. The "preferences" category you can use in the search of two year and four year institutions is also difficult to use. It does not allow you to make multiple selections in most cases. Once your search is finally underway, the statistics provided are minimal and do not give you any feel whatsoever for the college or the students. You'll find several other sites on the Web that do this job (college searches) much better.

WHERE TO FIND/BUY:

On the Internet at the URL: http://www.ctown.com.

College Quest

★★

Author/Editor:

Publisher: Educational On-Line, Inc.

Edition Reviewed:

Internet URL: http://www.edonline.com/demo/main.htm

Media Type: Internet

Price:

ISBN:

RATINGS (1-4 STARS):

Overall:	★★	Excellent narratives on careers, college prep; college search info minimal
Breadth Of Content:	★★★	Info on careers (many require subscription) and application process
Value Added:	★★	Checklists relevant and helpful; career/majors section useful
Ease Of Use:	★★	Font of narratives too small to read; amateurish graphics

DESCRIPTION:

Educational On-Line's website consists of the following sections: careers & majors (over 300), college preparation, colleges & universities, financial aid, faculty resources, scholarships, summer programs, and quick college tips. The last three sections are available only if you subscribe to College Quest ($30/month). The database of careers is grouped according to "college-degreed" (for example, "College of Architecture") and "non-degreed". A section entitled "Help - Choosing a Career" is also provided. This section along with many of the descriptions of careers are available only if you subscribe to College Quest. The website's focus is the section on college preparation. Here you will find narrative information on selecting a college, entrance tests, applications, interviews, a college planning calendar, and an index. Checklists are also included (self-evaluation, college selection, etc.). Searches for colleges are based upon these regions: Mississippi, southern states, United States, International, and historically Black. Eventually, you are given an alphabetical list of schools for your chosen region. Information about most schools consists of address, phone, enrollment, and tuition. Some listings are linked to the school's home pages.

EVALUATION:

Don't be misled by the home page of this website. Once you get through the clutter and confusion of their graphics and print, and into the heart of their website, you will be pleased with much of what they have to offer. In particular, the section on careers and majors may help any confused student as they decide which career or major path to explore. These narrative descriptions along with those having to do with the college preparation section are easy to understand; they state the main points, and offer valid suggestions and information. However, the font used is far too small to read on your screen; even though small when printed, it is worth the reading. We are not sure what basis Educational On-Line used to target their college searches upon the above-mentioned regions. But even still the information you glean from your search is minimal compared to other search resources. If you just need an address or phone for a school, then you'll be satisfied. Otherwise, use other sources for your college search. Use this website if you want in-depth and current information about specific careers or majors. Even though many careers are available only through subscription to College Quest, you may find what you need in this "demonstration" version.

WHERE TO FIND/BUY:

On the Internet at the URL: http://www.edonline.com/demo/main.htm.

College Counsel

Author/Editor:

Publisher:

Edition Reviewed:

Internet URL: http://www.ccounsel.com

Media Type: Internet

Price:

ISBN:

RATINGS (1-4 STARS):

Overall:	★	So far, the worst website we've found
Breadth Of Content:	★	There is no content, just their products for sale
Value Added:	★	None
Ease Of Use:	★	Look here for how NOT to do a website

DESCRIPTION:

This website is titled the "College & Scholarship Super Page." It's home page includes links to pages on Parental Advice, College & Universities, College Financing, College & Beyond, What's New, Marketplace, and Monthly Contest. The Parental Advice link describes a guidebook available on "all aspects of college financing & selection." The College & Universities link describes their College and University Advisor, a "40 page personalized report which recommends the ten most appropriate colleges based on each individual's interests, abilities, and goals," based on "an extensive database of over 2,500 accredited colleges." The College Financing link provides a similar description to a similar service, in this case providing information on college and private financial aid (based on "an extensive database of over 200,000 sources"). An ordering form for these and six other products is included, as are forms for requesting information and entering a monthly contest. All other links are "under construction."

EVALUATION:

This is one of the worst websites we've encountered. This appears to be a site focused solely on generating sales for this company's products, which appear based on several proprietary databases -- no other information for the college-bound is available. The site's shortcomings, apart from its focus, include a non-secure credit card order form (no encryption), more links under construction than finished, crude graphics, incomplete product descriptions, a contest using the same form as a request for information (and no indication of what the monthly "prize" is), etc. Stay away, don't bother, spend your time somewhere else.

WHERE TO FIND/BUY:

Find on the Web at the URL: http://www.ccounsel.com.

Internet College Exchange (ICX)

Author/Editor:
Publisher: US Mall, Inc.
Edition Reviewed:
Internet URL: http://www.usmall.com

Media Type: Internet
Price:
ISBN:

RATINGS (1-4 STARS):

Overall:	★	Of limited value in completing a first pass at college selection
Breadth Of Content:	★★★	Includes most colleges in U.S.; limited information available
Value Added:	★	Limited search criteria; very little descriptive material on colleges
Ease Of Use:	★	Design, navigation, and writing need improvement

DESCRIPTION:

A Web site that has as its principal feature a database that supports college searches/matches against several criteria. The criteria employed are limited to college type (2 or 4 year, public or private), geographic region or state, size, tuition cost, and field of study (not yet implemented). Short descriptions of colleges that are selected are available, as are (in some cases) email links, but require registration to access. Additional pages of information are offered for the college selection process and financial aid. A "Bulletin Board" offers a forum to ask or answer questions from visitors to the site. A newsletter, "The Dunce's Cap," is profiled and promoted on the site (it costs $25/year for 12 email issues); its stated purpose is to demonstrate that "getting into college should not be the hardest part of going to college." Other services are offered but are too sparse to mention, or are still under construction.

EVALUATION:

Their home page lists a number of awards from the usual assortment of award organizations -- we don't agree. This is not a quality website in a number of respects. It's not very polished in its presentation (design, navigation, and basic writing skills are lacking). Most of its features are under construction or not fully implemented. Registration is required to receive a user ID/password to view the results of a search; the registration process is intrusive and not optional. The site is sprinkled with promotions for their magazine ($25 via email, $75 via snail mail); this is symptomatic of a intrusive commercial slant to the site (the store and financial aid search service are other examples). Very little information is offered for colleges selected, so what you end up with is a simple list of colleges in a geographic region, which you'll need to more fully research elsewhere. Additional pages of information offered are pretty skimpy.

WHERE TO FIND/BUY:

Find on the WorldWideWeb using the URL: http://www.usmall.com

XAP.COM

★

Author/Editor: **Media Type:** Internet
Publisher: Xap Company   **Price:**
Edition Reviewed: **ISBN:**
Internet URL: http://www.xap.com

RATINGS (1-4 STARS):

Overall:	★	Only of interest if you want to use their computerized applications
Breadth Of Content:	★	About 141 schools are connected up to this software; none in Midwest
Value Added:	★	Pretty much standard fare; some links still under construction
Ease Of Use:	★★	Easy to navigate; difficulty accessing some highlighted schools

---

DESCRIPTION:

The Xap company provides you with basically two options at their website: 1) you can download interactive presentations about campuses you're interested in and take a "virtual tour", and 2) you can download colleges' computerized applications. These applications may be used by sending the school either a floppy disk of your completed application or a printed copy. Colleges and universities are located in this website either through an alphabetical listing or through a clickable U.S. map showing states that subscribe to the XAP software. There are approximately 141 schools that are listed. The benefit of using the "XAPplications" is that they purport that they will automatically check over your application to make sure it is complete and the answers are consistent. A 1-800 number is also provided if you need customer assistance. An on-line federal financial aid form is also provided for "demonstration purposes."

EVALUATION:

The virtual tours sound interesting at first but then require much time to download (often 10 minutes). They basically connect you up with the college's home pages and information commonly found in their catalog. The applications for colleges can be rather tedious to get through. You are given a screen asking you for very little information each time. You then need to scroll down and click on choices at the bottom of your screen to get to the next page. Error messages as XAP checks over the applications were rather ambiguous and not as helpful as we hoped; information was either "invalid or absent." This website leaves alot to be desired. It's ambitions are admirable, but it doesn't hit the mark.

WHERE TO FIND/BUY:

Find on the Internet at the URL: http://www.xap.com.

College Solutions

Author/Editor:

Publisher: College Solutions

Edition Reviewed:

Internet URL: http://www.college-solutions.com

Media Type: Internet

Price:

ISBN:

RATINGS (1-4 STARS):

Overall:	★	Must employ their services to get info on college selections, financial aid
Breadth Of Content:	★	Little to no info on admission/application process at this website
Value Added:	★★	Financial aid information primarily presented
Ease Of Use:	★	Must send and receive e-mail to receive the 8 seminars

DESCRIPTION:

College Solutions is a company founded by Dr. Charles Lord, a veteran college professor and now college planner. His team consists of a variety of consultants and specialists in areas such as essay critique, tax and financial planning, needs analysis, and more. They have a database of "the best 1000+ colleges in America." Their website consists primarily of a self-survey to determine whether or not you need their services, a calendar from the sophomore year through the senior year in preparation for college, and a set of eight seminars that you obtain through e-mail. The first seven seminars focus on the areas of financial planning for college and the variety of aid strategies available. The last seminar - "Choosing A College Wisely - Step One" - presents the various services that CS will provide for you for a fee ($500 - $1,500 depending upon which services you wish). Services include some of the following: a career assessment self-test, a college readiness self-test, an analysis of your academic record and financial situation, an initial list of colleges, monitoring of your application process, advice about essays, and more.

EVALUATION:

College Solutions certainly knows their marketplace and sells their services accordingly. They enlist concern about your child's future through scenarios that make you certain that you need this company's team of specialists. CS presents a different approach: rather than applying to a variety of colleges, and then seeing which ones you can afford, CS suggests that you can "counter-market" yourself. Knowing your financial situation, then selecting schools appropriate for your academic interests, and then renegotiating award letters, may lead you, they suggest, to schools you thought were out-of-reach financially. We have some reservation as to the criteria they use for their database of colleges; they cite a reference that we do not find much merit in. It may also be unwise to give high school students direction based upon a self-test of their career interests and a self-test of their readiness for college (40 questions). Using a test's results and matching a database of colleges to your child makes things all too simplistic. CS also states that they will be "monitoring" the paperwork you will be involved with. Does that mean they check it for you or do they actually do alot of the work for you? Something to consider before you spend the time and money.

WHERE TO FIND/BUY:

On the Internet at the URL: http://www.college-solutions.com.

National Association Of College Admission Counselors

Author/Editor:

Publisher: National Association Of College Admission Counseling

Edition Reviewed:

Internet URL: http://www.nacac.com/fairs.html

Media Type: Internet

Price:

ISBN:

RATINGS (1-4 STARS):

Overall:	NOT RATED
Breadth Of Content:	NOT RATED
Value Added:	NOT RATED
Ease Of Use:	NOT RATED

DESCRIPTION:

The focus of this site is to serve its members, largely high school and college admissions counselors. Nonetheless, the site includes a listing of College Fair dates; College Fairs sponsored by the NACAC bring dozens of college representative together to meet high school students throughout the country; it can be a cost-efficient way to learn about a number of college alternatives. College Fairs focused on the "Performing & Visual Arts" are listed as well.

EVALUATION:

NOT RATED

WHERE TO FIND/BUY:

Find on the Internet's World-Wide Web at the URL: http://www.nacac.com/fairs.html.

CollegeLink

Author/Editor: **Media Type:** Internet
Publisher: Enrollment Technologies, Inc.   **Price:**
Edition Reviewed: **ISBN:**
Internet URL: http://www.collegelink.com

RATINGS (1-4 STARS):

Overall:	NOT RATED
Breadth Of Content:	NOT RATED
Value Added:	NOT RATED
Ease Of Use:	NOT RATED

DESCRIPTION:

CollegeLink is a software program which collects information from the student, and then uses this input to generate multiple applications to colleges specified by the student (this program is not the "Common Application," another approach doing the same thing). Some 700+ colleges participate with CollegeLink; you can obtain a brochure which lists participating colleges. Most participating colleges also accept the program's common essay; those that don't are flagged. Unique input required by schools selected is gathered as well. After input is complete, a diskette is returned to the company (a prepaid mailer is supplied), which then produces laser-printed custom applications for signature and mailing. Electronic transmission of applications is an available option. The first application is "free" ($5.00 shipping); each application thereafter costs $5.00.

EVALUATION:

NOT RATED

WHERE TO FIND/BUY:

Call CollegeLink direct at 800-394-0404 for a list of participating colleges and a brochure, or to order the software.

U.S. News Getting Into College

Author/Editor:
Publisher: Creative Multimedia
Edition Reviewed: 1996
Internet URL:

Media Type: CD-ROM
Price: $24.95
ISBN: 1-57520-011-2

RATINGS (1-4 STARS):

Overall:	★★★	A useful resource, but not better, on balance, than the best printed books
Breadth Of Content:	★★★★	1,400 schools comprehensively profiled
Value Added:	★★★	Video/audio clips a plus, just the usual stats a minus
Ease Of Use:	★★	Well designed, but using the search engine is frustrating

DESCRIPTION:

For Mac and Windows (3.1+; 486SX/33+). This CD-ROM provides profiles on 1,400 schools and and a comprehensive search capability. The search process leads the student though choices on 12 variables used by the program to produce a rated listing. These variables are: location (state, region), size, campus setting (city, suburb, etc.), student diversity, co-ed or not, religious preference, available activities, sports programs, special programs (ROTC, etc.), student/faculty ratio, admissions selectivity, and available majors. A separate screen is provided for each variable, including sound/video clips discussing the alternatives provided. From the variables chosen, the program produces a sort of the database, prioritized by the "score" of each school against the variables. The student can re-sort the list by changing the weighting assigned each variable; schools can be substituted on the list. Profiles for each school are comprehensive, including pages of statistics and short descriptions. Pages of information and advice on the admissions process, finances, and what to expect are provided, as well as "To Do" lists for each of 10 schools targeted by the student.

EVALUATION:

The strength of this CD-ROM is that of all in this medium -- a comprehensive search capability of a large database, and the benefits of colorful graphics, good navigation design, and audio/video clips. All these should combine to make this a reasonable alternative to some of the large guidebooks, particularly at this price. The number of schools profiled is certainly adequate, as is the information and statistics provided for each school. The care with which the program leads students through the choices of variables is thorough and educational. However, the search engine ultimately provides a less effective search than just thumbing through the guidebooks. The principle problem is that all variables are used in making selections, and that no variables are absolute. Thus, a search which is supposed to select colleges in just one state produces a listing of colleges from all states. This makes the process of narrowing a list based on one or two key variables very cumbersome. The "advice" sections are well-written and helpful, but don't provide as thorough a treatment as specialized resources would. Design elements are quite good: context-sensitive help, pop-up menus, great use of audio/video clips, nice graphic and navigation design.

WHERE TO FIND/BUY:

Wherever CDs are sold, or direct from the publisher by calling 800-262-7668.

Kaplan On Campus '96

★★★

Author/Editor:
Publisher: Meetinghouse Technologies
Edition Reviewed: 1996
Internet URL:

Media Type: CD-ROM
Price: $49.95
ISBN: 0-671-05323-X

RATINGS (1-4 STARS):

Overall:	★★★	A useful CD-ROM; easy-to-use search engine helps with initial picks
Breadth Of Content:	★★★★	Basic information on 1,700 colleges provided, with 300 video clips, etc.
Value Added:	★★★	Great search engine; college data provided is limited
Ease Of Use:	★★★★	A really well-designed CD-ROM; effective use of multimedia

DESCRIPTION:

For Mac (7.1+; 68030+) and Windows (3.1+; 486/25+). This is Kaplan's new 5-disk CD-ROM set, with a database of 1,700 schools accessible by state, alpha, or search (5 regions are on different CDs). The search engine uses up to nine variables (selectivity, majors, location, cost, affiliation, size, setting, athletics, special services); choices are explained with a short video. As choices are made, the number of schools meeting the criteria are indicated. A separate facility is available to help select a major; nine major "clusters" are described, as are 100+ individual majors. Selecting personal abilities/tasks builds a list of suggested majors; a similar process is used to suggest career choices. Over 300 videos are available, as are campus maps. A financial aid reference includes an overview, details of federal and state sources of aid (for states, a listing of agencies is provided), and financial planning tools for estimating financial aid, loans, etc. Software to produce the Common Application (accepted at many schools) is included. Kaplan's "Guide To College Admissions" (print guidebook) is included.

EVALUATION:

This is an excellent tool for developing an initial list of college choices. The program indicates how many schools meet the criteria specified, an excellent way to fine-tune a search: for example, selecting no majors is better than two or three majors as possibilities, as the latter case requires that schools have ALL majors chosen to be listed. The videos are fun to watch, but basically convey no real information (not enough time); same for the campus maps (not enough detail); with a database this size, little else should be expected. Maneuvering within the database is eased by clicking on states or an alpha listing. College data provided is limited to statistics and lists. The processes provided to help identify majors or careers should be used just as a starting point at best; books focused on majors or careers will probably be more helpful. The financial aid section provides useful, but limited overviews. The financial aid estimator is a good tool for generating a quick estimate of expected student and parent contribution, given input for income, assets, etc. Helpful documentation is provided, as is online, context-sensitive video help. The "Guide To College Admissions" booklet is a useful additional resource; it's well organized, easy to read, and provides a lot of helpful information on essays, recommendations, interviews, etc.

WHERE TO FIND/BUY:

Bookstores and libraries, direct from the publisher at 800-527-4836, or on the Web at http://www.kaplan.com.

Interactive Fiske Guide To Colleges

Author/Editor: Edward B. Fiske

Publisher: Interactive Education, Inc. (Random House, Inc.)

Edition Reviewed: 1996

Internet URL:

Media Type: CD-ROM

Price: $49.99

ISBN: 0812-927-44-3

RATINGS (1-4 STARS):

Overall:	★★★	A great CD-ROM for evaluative input on colleges
Breadth Of Content:	★★★	Only 300+ colleges and universities covered
Value Added:	★★★★	Really outstanding insight; wholly original writing
Ease Of Use:	★★★	Excellent search engine, not deep on navigation design or multimedia

---

DESCRIPTION:

For Mac (System 7.0+, 68030+) & Windows (3.1+). The same product, less video clips, is available on floppy disk. The 800+ page guidebook contained on this CD-ROM offers original, evaluative essays on each of the 300+ colleges and universities covered, based primarily on in-depth feedback from students, supplemented by additional research, including campus visits. Each write-up (2-4 pages in length) includes comments on academics, the student body, financial aid, housing, food, social life, and extracurricular activities, with summary ratings (1-5 Stars) for Academics, Social Life, and Quality of Life. Typical statistics about the school are included; admissions practices, policies, and deadlines are summarized as well. Roughly 200 schools have short videos clips. A highly flexible search engine using 15 variables is available to generate a scored ranking of 10, 25, or all colleges. Choices within each variable can be expressed as positive (important to you), indifferent, or negative; rankings can exclude schools if they have any negatives. Criteria used in generating these ranked listings can be modified, saved, and printed.

EVALUATION:

This CD-ROM contains among the best, if not the best, source of original descriptions on the colleges included. The research done and questions asked of students and administrators alike are focused on issues that are relevant to selecting a college, and are responsive to the focus of both parents and prospective students. If you've got some of its 300+ schools on your list to evaluate, these profiles will be among the best resources you can use to pare down your list. That said, should you buy the CD-ROM or the printed guidebook? On the plus side, having a search engine this good and this flexible is a blessing. But, search engines can be misleading if not used with a great deal of care -- potentially great choices might be excluded inadvertently. So start with just a few criteria and refine the rankings carefully. The videos clips don't add much value: too small, too short, sometimes just pictures, frequently no narrative. Would we recommend the CD-ROM over the book? Probably not. The big minus is increased cost; the big plus is the search engine, if used carefully. But for refining a initial college list down to a dozen or so finalists, you'll have what you need in the print version.

WHERE TO FIND/BUY:

Bookstores or computer stores selling CDs, or direct from the publisher by calling 800-793-2665.

Profiles Of American Colleges

★★

Author/Editor:
Publisher: Laser Resources, Inc.
Edition Reviewed: 20th (1995)
Internet URL:

Media Type: CD-ROM
Price: $29.95
ISBN: 1-57288-000-7

RATINGS (1-4 STARS):

Overall:	★★	Buy Barron's printed version, unless you have to have full-text search.
Breadth Of Content:	★★★	Profiles on 1,650 schools included
Value Added:	★★	Multimedia additions are limited. Maps are useful.
Ease Of Use:	★★	Documentation is sparse; using the search engine is difficult for novices

DESCRIPTION:

For Mac (System 6.0.5+,68030+) & Windows (3.1+). This is a CD-ROM version of Barron's Profiles, one of several all-inclusive college guides that has been around for years. The CD-ROM contains all the college profile information contained in the printed version. The information for each of the 1,650 colleges profiled (roughly 3-4 pages each) includes the typical statistics, and separate sections on student life, housing, campus activities, programs of study, faculty/classroom statistics, admissions process/requirements, basic financial aid data, and other topics. Color maps are included, showing where schools are located in each state. Photographs of some 250 schools are included, as are short videos for 15 schools. The CD-ROM also includes school catalogs for roughly 40 schools, and printable applications for 60 schools. The principal feature of this media, and this CD-ROM, is the ability to search every word of each school profile, using multiple search criteria. One defined search criteria is available, supporting searches by either tuition cost and total cost.

EVALUATION:

CD-ROMs both give and take away relative to printed forms of information. This CD-ROM is a good example. It provides the addition features of maps, photographs, videos, applications, and a search engine. But, it gives up the essays contained in the printed version of this guide from Barron's, as well as other indexes and table summaries. Of course, the search engine can create any index you want, provided you're comfortable feeling your way by trial and error, with some help from the documentation provided. Much better would be to provide a listing of all the usual parameters helpful in selecting colleges, which could then be chosen in whatever combination was desired. What's required is to build multiple parameter search inquiries in a process that could be daunting to the novice. Note the caveat contained in the documentation: "information contained in Barron's Profiles..has been provided by the individual schools who retain responsibility for the accuracy of the content." Thus, this source is useful for creating a first cut at alternatives, not winnowing them down based on more subjective feedback. The maps are useful in visualizing where the schools are located. Less useful are the limited number of photos and videos provided. The applications included look crude when printed.

WHERE TO FIND/BUY:

Computer stores, or buy direct from Educorp (product code 50784) @ 1-800-843-9497.

College Where

★★

Author/Editor:

Publisher: McCabe Software Inc.

Edition Reviewed: 1995

Internet URL:

Media Type: CD-ROM

Price: $29.95

ISBN:

RATINGS (1-4 STARS):

Overall:	★★	Not as useful as other alternatives in helping target colleges
Breadth Of Content:	★★★	1,600 colleges included in the database
Value Added:	★★	Incredible breadth of variables too confusing; just basic stats on the colleges
Ease Of Use:	★★★	Works as advertised; out-of-date design, no multimedia

DESCRIPTION:

For Windows (3.1+; 386+). This is another of several CD-ROM alternatives offering a methodology to create an initial selection of colleges. This CD-ROM provides statistics on each of 1,600 colleges (but no video clips). The process of college selection begins with the student completing a profile (test scores, GPA, extracurricular/sports activities, etc.). Criteria for selection of colleges are comprehensive, with 11 general subject areas, each with multiple criteria to pick from -- each criteria can be weighted with one of 6 weights. The colleges in the database are listed by weighted ranking; the position of colleges on the list changes dynamically as input is changed. For each college selected, a "Report Card" can be generated showing its matches against the input criteria. In addition, an "Admission Estimate" can be generated, showing how the student profile compares to admission stats for the college; an overall rating is assigned ("reach, good fit," etc.). Statistics are available for each college. Letters to each college requesting information (customized by selecting various options) can be generated. Online help is provided.

EVALUATION:

The version we tested used a floppy disk to update the CD-ROM stats with current information (the installation went smoothly). This CD-ROM has some interesting wrinkles, both pro and con, compared to the alternatives we've tested. Its principal strength is also a significant weakness -- we've not seen any "initial college selection" resource which offers as comprehensive a set of choices for input (for example, over 30 input choices on financial aid preferences were available). This incredible array of alternatives (there must be 200+), EACH of which can be weighted differently, could provide very precise "targeting" for students who believe they know exactly what they want in a college. On the other hand, for the average high school student, this array of variables will baffle, bewilder, and eventually frustrate. Other resources which more effectively narrow these search alternatives are probably more on target; after all, the point of this resource is to generate an initial list, not the final answer. The estimate of the likelihood of being admitted to various colleges of interest is an innovative feature, but one that could inadvertently direct students away from alternatives where they might be able to get admitted. While this CD-ROM works as advertised, we think other alternatives available in this media would work better for the typical high school student.

WHERE TO FIND/BUY:

Bookstores, computer software stores, or direct from the publisher at 603-878-4432.

Lovejoy's College Counselor

★★

Author/Editor:

Publisher: InterMedia Interactive Software, Inc.

Edition Reviewed: 1993

Internet URL:

Media Type: CD-ROM

Price: $29.95

ISBN:

RATINGS (1-4 STARS):

Overall:	★★	Not as useful as their printed version; less effective than others of this ilk
Breadth Of Content:	★★★★	Basis stats on 1,600 colleges provided
Value Added:	★★	Not much more than stats and a few video clips
Ease Of Use:	★★★	Useful search engine; may be too flexible for some users

DESCRIPTION:

For Windows (3.1+; 386+). This is a CD-ROM based on the information contained in Lovejoy's College Guide, one of the large, all-inclusive tomes containing statistics on virtually all the 4 year institutions (1,600+). In addition to this basic information, this CD-ROM resource adds the power of a search engine, as well as some information on financial aid, majors, and careers. The search engine includes 7 basic variables (admissions, majors, campus characteristics, costs, location, sports, special services), with many choices for each variable, each assigned with one of 4 weights. When this selection process is complete, a ranking is produced of schools that meet the criteria. For each school, the usual stats are available (freshmen profile, admissions info, student body stats, financial aid, etc.); comparisons between schools can be made. The Careers section lists 120 career choices; rankings by increase in jobs, or numbers of jobs by 2005, are also available. The Majors section lists 150 majors in 6 broad categories (business, engineering, etc.); for each a brief description, plan of study, etc., are provided. The Financial Aid section provides a listing of 2,500 aid sources within 10 categories (sports, ethnic-specific, etc.); contact data and award information are provided. Multimedia features include pictures, video clips, and a "talking head" who explains what each section provides.

EVALUATION:

We are generally unimpressed by this kind of CD-ROM effort -- one that duplicates information found elsewhere in print, adds additional statistics, throws in a search engine, and sprinkles college profiles with primitive multimedia. This single distinguishing characteristic of this product, along with others of similar ilk, is the utility of the search engine. It can provide pretty good targeting of a very preliminary list of schools, provided the user is willing to undertake the considerable effort of reading and ranking dozens and dozens of choices. When all is said and done, however, the information provided on colleges selected is very basic; other resources will have to be used to flesh out a comparative picture among college alternatives. The design, navigation, and multimedia features of this CD-ROM fall below the standard set by some others we've reviewed. Finally, the additional information provided on careers, majors, and financial aid is so sparse as to be of little value compared to alternatives which treat these subjects in more depth. If you want Lovejoy's, buy their printed guidebook instead.

WHERE TO FIND/BUY:

Bookstores or computer software stores.

Peterson's College Database

Author/Editor: Peterson's Guides
Publisher: Peterson's
Edition Reviewed:
Internet URL:

Media Type: Online
Price:
ISBN:

RATINGS (1-4 STARS):

Overall:	★★★	Helpful to the initial search process; minimal college info provided
Breadth Of Content:	★★★★	Includes all 3,400 U.S. and Canadian two and four year colleges
Value Added:	★★★	Information provided is minimal; the search engine is really helpful
Ease Of Use:	★★★	Text-based with some improvements needed, but great search selectivity

DESCRIPTION:

Found on: CompuServe. This online site provides the same basic college profile information contained in Peterson's printed guidebooks on Two-Year and Four-Year Colleges. What's unique about this service is its ability to support searches of this large database, using up to 38 college characteristics, grouped within 8 primary categories: Location, Costs, Admission Difficulty, Majors Offered, Number of Students, Type of College (2/4 year, public/private), Campus Setting, and Student Mix (ethic, gender). Using this ability, you can produce as large or as small a list as you wish. For each college returned by a search, the database provides basic information on the college, its academic program, student life and housing, athletics, cost, and financial aid. None of the typical statistics or indexes are provided.

EVALUATION:

We've reviewed the printed version of this database, and Peterson's Internet Web Site as well. Of the three, this product is perhaps most limited in features. The printed version, for example, provides supplemental information on some 800+ colleges; these profiles enhance the limited pictures drawn by the basic information provided through this service. The printed version also provides numerous indexes and other materials. What distinguishes this service, and strongly recommends it, is the ability it provides for a college-bound student to spend some time building a list of choices on location, size, admissions difficulty, campus setting, etc. -- the resulting listing of colleges then produced by the database can save a student hours of flipping through pages, reading indexes, and creating list after list of alternatives. What this database provides is a shortcut to a student's initial list of target schools. That's very helpful. Nonetheless, when it's time to cut this initial list down to size, you'll still need to go other sources which provide some evaluative feedback on the college choices they review.

WHERE TO FIND/BUY:

Find on Compuserve, in the Education subject area.

College Board

Author/Editor: The College Board
Publisher:
Edition Reviewed:
Internet URL:

Media Type: Online
Price: $Varies
ISBN:

RATINGS (1-4 STARS):

Overall:	★★	Lots of information breadth and some useful features, but little depth
Breadth Of Content:	★★★★	It's a monster, and has basic information on all the colleges
Value Added:	★★	Their College Handbook provides just basic listings
Ease Of Use:	★★★	Interactive, easy to navigate; the search engine is not helpful

DESCRIPTION:

Found on: America Online (Keyword: College Board). The College Board is a national non-profit association which publishes a variety of information to "assist students making the transition from high school to college." This America Online site has 5 principal features of relevance to the college selection process. They include several short essays ("Tips") on choosing a college. The site includes a "Conference Hall" which provides live, interactive advice and information on college selection issues (when staffed). "Ask The College Board" is a bulletin board containing a wide variety of question and answer threads on a variety of topics (50 when we last checked). The "College Board Store" lists a variety of publications which you can order online, several relevant and potentially useful. The centerpiece of the site is an online version of their College Handbook, "the only one-volume guide to the nation's 3,200 two-year and four-year colleges." This guidebook can be searched by college name or by typing in key words.

EVALUATION:

This is an interesting site to browse, but it provides little value beyond the printed version of its principal publication, The College Handbook. The essays provided are very short and don't provide tips not encountered elsewhere. The interactive "Conference Hall" has potential for being very useful, depending on load, but was not in operation when we visited. The bulletin board feature has the typical pros and cons: lots of suggestions and information from users of the site, but difficult/time-consuming to navigate and of inconsistent quality. Their store offers some relevant publications, and you can order them online. Where the site really falls down is when you try to do a search on the information available for some 3,200 schools -- the search engine can find you anything, but you can't do searches on multiple criteria, even if you understood what the most important factors were. The information a search gives you back is typical of the large, all-inclusive tomes: namely, the basic profile provided by the colleges themselves.

WHERE TO FIND/BUY:

On the America Online ("AOL") online service (Keyword: College Board).

Princeton Review Online

★★

Author/Editor:	
Publisher:	
Edition Reviewed:	
Internet URL:	

Media Type: Online
Price:
ISBN:

RATINGS (1-4 STARS):

Overall:	★★	Not as useful or as comprehensive as the publication replicated in part here
Breadth Of Content:	★★	Only 309 colleges included in their database
Value Added:	★★★	Some original narrative on colleges; the essays are really abbreviated
Ease Of Use:	★★★	Nicely organized service, but their database is not searchable

DESCRIPTION:

Found on: America Online (Keyword: Princeton Review). This online service reflects much of the scope of the Princeton Review's print publications. Of principal value to those undertaking the college search process will be the database included on the site; this is some of the same material contained in their publication "Guide To The Best 309 Colleges". The best colleges (according to Princeton Review) included in the database are listed alphabetically. Selecting a college retrieves a narrative addressing academics at the school, and a host of statistics formatted in several categories, Campus Life (including What's Hot and What's Not), Academics, Admissions Facts, and Financial Facts. Also available are a number of rankings within this population of schools (selected mostly for fun). Short essays on typical admissions topics are included as well. A section listing their publications (concentrated mostly on SAT and other test preparation) is also available. A student message board and forum is available as well.

EVALUATION:

This is a useful service, within the context of an online service you might already be using. The primary focus of The Princeton Review is test preparation, covering the entire spectrum from the SAT to graduate school exams; thus, this service is light on college admission and selection information. If you have a list of schools already, their database can provide you with some original information; however, the database is not searchable. This database is included in their publication "Guide To The Best 309 Colleges," which we like very much and would recommend over this site. The printed version contains many more narrative insights, is easier to use, and includes features not available online.

WHERE TO FIND/BUY:

Find on AOL with the keyword: Princeton Review.

Money Magazine's College Finder ★★★

Author/Editor:
Publisher: Wintergreen Orchard House, Inc.
Edition Reviewed: '95-'96
Internet URL:

Media Type: Software
Price: $39.95
ISBN:

RATINGS (1-4 STARS):

Overall:	★★★	A strong contender among alternatives to generate initial lists
Breadth Of Content:	★★★	Database includes 1,150 schools, with stats for 13 areas of interest
Value Added:	★★	College info limited to basic statistics
Ease Of Use:	★★★★	Nicely designed program; very easy to use and navigate

DESCRIPTION:

For Windows (3.1+; 386+). This software program, from the organization that provides many guidebooks with their basic college data, provides a search engine and basic information on 1,150 colleges. The program has four principal sections: questions (to select search variables), importance (to assign weights to variables selected), regions/states (to narrow searches geographically), and fit (which compares specified variables to characteristics of colleges selected). Variables available are organized into 13 major areas, with multiple choices within each area (majors, sports, rankings, selectivity, school size, affiliation, city size, % men/women, minorities, cost, programs, activities, student/faculty ratio). Weightings are used to generate rankings for the schools matched to specified criteria. A "fit" analysis is available for each school selected. Reports can be printed as various scenarios are tried, or can be saved for a later, complete report. Basic information on schools selected is available. Letters to college admissions offices requesting materials can also be generated.

EVALUATION:

This is a useful software program, priced higher than the guidebooks but less than most CD-ROMs. It provides an easy to use search engine to select and rank colleges, using 13 basic criteria relevant to most students creating an initial cut at college alternatives. The number of variables available to use in generating lists is large, equal to or better than most search engines available on CD-ROM or other resources (they include Money Magazine's annual ranking as a variable). Information available on each school is limited to the statistics used to support searches among the 13 sets of variables, and thus is of help only for a very coarse initial cut among college alternatives. This is a basic weakness of all similar resources; students need to be very cautious in using these tools, and ensure good alternatives are not omitted inadvertently. Nowhere in the program does it explain how colleges were selected to be included in their database; one wonders which were left out, and why. Online, context-sensitive help is available from any screen. The help screens can be printed; they are well written and help the user understand how to select variables and use the program to test different scenarios.

WHERE TO FIND/BUY:

Order from the company by calling 800-321-9479.

CollegeLink

Author/Editor:	**Media Type:** Software
Publisher: Enrollment Technologies, Inc.	**Price:** $5.00
Edition Reviewed:	**ISBN:**
Internet URL: http://www.collegelink.com	

RATINGS (1-4 STARS):

Overall:	NOT RATED
Breadth Of Content:	NOT RATED
Value Added:	NOT RATED
Ease Of Use:	NOT RATED

DESCRIPTION:

CollegeLink is a software program which collects information from the student, and then uses this input to generate multiple applications to colleges specified by the student (this program is not the "Common Application," another approach doing the same thing). Some 700+ colleges participate with CollegeLink; you can obtain a brochure which lists participating colleges. Most participating colleges also accept the program's common essay; those that don't are flagged. Unique input required by schools selected is gathered as well. After input is complete, a diskette is returned to the company (a prepaid mailer is supplied), which then produces laser-printed custom applications for signature and mailing. Electronic transmission of applications is an available option. The first application is "free" ($5.00 shipping); each application thereafter costs $5.00.

EVALUATION:

NOT RATED

WHERE TO FIND/BUY:

Call CollegeLink direct at 800-394-0404 for a list of participating colleges and a brochure, or to order the software.

Apply

Author/Editor:	**Media Type:** Software
Publisher: Apply Software Systems, Inc.	**Price:** $15
Edition Reviewed:	**ISBN:**
Internet URL: http://www.applysft.com	

RATINGS (1-4 STARS):

Overall:	NOT RATED
Breadth Of Content:	NOT RATED
Value Added:	NOT RATED
Ease Of Use:	NOT RATED

DESCRIPTION:

Apply is a software program which collects information from the student, and then uses this input to generate multiple applications to colleges specified by the student (this program is not the "Common Application," another approach doing the same thing). Some 120+ colleges participate with Apply; you can obtain a brochure which lists participating colleges. A "personal information" feature allows the student to enter information once that will be used in all applications. An exact duplicate of the applications specifed are included in the diskette; requirements unique to each college are entered directly into their application. When complete, applications are printed by the student (preferably on an inkjet or laser printer). Ordering a single application costs $15. Up to 6 applications cost $50; additional applications cost $5 apiece. Shipping is $6.

EVALUATION:

NOT RATED

WHERE TO FIND/BUY:

Obtain the software, or a brochure, by calling Apply Software at 800-932-7759 or 212-245-4558.

Search By Video

Author/Editor:
Publisher: Search By Video
Edition Reviewed:
Internet URL: http://www.searchbyvideo.com/

Media Type: Videotape
Price:
ISBN:

RATINGS (1-4 STARS):

Overall:	★★★	A useful service for getting a "feel" for a college on your short list
Breadth Of Content:	★★★	Videos for 300+ colleges are available
Value Added:	★★	The videos are prepared by colleges for recruitment purposes
Ease Of Use:		Not applicable

DESCRIPTION:

This company provides a service which compiles videos of colleges you select onto a single videotape (up to 8 videos). They charge $6/video selected, plus $2.95 for shipped/compiled videotape. The videos you select are those provided by whatever colleges are participating (currently over 300).

EVALUATION:

If you're down to a short list, and you'd like to see what your choices look like on videotape, this can be a very useful service and a cost-effective alternative to a college visit. Recognize, of course, that the videos are created for recruitment purposes, and will highlight each institution's strong points. Nonetheless, this visual tool can be useful in your initial selection process, in providing a first impression of the "look and feel" of a campus.

WHERE TO FIND/BUY:

Visit on the Web at the URL: http://www.searchbyvideo.com/. Obtain a brochure listing college videos available, and place an order, by calling 800-248-7177.

Getting Into College

Author/Editor: R. Fred Zuker (Consultant)
Publisher: College Admission Productions
Edition Reviewed: 1989
Internet URL: http://www.dn.net/NACAC

Media Type: Videotape
Price: $32.95
ISBN:

RATINGS (1-4 STARS):

Overall:	★★★	Good introduction to the process and terminology; positive tone & style
Breadth Of Content:	★★★	Strong on all elements of getting into college, except financial aid
Value Added:	★★★	Broad, effective coverage of college selection & admission
Ease Of Use:		Not applicable

DESCRIPTION:

This videotape runs roughly 45 minutes; it follows a high school student through the college selection and admissions process, A-Z (junior year through acceptance), with the student's college counselor giving advice and instruction throughout. Five "real" (not actors) college admission counselors also provide advice and counsel in short clips interspersed throughout the video. Subjects covered include the gamut: what's important during high school, how to decide which schools to apply to, the college visit and interview, the application (including what's important and how to write an effective essay), and how to make a final decision.

EVALUATION:

This videotape provides a very good overview of the college selection and admissions process. The narrative is well written and delivered at a pace which can be followed easily. The student, his family, and his high school counselor are presented in a positive, caring, constructive light. The information content of the video is thorough in its breadth, and provides many lists, tips, hints, questions, and instructions along the way. By its nature, however, the information provided is not as deep as can be provided by the better print options available. This video provides value as a "starting point" for students and families starting the college selection and admissions process. It includes a good overview of each stage of the process, introduces much of the terminology likely to be encountered, and provides reassurance, with its positive style, that "Getting Into College" can be a positive experience readily managed by the typical high school student.

WHERE TO FIND/BUY:

Order from the National Association Of College Admission Counselors @ 703-836-2222.

Collegiate Choice Walking Tours

★★★

Author/Editor:
Publisher:
Edition Reviewed:
Internet URL: http://www.register.com/collegiate/

Media Type: Videotape
Price: $15
ISBN:

RATINGS (1-4 STARS):

Overall:	★★★	A pretty good idea, one that may help families save some time and $
Breadth Of Content:	★★	Just 400+ college videos are available, concentrated in the East
Value Added:	★★★	The advisors ask the questions and provide an "informal" look at colleges
Ease Of Use:		Not applicable

DESCRIPTION:

This is a service set up by several independent college advisors "who work with families in Bergen County, New Jersey." Since 1988, these advisors have taken amateur videos of the tours offered by some 400+ colleges throughout the country. Their intent in doing so has been to provide those families they work with an opportunity to "visit" colleges of interest that they aren't able to visit in person. They charge $15 per video plus a $6 handling/shipping fee per order (videos are ordered via mail or toll phone call; the website does not support online purchases). The website includes information explaining the service; these pages make it clear that these videos have been made by amateurs using hand-held video cameras, and that they are not intended to replace viewbooks and catalogs available from the colleges. Their value, the site explains, is found in the experience of the advisors taking the college tours -- in the questions asked, and the "feel" for the school created by an informal, unbiased approach. The videos vary in length from 20-100 minutes in length (average roughly 60+ minutes). A brief essay on making a college visit is included on the site, as are simple lists of "best colleges" from U.S. News, Money Magazine, etc.

EVALUATION:

This is a useful service. We've ordered and viewed several sample tapes. Each tape provides a "real" tour of the college, lasting roughly 60 minutes. You get to see lots of buildings, students in informal, unrehearsed settings, and hear the Q&A of the tour participants and the guide. The questions asked by these college advisors are useful (and consistent from tour to tour); the answers given by the guides are not commented on (judgments are left to the viewers). The video quality is quite good, the audio quality less so. Guides can be good (enthusiastic, well-informed) or bad (dull, ill-informed). One video we saw on a college we know well was 3 years out-of-date and the answers given by the guide in some cases were inaccurate. The price of $15/video may seem steep (Search By Video charges $6/video for their collection of college video viewbooks), but value added, measured by an unbiased view of the schools toured, should be higher than the standard "canned" college viewbook. When each video was taken is not revealed in their listing, but an email inquiry brought a response that they try to update each video at least every 5 years. There are a healthy number of colleges from each state listed (albeit with an East Coast concentration), and these videos could serve as a practical alternative to a college visit for those families whose budgets or schedules prohibit a visit to all colleges of interest.

WHERE TO FIND/BUY:

Find on the Web at the URL: http://www.register.com/collegiate/; order videos by calling 201-871-0098.

Rugg's Insights On The Colleges

★

Author/Editor: Frederick E. Rugg
Publisher: Rugg's Recommendations
Edition Reviewed: 1993
Internet URL:

Media Type: Videotape
Price: $29.95
ISBN: 1-883062-02-0

RATINGS (1-4 STARS):

Overall:	★	Entertaining, but directed at high school counselors
Breadth Of Content:	★★	Not too many schools mentioned by name
Value Added:	★★	The author's experience shines through; highly subjective opinions do too
Ease Of Use:		Not applicable

DESCRIPTION:

Fred Rugg is the author of the highly rated Rugg's Recommendations On The Colleges; this is a videotape (roughly 20 minutes long) consisting of excerpts from one of the seminars he puts on for high school counselors. The videotape can be purchased separately or as part of his seminar "package" which includes the videotape and a number of college lists and seminar transcripts. Those portions of the seminar captured on this videotape cover a variety of topics, some part of his seminar outline, many in response to questions. The many topics covered are quite diverse (from comparing the Ivy League schools to guidebook recommendations for counselors); a structured approach to his comments is not evident. Careful note taking on the part of the viewer could generate a list of several dozen colleges recommended for one reason or another.

EVALUATION:

It's fun, in this tape, to see the man behind "Rugg's Recommendations" in action. The author is obviously very knowledgeable, and very opinionated, about various colleges across the country. Most of the observations on colleges selected for this tape are positive, some are not. The seminar is obviously directed at a group of experienced high school counselors, and as such assumes a level of knowledge not found among typical high school students or their parents. Thus, this resource, while entertaining, will be of little practical value to students and parents in their search.

WHERE TO FIND/BUY:

Contact the publisher at 805-462-2503.

America's Best Colleges

Author/Editor:
Publisher: U.S. News & World Report, Inc.
Edition Reviewed: 1996
Internet URL: http://www.usnews.com/usnews/fair/home.html

Media Type: Misc.
Price: $7.95
ISBN:

RATINGS (1-4 STARS):

Overall:	★★	Statistically comprehensive, but not credible as a shortcut to real research
Breadth Of Content:	★★★	1,400+ schools are analyzed, profiled, and ranked
Value Added:	★★	Lots of computer time went into this, but in the end its just data
Ease Of Use:	★★	The type is tiny and the selectivity/regional tiers a bit confusing

---

DESCRIPTION:

The U.S. New's annual ranking of 1,400+ colleges is based on a comprehensive statistical survey. This universe of colleges is divided into four major groups, "National" universities and liberal arts colleges (more selective), and "Regional" universities and liberal arts colleges (less selective); selectivity is determined by a combination of freshmen accepted and enrolled, average scores on the SAT/ACT, and high school class standing of entering freshmen. The rankings, in quartiles, are derived from the weighted opinions of 2,700+ college presidents, deans, and admissions directors on "academic reputation", combined with statistical rankings of selectivity, faculty resources (5 factors), financial resources, retention (returning freshmen and % graduated in 4 years), and alumni satisfaction (% who contribute to fund drives). All these figures come together in the rankings. The "best" business schools and engineering programs are highlighted as well. Following the rankings comes a 130+ page directory of the schools, with basic stats for each school provided. A number of articles are sprinkled throughout, from managing student debt, to determining whether a college is "technologically savvy."

EVALUATION:

This magazine's annual ranking of colleges is well known and widely available. As such, it garners considerable interest and press, both pro and con. For many people, its convenience, low cost, and strict rankings present an alluring alternative to more exhaustive research. For many professionals in the field, the largely numbers-based rankings are exactly the wrong way to go about deciding which colleges to apply to. For each of the measures used to derive these rankings, it could be argued that there is a relationship between the variable and the quality of the school. It could also be argued that any ranking that is based on so FEW variables cannot possibly represent an accurate guideline for most prospective applicants. And therein lies the difficulty. Selecting a college is a process that has many steps, some introspective, some research-based, and some based simply on "look and feel." Thus, to imply that any ranking can be taken as conclusive, even one as statistically comprehensive as this, is fundamentally misleading. Where we come out on this research tool is this: Hey, it's cheap, buy one, have some fun looking at the rankings, maybe even take down some names of schools that you hadn't thought of before, but DON'T view this as anything more than just a starting point for your research.

WHERE TO FIND/BUY:

For sale from the fall until late spring each year, wherever magazines are sold. Can be ordered direct by calling 800-836-6397.

College Visits (Tours Of Colleges & Universities)

Author/Editor: Robert Rummerfield, Director
Publisher:
Edition Reviewed:
Internet URL:

Media Type: Misc.
Price:
ISBN:

RATINGS (1-4 STARS):

Overall:	NOT RATED
Breadth Of Content:	NOT RATED
Value Added:	NOT RATED
Ease Of Use:	NOT RATED

DESCRIPTION:

This specialized travel business, located in Charleston, South Carolina, was founded by Robert Rummerfield, "previously assistant director of admissions at The Johns Hopkins University." Most trips have been arranged for visits to schools in the eastern 1/3 of the country, although the company claims it can arrange such trips anywhere. All trips are supervised. Some trips take a group of students from the same high school on a tour of colleges; others put together individual students for similar trips. We talked to Mr. Rummerfield at the 1995 NACAC Conference in Boston; among the benefits he listed for this service were: lower overall travel costs; more informed itinerary and better questions asked; more freedom to ask important questions without parents in attendance (this from the students' perspective), and exposure to more college alternatives in a shorter period of time.

EVALUATION:

NOT RATED

WHERE TO FIND/BUY:

Call College Visits at 803-853-8149.

Section IV Title Index

How To Send Your Suggestions To Resource Pathways

We want to hear from you! Your feedback has always been, and will always be the most important factor we use in creating new products to meet your needs and improving the quality of our existing guidebooks!

So, please tear out (or copy) the form below, fill it out with your comments and suggestions, and send it to us at the address noted below.

I am a:
- ◯ High School Student
- ◯ College Student
- ◯ Parent

- ◯ High School Counselor
- ◯ College Counselor
- ◯ Publisher

My feedback or suggestion is:

_____

_____

_____

_____

_____

_____

_____

_____

_____

_____

Mail this form to us at this address:

College Information Community Editor
Resource Pathways, Inc.
22525 S.E. 64th Place, Suite 253
Issaquah, WA 98027-5377

You can also send us email at:

counselorfeedback@sourcepath.com
studentfeedback@sourcepath.com
publisherfeedback@sourcepath.com

Thanks, in advance, from Resource Pathways!

Notes

Notes